G000164945

Folk Song Papers, No. 1

Proceedings of
The English Folk Dance and Song Society
Folk Song Conference 2013

Edited by David Atkinson and Steve Roud

Individual articles © 2015 by their authors.

Produced by:

CAMSCO Music
www.camscomusic.com

Loomis House Press
www.loomishousepress.com

ISBN 978-1-935243-85-4

Cover photo: Charity Farm, by Paul Burgess

Contents

I. Singers and Collectors

II. Songs

III. Tunes

IV. Revivals

I. Singers and Collectors

Miss Wakefield's Folk Song Competition, 1902–1906, and its Legacy

SUE ALLAN

Few people today regard Cumbria as a repository of traditional music, perhaps because the landscape of the Lake District and the Romantic heritage of the Lakes Poets have historically outshone any musical heritage.[1] Writing shortly after the administrative county of Cumbria came into being in 1974, amalgamating the former counties of Cumberland and Westmorland with Lancashire-above-the-Sands and a small corner of the Yorkshire Dales, Paul Adams of Fellside Recordings in Workington bemoaned the fact that Lancashire, the Borders, and Northumberland were all areas rich in musical traditions, whereas those of Cumbria seemed to have been 'virtually extinguished', leaving only scraps of Border ballads, industrial songs, 'local songs' (a term he does not define), and hunting songs.[2] As a singer and musician looking for Cumbrian material to perform, I took this as a call to arms and subsequent research has demonstrated quite clearly that Cumbria actually has a rich musical heritage, with a substantial corpus of folk songs, including a specifically local repertoire of hunting songs and songs in dialect.

The record of folk song in Cumbria shows two notable 'spikes', or clusters in numbers of sources, indicative of two periods of interest: in the 1970s, when as part of a general revival of interest in folk song, young Cumbrian folk singers were seeking a local repertoire to perform, and in the early twentieth century, during the 'first' folk song revival.[3] Although

1 Although use of the term 'Cumbria' may seem anachronistic, the region's cultural coherence has long been recognized. J. D. Marshall and John K. Walton, *The Lake Counties from 1830 to the Mid-Twentieth Century: A Study in Regional Change* (Manchester: Manchester University Press, 1981), pp. viii, 14, observe that 'the overall concept of "Cumbria" is of more consequence than a mere administrative boundary or two'.

2 Paul Adams, 'The Neglected Corner', *Folk Review*, 4 (1975), 6–7.

3 The Cumbrian corpus includes some 519 folk songs from 1,007 different sources, around 30 per cent of them being versions of broadside ballads widely circulated elsewhere in Britain, along with a few songs about the

they do not comprise a large part of their collections, many of the big names of Edwardian folk song scholarship and collecting, including Lucy Broadwood, Frank Kidson, Cecil Sharp, Percy Grainger, Anne Gilchrist, and Ralph Vaughan Williams, did collect songs in Cumbria. Broadwood did this via correspondents in Cumberland and Westmorland; Vaughan Williams paid two very brief visits to the area; and Kidson and Sharp visited the region primarily as adjudicators at the Folk Song Competition instituted by Mary Wakefield in 1902, as part of the Westmorland Music Festival held in Kendal.[4]

Born into a well-known and well-to-do local Quaker family at Kendal, Mary Augusta Wakefield (1853–1910) was a talented singer, who had trained as a musician in London. A friend of John Ruskin, and of other notable families including the Somervells who founded K Shoes of Kendal, Wakefield is best known as one of the founders of the competitive music festival movement, having started the Kendal Musical Competition—later the Westmorland Festival—which rapidly became a major fixture in the regional musical calendar.[5] Her life, typical of a middle-class Victorian lady in its combination of privilege with restriction, meant that despite her training a career as a professional musician was not open to her. 'Thwarted in her ambitions to become a professional musician by the exigencies of her class and the moral scruples of her father, to whom music and the theatre were closely and unsuitably linked, she then turned her considerable energies to projects that combined music and philanthropy.'[6]

Believing that she was working in the cause of national musical regeneration, Wakefield regarded music as a serious art which, as a prerequisite to its being appreciated and understood as much as it was in Germany, needed an educated enlightened public. To achieve this, 'most surely the root of the matter will prove to be the cultivation and encouragement of the musical amateur'.[7] Music festivals, she believed, could form 'a social platform whereon everyone, irrespective of religion, politics, class or education, can meet freely with a common cause, ideal and interest'.[8] To this end, she went on to found and train choirs in Westmorland villages,

county published in the region. A distinctive regional repertoire emerges, however, with 30 per cent of the total being hunting songs, and 23 per cent songs in Cumberland and Westmorland dialect. These figures come from my as yet uncompleted doctoral thesis, 'Cumbrian Folk Songs and Regional Identity'.

4　Vaughan Williams visited the village of Dent, then in Yorkshire, on 10 August 1904, noting four tunes and a song from John Mason; and visited Carlisle, at the invitation of the acting organist of Carlisle Cathedral, Sydney Nicholson, on 9 August 1906, noting down seven songs from Mr Carruthers.

5　The festival, now known as The Mary Wakefield Westmorland Music Festival is still a feature of the musical life of Cumbria, held at Kendal bi-annually.

6　Christine Cathrow, *Mary Wakefield, Westmorland Centenary Festival, History, 1885–1985* (Kendal, 1985).

7　'Amateur Music as It Should Be', *Musical Times*, 25 (1 March 1884), 143–44 (p. 144).

8　Rosa Newmarch, *Mary Wakefield: A Memoir* (Kendal: Atkinson & Pollitt, 1912), p. 86.

bringing them together in 1885 to take part in a singing competition at her home, Sedgwick House, a few miles outside Kendal, to raise money for Crosscrake church. This was the nascent Westmorland Music Festival.

The event proved so successful that the following year it had to move into bigger premises. Wakefield was still organizing the festival, but with the support of her wide network of relations and friends. These included Dr Arthur Somervell and Dr McNaught, both of whom would join the Folk-Song Society in due course, Somervell's brother, Gordon, and his son, Charles, as well as Colonel Mason, Miss Cropper, and the Rev. T. Heelis—all of whom entered the Folk Song Competition that was inaugurated as part of the festival in 1902. The *Musical Times and Singing Class Circular* published an appreciation of Mary Wakefield's work when she retired from conducting at the festival in 1900, noting, rather patronizingly, that: 'A district reputed to be unmusical has, in this way, gained an almost national reputation for its enthusiasm for musical study and ability in execution.'[9]

An early member of the Folk-Song Society, Wakefield was a friend and correspondent of both Lucy Broadwood and J. A. Fuller Maitland, in whose house she sometimes stayed when visiting London.[10] Her biographer, Rosa Newmarch, reveals that Wakefield had learned traditional Border songs from her nurses when she was a child; that she had published a book of 'Northern Songs', comprising songs written in a folk style on a range of 'quaint' topics, such as Grasmere Rushbearing; and that she frequently included northern dialect songs in her recital repertoire, including her own arrangement of what Newmarch mistakenly calls a 'Westmorland dialect song', Robert Anderson's 'Sally Gray'.[11]

As John Francmanis describes, the musical establishment of the time perceived a need for a characteristic English art music, thus imbuing folk song with great significance, as both theory and practice in Europe seemed to suggest that folk song was an essential ingredient of national music.[12] This was a message that Mary Wakefield took very much to heart, and it

9 W. G. McN., 'Miss Wakefield', *Musical Times*, 41 (1 August 1900), 529–30 (p. 529).

10 Newmarch, *Mary Wakefield*, p. 23.

11 This song was written by Carlisle dialect poet Robert Anderson and published in his *Cumberland Ballads* in 1805, with subsequent editions throughout the nineteenth century. Lucy Broadwood and J. A. Fuller Maitland, eds, *English County Songs* (London: Leadenhall Press; J. B. Cramer; Simpkin, Marshall, Hamilton, Kent, 1893), included 'Sally Gray' as a Cumberland song, with a tune submitted by Miss Wakefield that is not the one to which the words are usually sung, in the north of the county at least.

12 John Francmanis, 'The "Folk-Song Competition": An Aspect of the Search for an English National Music', *Rural History*, 11 (2000), 181–205. Francmanis's excellent paper has informed and inspired much of my own research into the Kendal competition.

provided a rationale for her instituting a Folk Song Competition as part of the festival in 1902. Although hers was not the first competitive music festival, it was certainly the first to include a folk song competition.[13] Roy Palmer has written about other such competitions, at Frome (1904), Brigg (1905–6, 1908), Retford (1907), and Stratford-on-Avon (1911), although he does not mention the one held at Carlisle in 1906, which was undoubtedly the direct descendant of the Kendal Folk-Song Competition.[14]

Wakefield's obituary in the *Journal of the Folk-Song Society* in 1910 describes her as 'the greatest force in the musical competition festival movement in this country', and goes on to add that while she may not have been an important collector of folk songs, she was nonetheless one who 'took an active part in making them known'.[15] As Francmanis points out, her Folk-Song Competition was her inspired method of gathering this raw material—no need to go out collecting songs if you could get the singers to come to you.[16]

A Folk Song Competition—Open to the Six Northern Counties

The Folk Song Competition was instituted as a part of the festival programme in 1902. The class details in the 1904 prospectus outline its aims:

> Folk-Song, unaccompanied. Open to the Six Northern Counties.
>
> The best unpublished People's Song of which the words or music must be unpublished and which has been handed down traditionally and orally in any one of the Six Northern Counties. The award will be made for the most interesting, curious, and best among the old fashioned songs entered; songs which are rapidly becoming more and more rare. A copy of the words must be submitted to the Secretary for approval when entry is made, with particulars as to origin etc. The judge will be at liberty to withhold the awards should the songs be deemed unworthy of them.[17]

Frank Kidson, judge of the 1902 competition, expressed the objectives in the *Westmorland Musical Festival Folk-Song Book* of 1903 in rather more Romantic fashion, as being 'to elicit and rescue some of the unpublished Folk Songs, most of which are held only in that fragile

13 The first competitive musical festival was that instigated by composer and conductor Henry Leslie, a friend of the Wakefields with whom Mary Wakefield stayed in 1884, who founded the Oswestry Festival of Village Choirs in 1879 (Newmarch, *Mary Wakefield*, p. 79).

14 Roy Palmer, 'An Era of Song, Ninety Years Ago', *English Dance & Song*, 56.3 (1994), 14–16.

15 'Augusta Mary Wakefield', *Journal of the Folk-Song Society*, 4.2 (no. 15) (1910), 141.

16 Francmanis, 'Folk-Song Competition', p. 186.

17 Kendal, Cumbria Archive Centre, WDSO/11/1/12, Letter Books of Mary Wakefield.

keeping—the memories of old people fast passing away [. . .] It is well known that many of these ditties still linger in the Northern Dales.'[18]

With its prime concern being 'the most interesting, curious, and best' songs, the Folk-Song Competition was the only part of the festival not to be judged on quality of performance. In seeking only those songs that were unpublished, it became incumbent upon the organizers to appoint a judge who had a thorough knowledge of printed sources. This they certainly did in the person of antiquarian and folk music scholar Frank Kidson, who gave a long introduction about the nature of folk songs before going on to outline his judging criteria. The song, he said, must be old enough to have been sung in the northern counties for at least two generations, and must have an old tune, unpublished to the present. The most interesting song to fulfil these criteria would win first prize, especially if the words as well as the tune had not been published before, although the words 'might be found on some early ballad sheet'.[19]

Of the ten entries in the first year, only three matched Kidson's criteria, the others being disqualified on account of prior publication, including Mr Henderson's 'Bleckell Murry Neet' and Mr Turnbull's 'Canny Auld Cummerlan', both written by Robert Anderson. The winner was Miss Hayhurst of Milnthorpe with 'Sledburn Fair', second was Miss Germain's 'Holm-Bank Hunting Song', and third Mr C. J. Cropper's 'A Hunting Song' (not actually a specifically local song).

In 1903, the competition was held again, once more with Kidson as judge, and with nine entrants, of whom just six turned up. The *Musical Times* reported: 'The folk-song competition, begun last year, was resumed with good results, Mr. F. Kidson, of Leeds, a specialist in this matter, disqualifying some excellent songs as having been published, but finding three excellent ones well worthy of prizes—"Poor Old Horse", "Swarth Fell Rocks", and "The Cartmel Hunting Song".'[20] All three songs later appeared in the *Journal of the Folk-Song Society*.[21] In a letter to fellow musician and collector Anne Gilchrist in May 1903, Kidson wrote: 'The Folk Song thing passed off very nicely but unfortunately some who were put down for songs didn't turn up. I gave the first prize to a very nice set of "Poor Old Horse" with a very marked "flattened seventh".'[22]

18 A. M. Wakefield and Frank Kidson, *Westmorland Musical Festival Folk-Song Book* (Kendal, 1903).

19 Francmanis, 'Folk-Song Competition', p. 189.

20 'Competitions: Westmorland Musical Festival', *Musical Times*, 44 (1 June 1903), 404.

21 *Journal of the Folk-Song Society*, 1.5 (1904), 258–61; *Journal of the Folk-Song Society*, 2.4 (no. 9) (1906), 267–69.

22 London, EFDSS Archives, Anne Gilchrist Collection, AGG/8/167, Frank Kidson to Anne Gilchrist, 31 May 1903.

A *Westmorland Musical Festival Folk-Song Book*, price threepence, was also published that year, containing the words and music of the three winning songs from 1902 and the words of all the 1903 entries, including the three that had not been sung, 'Axes to Grind', 'It's Nobbut Me', and 'Ground for the Floor'. In her foreword, Wakefield wrote that she had decided to continue the competition partly because of the encouragement it had received the previous year, and also because it had produced 'two hitherto unpublished tunes'. Several people, she says, had asked for copies of the book of words, including Cecil Sharp, who had written to say he had taken down the three best songs and, had his *A Book of British Song* not already been published, would have included the 'Hunting Song', adding that there were 'few good genuine hunting folk songs in England'. The comment shows either how little he knew of hunting songs in Cumberland and Westmorland, or that, because most of them had known authors, he did not consider them folk songs. Wakefield concludes by exhorting her readers to 'ransack their country surroundings' in the attempt to collect more old tunes and verses.

The following year, 1904, saw Kidson reappointed as judge. The *Westmorland Gazette* noted that he 'expressed pleasure that the competition still held on, though he would like to hear a better selection, because he was sure that in Kendal they had a lot of good songs if they could only get the right people to come forth and sing them', adding that the main thing he was looking for was the melody, as 'the words generally were not very good'.[23] The 'right people' whom Kidson was envisaging were, of course, the rural working classes, not the educated middle classes who almost exclusively entered the competition. However, that year did bring a breath of fresh air in the form of the blacksmith John Collinson from Casterton, near Kirkby Lonsdale, who sang three songs, one of which, 'In Yon Land', won second prize. The *Musical Times* was not over-impressed with the competition, however, reporting that 'The speculative and highly interesting folk-song competition produced six competitors. None of their "finds" were of exceptional interest, but Mr. Frank Kidson, of Leeds, who acted as judge in this class, had no difficulty in awarding the prize to the Rev. T. Heelis, Vicar of Crosthwaite.'[24] His winning song was 'The Old Dun Cow'.

In July 1904, at the General Meeting of the Westmorland Festival, Wakefield proposed that money prizes should be offered in order to stimulate more entries for the 1905 competition. This was quite astonishing given her well-known distaste for what she called 'pot-hunting', and was perhaps a sign of desperation that so few suitable songs and singers were coming

---

23 'Westmorland Musical Festival', *Westmorland Gazette*, 16 April 1904.
24 Herbert Thompson, 'The Westmorland Musical Festival', *Musical Times*, 45 (1 May 1904), 315.

forward. The incentive appeared to work, however, as in 1905 ten songs were entered by eight singers. At the meeting it was also decided to appoint Cecil Sharp as judge, although it is not clear whether this was because Kidson was unavailable or because Sharp's national profile as a collector, publisher, and educationalist was high in 1905.[25]

The *Westmorland Gazette* reported that Sharp found the entries a 'most interesting' lot of songs, far better than the printed words had led him to expect—once again showing that it was the tunes that were of most interest. His comments tend towards either damning with faint praise—'a popular theme, but there was nothing much about the tune'—or outright condemnation—'this is not a folk song', or, in the case of one song, it was 'not of the type that the folk really cared about'.[26] As Francmanis notes, Kidson's level of clarity and knowledge of the repertoire was hardly emulated by Sharp, whose remarks reveal that he knew far less about printed sources than Kidson and include derogatory comments about published songs or songs he perceived as being 'popular', in the sense of 'common'.[27] In the end, he awarded first prize to John Collinson for his 'Walney Cockfighting Song', the tune of which was, he thought, 'a very find one indeed'. Also for its fine tune, he gave second prize to the Rev. Heelis's 'Bonny Boy', and both songs were published in the *Journal of the Folk-Song Society* that year.[28]

In 1906, Sharp was once again invited to be judge, the committee minutes revealing that Lucy Broadwood was second choice. The Rev. T. Heelis was appointed Honorary Secretary of the Folk-Song Competition. In his introductory remarks, Sharp said that he believed there were a large number of uncollected folk tunes in the neighbourhood and appealed to the audience to get hold of them before it was too late. There were eight entrants for the competition, two of whom scratched on the day, with the remaining six singing nine songs between them. Miss Cookson's song, 'Early Early', was sung in her stead by the Rev. Heelis, who also sang 'Sweet Primeroses' and 'The Seeds of Love'. None were specifically local songs, but Sharp awarded first prize to Heelis's 'Sweet Primeroses'. The other competitors that year were John Collinson, Mr Barrow of Brathay, and Mr Sisson of Leasgill, who gained second place with 'The Squire's Daughter'. It was not the extensive field of folk songs hoped for, however, and

25 Kendal, Cumbria Archive Centre, WDSO/11/1/11, Westmorland Musical Festival, Minute Books of Committees.
26 'The Westmorland Festival', *Westmorland Gazette*, 6 May 1905.
27 Francmanis, 'Folk-Song Competition', pp. 196–97.
28 *Journal of the Folk-Song Society*, 2.2 (no. 7) (1905), 84–85, 82.

the *Westmorland Gazette* opined that perhaps the pool of unpublished folk songs awaiting recovery was nearing exhaustion.[29]

There were no further Folk Song Competitions in subsequent years. The Westmorland Festival became a biennial event and when it resumed in 1908 there was no Folk Song Competition in the programme. It had been discontinued without, it seems, a murmur of complaint, due partly to the perception that there were few songs left to be found, and also because Mary Wakefield had no personal involvement in the festival during the last few years of her life.

Legacy of the Folk Song Competition

Although it ran for just five years, the Westmorland Festival's Folk Song Competition had yielded some thirty-six songs, from nineteen different singers. Five of the songs had appeared in the *Journal of the Folk-Song Society*, the festival had brought the singer John Collinson to the notice of collectors, and it had inspired a similar competition in Carlisle.

John Collinson was evidently a man with a fine ear for a song, 'some education', and a keen interest in singing. As we have seen, he entered three songs in the Folk Song Competition in 1904, gaining second place with 'In Yon Land', and two songs in 1906. His greatest triumph came in 1905 when he won first prize with one of his two songs, 'The Wa'ney Cockfeightin' Song' ('Walney Cockfighting Song'), a localized version of the broadside ballad *The Charcoal Black and the Bonnie Grey*.

Anne Geddes Gilchrist (1863–1954), of Southport, who, like Mary Wakefield, was a trained singer, collected songs, tunes, and children's games from her native Lancashire and further afield. Persuaded by Frank Kidson to join the Folk-Song Society in 1905, she became a prolific contributor to (and later editor of) the *Journal of the Folk-Song Society*. Mixing in the same circles as Mary Wakefield, Gilchrist would undoubtedly have taken a keen interest in the Kendal Folk Song Competition, and she heard John Collinson sing there in 1905. It was not until 1909, however, that she went to the Kirkby Lonsdale area to visit Collinson at his home at Casterton. He was then aged just forty-seven, much younger than the other singers she visited at the same time—Mrs Carlisle, aged eighty-eight, and James Bayliff, aged seventy, both of Barbon. She collected some twenty songs in all from these three singers.

Collinson told Gilchrist that he had learned his winning song specially for the competition from his wife's father, as he was quite determined to win:

29 'Westmorland Music Festival Report', *Westmorland Gazette*, 5 May 1906.

Thinking this old song would have a good chance of obtaining a prize, he set off on foot from Casterton to Hutton Roof [. . .] Alas, when he arrive the old cocker had forgotten the song. It was three days before his son-in-law's patience was rewarded by the return of the old man's memory. Then, secure with it in his own, the blacksmith brought the song home. But, as he remarked, it cost him more than the value of his prize in loss of work through absence.[30]

She notes in the same article that Mrs Carlisle was rather jealous of John Collinson, whom she regarded as a rival, asking, 'Does John Colli'son know this or that one?' Collinson was very well known locally, as a farmer and dealer as well as a blacksmith, an autodidact, a keen singer and also a poet, who, according to his grandson, sent his poems regularly to both local and national newspapers, and also wrote verses 'Inscribed to the 21st Westmorland Musical Festival'.[31]

Gilchrist was not the only person to collect songs from John Collinson. Four years earlier, in October 1905, he had been visited by composer, pianist, and folk song collector Percy Grainger (1882–1961), well known for his pioneering work in recording singers with an Edison phonograph. Unfortunately, it seems he did not take his machine on this occasion, instead transcribing into his notebooks Collinson's songs 'Ah Teaks efter me Feyther', 'Apron Strings', 'The Beadle of the Parish', 'Ga wi' Me t' Farleton', 'Hoo Happy We Lived Then', 'I Wonder What's Keepin' my Love', 'In Yon Land', 'Middleton Ha' Clipping', 'Peace Eggin' Song', 'Up Step'd Jack', and 'Wa'ney Cockfeightin' Song'.

The influence of Mary Wakefield's Folk Song Competition also spread further north, to Carlisle in Cumberland, where it caught the attention and engaged the interest of Sydney Nicholson (1875–1947), then acting organist at Carlisle Cathedral.[32] Nicholson would have known about the festival in Kendal through his musical contacts, some of whom were probably members of the Westmorland Festival committee, and in 1907 and 1908 he was invited to the festival to judge the sight-reading classes.[33] He had become interested in folk song a few years earlier, corresponding with Lucy Broadwood about the Folk-Song Society, which he

30 Anne Geddes Gilchrist, 'Some Old Westmorland Folk-Singers', *Journal of the Lakeland Dialect Society* (1942), p. 8.

31 John Collinson (the singer's grandson), interview with Sue Allan, Kirkby Lonsdale, 1 October 2013.

32 Nicholson was also conductor of the Carlisle Choral Society, and went on to become organist of Manchester Cathedral in 1908 and of Westminster Abbey in 1919. In 1929 he founded the Royal School of Church Music, and in 1938 was knighted for services to church music.

33 Kendal, Cumbria Archive Centre, WDSO/11/1/11, Westmorland Musical Festival, Minute Books of Committees.

joined in 1905.[34] He sent Broadwood some Cumberland songs that same year, sung for him by James Walter Brown, a lay-clerk at the cathedral and member of Carlisle Choral Society. He was evidently unsure of his ability to notate the songs accurately, writing: 'In taking them down it is hard to give the exact notation as they are sung in a very jaunty fashion with many pauses &c, but I have done the best I could. The notes are certainly correct.' He then adds, rather tellingly, 'Robert Anderson the Cumberland poet wrote a large number of dialect songs to the old tunes & these have taken the place of the old words entirely.'[35] In fact, Anderson tended to designate well-known, often Scottish, airs for all his ballads, much as Burns did, and most of the songs sung by Brown had retained their local popularity throughout the nineteenth century, especially 'Sally Gray'.[36]

Six of the tunes Nicholson sent to Broadwood — 'Elizabeth's Birthday', 'Sally Grey' (Gray), 'The Worton Wedding', 'Barbary Bell', 'Bleckel Murry Neet', and 'Geordie Gill' — are by Robert Anderson, and Nicholson promised to send Anderson's book for the words. The remaining two songs are 'King Henry my Son' and a version of a 'Pace Egging Song'. 'Bleckell Murry Neet', 'Sally Gray', and 'King Henry my Son' all appeared in the *Journal of the Folk-Song Society* in 1907, along with another Anderson ballad, 'Canny Cummerland'.[37] This latter, however, came not from Nicholson, but from a transcription made by Ralph Vaughan Williams, who paid a brief visit to Carlisle Cathedral in August 1906 to note down the tunes of some of the same Anderson ballads from a Mr Carruthers, presumably at the behest of Nicholson, whom he might well have known from church music circles.[38] It is interesting to note the difference in attitude to Anderson's songs, which Kidson had disqualified from the 1902 Kendal Folk Song Competition, but which Broadwood and Vaughan Williams now apparently regarded as worthy of inclusion in the Folk-Song Society's journal.

34 London, EFDSS Archives, Lucy Broadwood Collection, LEB/5/359, Sydney Nicholson, to Lucy Broadwood, 11 October 1905.

35 Robert Anderson (1770–1833) was the most popular and prolific of Cumberland dialect poets and a number of his songs entered into tradition and were still performed as late as the 1960s. See also Broadwood Collection, LEB/5/351.

36 Robert Anderson, *Ballads in the Cumberland Dialect, with notes and a glossary* (Carlisle: W. Hodgson, 1805 [and many subsequent editions]).

37 *Journal of the Folk-Song Society*, 3.1 (no. 10) (1907), 40–44.

38 London, British Library, Additional MS Add MS 71700, Ralph Vaughan Williams to Ralph Wedgwood, 20 August 1906 (copy kindly supplied by Hugh Cobbe). The seven songs Vaughan Williams transcribed were: 'Bleckell Murry Neet', 'Rob Lowry', 'King Roger', 'Barberry Bell', 'A Wife of Willy Miller', 'Rossler Fair' (Rosley Fair), and 'Geordie Gair' (Geordie Gill).

Earlier in 1906, whether inspired by Broadwood's positive reception of the songs or by the success of Mary Wakefield's folk song competition—or both of those things—Nicholson was encouraged to start a folk song competition of his own. Thus we find the Carlisle and District Musical Festival of 1906 offering a prize of £1 (donated by Nicholson) for 'the best genuine folk-song from the six northern counties'.[39] The *Carlisle Patriot* reported that the adjudicator, Mr A. Foxton Ferguson, opened the event with a talk on 'Songs of the People', and that the competition attracted seven singers, who sang between them nine songs, seven of them by Robert Anderson. There are some familiar names: Mr J. W. Brown sings Anderson's 'The Worton Wedding', while Mr J. Carruthers contributes 'Barbary Bell' and 'Gwordie Gill'. The first prize, though, went to 'King Henry, my Son', sung by a young chorister, Master T. Grierson.[40]

The following year, however, the *Carlisle Patriot* reported that Sydney Nicholson's efforts at collecting folk songs 'have scarcely met with the success they merited', and although the prize he offered at the previous year's festival had drawn several competitors, the competition had to be abandoned in 1907 because there were so few entries. The article ends with a plea from Nicholson, who was 'especially interested in saving from oblivion such examples of music as were known to our forefathers', and would be pleased to meet singers of old tunes, even if they were 'uncultured' singers, as 'by far the greatest number and finest examples of folk songs have been obtained from people who knew nothing of the art of the music'.[41] It is somewhat ironic, then, to note that the songs Nicholson collected were not actually from 'uncultured' singers at all, but mostly from members of the Carlisle Choral Society—notably Messrs Brown and Carruthers, and a former member, the late Robert Lattimer (*sic*), from whom all the songs submitted to the *Journal of the Folk-Song Society* had apparently been learned.[42]

And so the Carlisle Folk Song Competition sinks without trace—although Lucy Broadwood did publish 'King Henry, my Son' in *English Traditional Songs and Carols* in 1908, its air noted by Miss M. B. Lattimer, sister of Robert.[43] Also, in a not unrelated development, two years later, in 1910, Carlisle-born musician John Graham, doyen of the music festival scene, friend of Mary Wakefield, Anne Gilchrist, and James Walter Brown, and 'one of many collectors of folk-song before Cecil Sharp', according to his obituary in the *Musical Times* in 1932,

39 'Carlisle and District Musical Festival', *Carlisle Patriot*, 19 January 1906.
40 'Folk Song Competition', *Carlisle Patriot*, 23 February 1906.
41 'Folk Songs in Cumberland', *Carlisle Patriot*, 28 June 1907.
42 *Journal of the Folk-Song Society*, 3.1 (no. 10) (1907), 39.
43 Lucy E. Broadwood, *English Traditional Songs and Carols* (London: Boosey, 1908), pp. 96–99.

published his *Dialect Songs of the North*, which includes three Robert Anderson songs as well as 'The Rushbearing', a two-part song by Mary Wakefield.[44]

In conclusion, although some very good folk songs were brought into the spotlight at both the Kendal Folk Song Competition and its offspring in Carlisle, it does seem that the pool of singers and songs in Cumbria in the first decade of the twentieth century was very limited. Appearances, however, can be deceptive. It is certainly the case that the collectors of folk songs, all professional musicians, in Cumberland and Westmorland were few and far between. And it was unfortunate that their informants and singers were few in number, predominantly middle-class and mainly amateur musicians—that is to say, just the sort of people who would be attracted to enter a competition at a music festival—with the possible exception of the blacksmith John Collinson, although as an aspiring poet and keen performer he could not be described as 'uncultured'. What is also clear, however, is that the folk song competition organizers, and judges, failed to tap into popular rural gatherings such as hunt suppers, shepherds' meets, clippings (communal sheep-shearings), kurn (harvest) suppers, and 'merry neets'. Had they done so they would have heard a whole raft of other songs—predominantly hunting songs, along with the obligatory sprinkling of popular Anderson songs.

As Lyn Murfin notes in her *Popular Leisure in the Lake Counties*: 'Elsewhere, Cumbrian singers and their audiences eschewed the distinction drawn by the Edwardian collectors between "folk-song" and other, in their view, less worthy forms of popular song, and the competitions which were sometimes held at sports days made no such value judgement.'[45] One such event was the annual song competition at Egremont Crab Fair, where in 1926 prizes were awarded to songs in each of four categories: best sung Scotch song (for lady competitors only), £1; best sung old hunting song, 10 shillings; best sentimental song, 5 shillings; and best comic song, 5 shillings and a box of kippers.

44 John Graham, *Dialect Songs of the North* (London: Curwen, 1910).

45 Lyn Murfin, *Popular Leisure in the Lake Counties*, (Manchester: Manchester University Press, 1990), p. 175.

Cecil Sharp and Photography

C. J. BEARMAN

Between 1904 and 1918, Cecil Sharp took several hundred photographs in a process that began in Somerset and ended in the Appalachian mountains. Despite the recent appearance of some of these photographs, this remains among the least known, and certainly the least discussed, aspects of his work. I began to use the photographs in the 1990s, but the real foundation of this paper was cooperative work with Yvette Staelens in preparing the Somerset Folk Map in 2006 and our work on The Singing Landscape project between 2008 and 2010. I have been working on a catalogue of the photographs since 2009. The first part of this paper will be a general discussion of how and why Sharp went into photography. In the second I will try to analyse its significance in the context of his life and work in folk music, and in the third I will discuss the many difficulties the collection presents.

Sharp began to take photographs in 1904, either in April or July. For example, he collected from the miller William Spearing twice, the last time on 6 April 1904. I believe the two photographs of him and his family date from then. True, they might be later, because Sharp's collaborator Charles Marson regularly fished Spearing's mill pond, but in one of the photos Spearing's son is holding a pet lamb which would seem to indicate the April date (Figure 1).

The camera Sharp used in England was a Kodak No. 1 folding half-plate, bought on the recommendation of G. O. Smith, his colleague at Ludgrove School. Its roll film provided negatives almost the same size as lantern slides. This provides the clue to Sharp's motivation, which was to get illustrations for the lectures he was beginning to give. In the Appalachians, Sharp took some photographs on his first collecting trip in 1916, but these did not come out well, and with one possible exception all of the present collection dates from 1917 and 1918. For these, he used a 'vest pocket camera' bought in April 1917. This would have been of the

Figure 1. *William Spearing and family (Cecil Sharp Photograph Collection, B21b)*

open-out bellows type. This type of camera produced generally poor-quality photographs, and that is the reason why, in general, the Appalachian photographs do not match the quality of those taken in England.

Sharp's main motivation for the Appalachian photography was the same as in England. His 1916 collecting expedition had more than confirmed the promise of the material shown him by Olive Dame Campbell. That expedition had been made possible by financial support from Helen Storrow. Sharp managed to place a volume of his own and Campbell's work with the American publishers Putnam. But to investigate properly, and to publish his collections in full, he would need backing, either from universities or from a group such as the Russell Sage Foundation, and his means of attracting their attention would have to be public lectures. He also wanted the material for the classes and summer schools, the income from which kept Sharp and Maud Karpeles going while in America.

In connection with these summer schools there is a tantalizing mystery. When Sharp went to America for the third time in 1916, he brought out two 'cinema' or 'cinematograph' films. These were not the 'Kinoras'. One was of 'Pittsburgh'. Perhaps his most successful engagement in 1915 was the three weeks he spent at the Carnegie Technical Institute, which, despite its name, had a drama department and therefore had a use for dance. The film must have been made then. The other was 'Handsworth'. Sharp showed the film and taught the Handsworth sword dance at the summer school at Amherst, Massachusetts, in 1916. But there is absolutely no information about what happened to these films afterwards.

The photograph collection is near unique from two points of view. In the first place, no other collectors are known to have taken photographs of their sources, except Harry Albino and Clive Carey, and to my knowledge only one each of their pictures survives. Other scattered photographs survive, such as those of a few of George Gardiner's singers in Hampshire Record Office, and one of Percy Grainger with singers from in and around Brigg, supplemented by what can be gleaned from family collections, books, and newspapers. Some other collectors are alleged to have been keen photographers, including Frank Kidson and Charles Marson, but if they took any photos of their sources, none have come down to us.

The other major point is that the collection is composed largely of portraits, taken for the most part outdoors, un-posed, with the subjects in working clothes. Other contemporary photographers such as Francis Frith and Fred Spalding concentrated on town- and village-scapes. The only parallel I know of is the work of Frank Meadow Sutcliffe in Whitby and the Esk Valley, beginning in the 1880s or 1890s. The range is extraordinary, from the photo of Lily Porter of Bridgwater, aged about eleven (Figure 2), to that of James Creedy, also of Bridgwa-

Figure 2. *Lily Porter (Cecil Sharp Photograph Collection, B68-a)*

Figure 3. *James Creedy (Cecil Sharp Photograph Collection, A10-d)*

Figure 4. *George Templeman (Cecil Sharp Photograph Collection, B48-b)*

Figure 5. *Oliver Shutler (Cecil Sharp Photograph Collection, B46b)*

ter, who was born in 1811 and claimed to remember news of the Battle of Waterloo coming to town (Figure 3). Photographs of prominent people in local society, such as Sharp's clergymen collaborators and prosperous farmers like George Templeman in Hambridge (Figure 4), are mingled with portraits of the very poorest and most obscure, like Oliver Shutler who spent his summers stone-breaking on the roads and his winters in High Ham Workhouse (Figure 5).

Both Sharp's friends and his critics have been curiously silent about his photography. Although some of his pictures were used in the 1933 biography, A. H. Fox Strangways and Maud Karpeles did not discuss it. This omission continued into the second impression of 1955 and the rewrite that Karpeles published in 1967. It was not discussed even during the centenary events in 2003. The only attempt at public discussion has been a seminar presented by Yvette Staelens at the Wallace Collection in 2012.

Harsh and destructive criticisms of Sharp began in the 1970s, continuing into the 1990s and even to this day, but there has similarly been no mention of his photography, even though the collection challenges many of the highly politicized and pejorative assumptions made in this literature. Most revolve around the doctrine of class separation and the idea that folk music collecting was therefore an act of 'expropriation', meaning that the collectors, Sharp in particular, were not really interested in folk music itself or in the people who sang, played, or danced, but were only concerned with it as a 'commodity', for its uses for political propaganda, personal prestige, and financial gain.

True, Sharp began his photography to provide material for his lectures and what was sometimes published in the musical press: for example, the interview 'Mr Cecil Sharp' that the *Musical Times* published in 1905. But if that were the case, he would only have needed to take one photograph of each performer—though possibly 'bracketing' them to take account of under- or over-exposure, because light meters did not exist in those days. It cannot explain why he took so many pictures of particular people and their families, such as the six photographs of Betsy Holland, including the extraordinary ones of her children in their tent or 'bender' (Figure 6), or the nine of Robert Parish and his family, or the ten of Emma Glover and hers. Still less does it explain why Sharp often sent his subjects their photographs. In a letter to his wife about his first meeting with Betsy Holland, he writes, 'They are wild to have the photo-

Figure 6. *Betsy Holland (Cecil Sharp Photograph Collection, A20–b)*

graphs'—which were probably delivered at their second meeting, a few days later, when the 'bender' photos were taken. The photograph of Joseph Cornelius survives only as a lantern slide, but Yvette Staelens has spotted a reproduction in a local history magazine that can only have come from his family. On at least four occasions in his American diaries, Sharp mentions giving or sending prints to singers or people who had helped him, such as the one of his namesake Mrs Sharp's children. The evidence of the photograph collection reveals the reverse of the image of a ruthless expropriator. Here, quite evidently, was a man with a deep interest in people.

The further implications of the charge of expropriation range from seeing folk singers as shy, passive vessels, there only to be milked of their culture by the class enemy, to the idea that this process was somehow systematically 'de-humanizing and de-individualizing'. This aspect was given pace by the idea, first adumbrated in 1980 and developed in 1993, that the whole folk music movement represented no more than an attempt to heal, or at least to conceal, the divisions in an industrial society by romanticizing its sources and creating a 'construct', an

Figure 7. *Eliza Hutchings (Cecil Sharp Photograph Collection, B13-e)*

'Imagined Village', through which the nation could forget its discontents and conceive of itself as an idealized rural community.

Some of the photographs, especially those of women, show all too clearly the effects of lives spent in poverty and hard work—women such as Eliza Hutchings (Figure 7) or Betsy Pike, who was completely bald and only recognizable as a woman because of her dress. A case of romanticization, the creating of a rural idyll? I think not. I think that Sharp recognized the other side of the coin, that the human spirit, with its capacity to create and its need to express, can rise above disasters and attain a dignity all its own. Do Walter Locock (Figure 8) or Emma Overd (Figure 9) look like people who were systematically dehumanized and de-individualized? Once again, I think not—and perhaps I may be permitted the possibly sentimental point that without Sharp's work we would not even know these people's names, still less what they looked like.

The collection is in three parts: negatives; prints; and magic-lantern slides. Some photographs exist only as negatives, some only as prints, and some only as slides. This, and other difficulties I will discuss, make it very difficult to give exact numbers, or even reliable estimates. All that can be said is that there are more than 450 negatives and/or prints, and some 180 lantern slides. Excluding duplicates, Sharp probably took about three hundred photographs. Not all of these are 'source' photos. There are landscapes, town- and village-scapes. Besides singers,

Figure 8. *Walter Locock (Cecil Sharp Photograph Collection, B58-b)*

musicians, and dancers, Sharp also photographed relatives, non-singers, and even boys at Ludgrove School.

The only identification system is the negative card index, said to have been compiled by David Bland, though he says he does not remember doing so. The index is divided into five sections. 'A' and 'B' represent English scenes, most of them in Somerset. 'D' contains dance and folk customs. 'AD' includes some of the Appalachian lantern slides, and 'AC' the American negatives in general.

All that can be said about the present system of indexing is that it is a mess, and one that presents something of a mystery. Where we have the direct evidence from his American diaries, Sharp

Figure 9. *Emma Overd (Cecil Sharp Photograph Collection, B19-b)*

was very meticulous about indexing his negatives and prints and putting them into books. For example, in the entry for 16 October 1918, he writes, 'and in the afternoon have a long spell at my photos, getting copies into my book, negatives filed away and indexed'. He was at it again next day. There is no reason to believe that he was any less meticulous in England. So why are there so many missing photographs and pictures of unidentified people, of which there are perhaps sixty or seventy in the whole collection?

I believe that David Bland only worked on sections 'A' and 'B'. He says he found the photographs in a tin trunk with 'M. Karpeles' painted on the lid, and he must have had access to Sharp's own arrangement and indexing, because these sections contain references to photographs of Sharp's family that are no longer present. But at some time his arrangement was upset when section 'D' was formed and the photographs removed, usually without any indication of where they came from. From that time, the collection suffered from being treated in a piecemeal and arbitrary way. A decision seems to have been made not to include in the card index photographs that exist only as lantern slides. Some of these were twenty-two landscapes and 'context' scenes from the Appalachians.

The same policy was applied to section 'D', which seems to promise sixty-six items. However, several record cards have been removed, and there are only thirty-nine negatives or prints. The missing record cards probably referred to twenty-seven lantern slides, including Sharp's photos of the Earsdon and Swalwell sword sides and the Abbots Bromley Horn Dance. The overwhelming need is for an itemized catalogue, which would also take account of recent research, particularly census and other work on English singers and dancers, and the information that has become available from transcription of the American diaries. It is possible now to identify new people, such as Alice Snow, and to clear up confusion surrounding Appalachian photographs such as those of the Coffey family and Delie Hughes.

In conclusion, I would say this. Sharp's photograph collection deserves to be much better known to the outside world. The photographs need to be on public display, as Frank Meadow Sutcliffe's are in Whitby's art gallery. The photographs offer countless stories: personal ones; those of groups like Emma Overd and her neighbours in Knapp's Lane, and those of Lily Porter and her neighbour 'Jack Barnard'; and the great epic stories of Sharp's work in England and in the Appalachians. Many of you will have photographs like this one. This is me at primary school, aged ten (Figure 10). The eyes seem to look at you with the question: What have you done? What have you achieved? In the same way, in the collection the eyes seem to look out and ask: What have you done? What have you achieved in our cause?

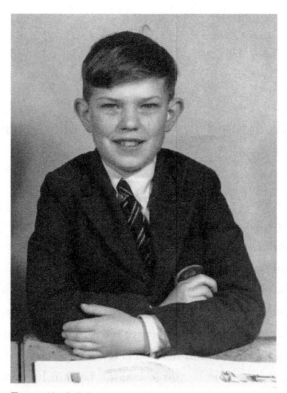

Figure 10. *C. J. Bearman, aged ten*

Eliza Wedgwood and Folk Song Collecting in Gloucestershire

PAUL BURGESS

Much has been written about the folk song collecting activities of Percy Grainger and Cecil Sharp in Gloucestershire,[1] but little has so far been heard of one of the most important figures who enabled this work. Eliza Wedgwood was a fascinating character who was responsible for finding all the singers from whom Grainger recorded songs in Gloucestershire, and several of those from whom Sharp obtained material. She was an important part of the John Singer Sargent artistic circle, and later put her formidable organizational skills at the disposal of the villagers in her adopted home of Stanton (Figure 1).

Robert Wedgwood, great-grandson of Josiah, was born in Etruria, the Wedgwood firm's suburb of Stoke-on-Trent. By the early 1850s he was rector of the parish of Dumbleton, in Gloucestershire, where he lived with a large household headed by his second wife, Mary Halsey, and including his five young daughters, the youngest of whom was born in 1860 and christened Eliza Melicent. He then built a new, more spacious rectory by the church at a location called Nutmeadow, into which the family moved around 1870 (the building has now been demolished). Following Robert's death in February 1881, Mary moved, along with her unmarried daughters, to The Manor at Stanton, an imposing Jacobean building dating from 1577.

Little is known about Eliza's early years, although as early as January 1879 a 'Miss Wedge-wood' (*sic*) provided the Folk-Lore Society with a full transcription of the Dumbleton mummers' play, taken down from one of the participants.[2] It may be that the mummers had includ-

---

1 Gwilym Davies, 'Percy Grainger's Folk Music Research in Gloucestershire, Worcestershire, and Warwickshire, 1907–1909', *Folk Music Journal*, 6.3 (1992), 339–58.

2 London, Folklore Society Archives, Thomas Fairman Ordish Collection, photocopy of typewritten transcription by Alex Helm (the original is missing) [Full English Digital Archive: TFO/1/10/2].

Figure 1. *Jane Emmet de Glehn*, Eliza Wedgwood, Frascati, *1908 (pencil, signed with initials, 23 × 20 cm). Courtesy of David Messum Fine Art*

ed the rectory in their tour the previous Christmas. According to census records, only three of the Wedgwood sisters were living at home at that time, and although any of the three would be a candidate for having undertaken this work, it is possible that the nineteen-year old Eliza was responsible. A note to the manuscript reads as follows:

> Note: the above has been acted at Dumbleton from time immemorial. There is no written record but it is handed down verbally from generation to generation. The mummers get themselves up in any bright coloured articles they can get given to them and they always wear a High sugar loaf hat covered with ends of ribbon etc.

This shows that the young author was quite aware of the kind of questions that collectors should ask traditional performers.

In 1885, the famous American artist John Singer Sargent had moved from Paris (where he had painted Monet) to London, but subsequently needed to recover from a bad head injury occasioned when he dived into a weir. To aid his recuperation, his friend Edwin Austen Abbey invited him to stay with the painter G. F. Millet in the secluded village of Broadway, three miles from Stanton. While he was there, Sargent painted two well-known canvases, *At Broadway, 1885* and *Carnation, Lily, Lily, Rose*.[3] The artistic community at Broadway included several expatriate Americans, who were well known to the Wedgwood family. After Sargent had painted a portrait of her cousin, Lancelot Allen, in 1894, Eliza approached one of the Broadway artists, Alfred Parsons, to act as an intermediary in delivering her request that Sargent paint her mother. Sargent replied that he would be delighted to do so, and quoted a fee of £250.

Following this, Mrs Wedgwood sat twelve times for a first version of the portrait, although Sargent found himself unable to complete the beautiful but 'headless' portrait, as 'the charm he tried to catch on canvas was so variable and fleeting'.[4] Soon, however, 'Sargent was struck by a new possibility as he was talking to Mrs Wedgwood in her garden, and asked her to do it again', which led to the successful completion of the portrait. In the course of creating these two paintings of *Mrs Robert Wedgwood* in 1896, Sargent 'began a close and life-long friendship with her daughter Eliza'. This would include annual travels with the group of artists to destinations such as Florence, Frascati, Majorca, and Corfu, where they would spend their time painting:

> Every autumn we spent together the routine was the same — breakfast generally 7.30, afterwards work literally all day till the light failed. At rare intervals an excursion — if very hot a siesta after the midday meal, but work was the order of the day — when possible, a bathe the end of the morning. After dinner duets and chess — & early to

---

3   A number of Sargent's paintings from this period can be viewed online:
    At Broadway, 1885 <http://www.wikipaintings.org/en/john-singer-sargent/landscape-at-broadway-1885>
    Carnation, Lily, Lily, Rose <http://www.tate.org.uk/art/artworks/sargent-carnation-lily-lily-rose-n01615>
    Millet's Garden <http://www.wikipaintings.org/en/john-singer-sargent/millet-s-garden-1886>
    Mrs Robert Wedgwood <http://www.bbc.co.uk/arts/yourpaintings/paintings/mrs-robert-wedgwood-d-1906-20307>
    Miss Eliza Wedgwood and Miss Sargent Sketching <https://www.tate.org.uk/art/artworks/sargent-miss-eliza-wedgwood-and-miss-sargent-sketching-n03658>
    Mosquito Nets <http://www.wikipaintings.org/en/john-singer-sargent/mosquito-nets-1908>
    Portrait of Miss Eliza Wedgwood <http://www.encore-editions.com/john-singer-sargent-portrait-of-miss-eliza-wedgwood>.
4   E. Wedgwood, 'Memoir' [in the form of a letter to Sargent's biographer, E. Charteris, 22 November 1925], pp. 6–7.

bed. I was the drone of the party, but allowed to sit and watch John for hours at a time; I don't think he was conscious of my presence, or if he were he didn't mind, but I incline to the first—he was so absorbed in his work that he was oblivious of all else.

Although most of her sisters had left the family home, Eliza continued to live with her elderly mother until the latter's death early in 1906. Mrs Wedgwood always treated her youngest daughter as though she were still a child, albeit an exceptionally useful and industrious one, to the extent that so long as her mother lived, Eliza was primarily—indeed, almost professionally—a daughter, and can scarcely be said to have been allowed to become a person in her own right.[5] She was forty-seven when her mother died and she found herself 'in the same department as Emily [John Singer Sargent's sister] [...] a spinster landed with freedom for the first time in advanced middle age'.

The following year, the Stanton estate was sold, and Eliza had to look for new lodgings. These she found at Charity Farm, towards the top of the hill in Stanton (known as 'Above Town'), described as 'that orchard-set, grey-gabled cottage which became so dear to numbers of people, both for its own Cotswold charm and as the very personal setting of a much-loved friend' (Figure 2). The building next door to Charity farmhouse was a beer-house called The Bank—known popularly as 'The Five Elms', due to its not having an indoor licence and therefore requiring its customers to drink their beer and cider, which were served from an outhouse, on the other side of the gate, next to five elm trees.[6] (At a later date, the proximity of refreshment was perhaps used as an inducement to persuade the singers to visit.) It had been thought that when she left The Manor, Eliza would be leaving the village altogether, so a subscription was raised and the villagers presented her with a silver cup, rather unfortunately inscribed 'Presented to Miss Eliza Wedgwood in token of gratitude on her leaving the village of Stanton'.[7]

At this time, Eliza held the position of secretary to Mary Wemys, Lady Elcho, wife of the third Baron Wemys, of Stanway House, near Winchcombe, Gloucestershire. Although in paid employment, Eliza was also one of the family's dearest friends. Mary Elcho's daughter, Cynthia Asquith, wrote: 'The great devotion of Eliza's life was to my mother; and to a share of this devotion all my mother's children and their children too succeeded by mere hereditary right. I can remember no phase of family life certainly no crisis of any note in which she did

5   Cynthia Asquith, *Remember and Be Glad* (New York: Charles Scribner's Sons, 1952), p. 152.

6   <http:themountinn.co.uk/history.php>.

7   Asquith, *Remember and Be Glad*, p. 155.

Figure 2. *Charity Farm, Stanton, Gloucestershire (photo Paul Burgess)*

not take intimate part.'[8] Mary Elcho and her husband were interested in the arts and were members of the group known as The Souls. Jane Ridley describes this as 'a late Victorian aristocratic clique loosely linked to the Conservative politician [and ex-prime minister, Sir] Arthur James Balfour [. . .] cultivating personal intimacy and friendship rather than field sports and ostentatious display [. . . they] combined the characteristics of the Holland House set and the Bloomsbury Group.'[9] Mary Elcho and Arthur Balfour were very close and conducted an *amour aimable* for many years. Eliza herself, through her friendship with Sargent, was also associated with the Chelsea Set, and the two groups often combined to attend artistic evenings at the London home of William Gair Rathbone.

---

8   Asquith, *Remember and Be Glad*, p. 155.
9   Jane Ridley, 'Souls (act. 1886–1911)', *Oxford Dictionary of National Biography*, online edn <http://www.oxforddnb.com/view/theme/42005> [accessed 17 February 2015].

William Gair Rathbone (1849–1919) was a wealthy Liverpool industrialist.[10] As well as being a partner in Rathbone Brothers, an investment management company that originally traded in cotton and later became the Liverpool agents for the East India Company, he was also a director of the London and County Bank, the Hong Kong and Shanghai Bank, and the Royal Exchange Corporation. In keeping with his family's long history of supporting the arts, he was responsible for sponsoring and substantially aiding the careers of the Hungarian composer Zoltán Kodály and the American painter John Singer Sargent, as well as the Australian pianist and composer Percy Grainger. He had been introduced to Grainger by the actor Ernest Thesiger, and it was also via this route that he had met Sargent. Rathbone held musical soirées at Cadogan Gardens. These were much appreciated by Grainger, who felt that at Rathbone's gatherings he was appreciated by artistically sensitive companions—rather than being 'tortured', as was the case at other society 'at-homes'. It was there, too, that Grainger and his mother, Rose, met Eliza Wedgwood and Lady Elcho.

It may well have been at one of Rathbone's soirées that they learned of Grainger's folk song collecting, which seems to have inspired them to see whether there was anything of interest in their own area of Gloucestershire. By September 1906 they had collected some sets of words of folk songs from Mrs Hawker at Broad Campden, a village about halfway between Stanway and the larger village of Chipping Campden. However, neither Wedgwood nor Elcho was sufficiently musically literate to transcribe a melody from the singing of a traditional singer, so they were keen to enlist some help. Rose Grainger was also enthused with the prospect of folk song collecting, and together they drafted in Percy to assist. Rose stayed with Wedgwood in November 1907 and arranged for Percy to join them following a concert performance at Cheltenham.

Wedgwood, whom Grainger described as 'a dear old maid',[11] took Grainger to Broad Campden, to visit the 71-year-old Mrs Hawker, who sang him 'The Drummer Boy' (Roud 226) and 'The Spotty Cow' (Roud 956), the words of which Wedgwood and Elcho had collected two months previously.[12] She then arranged for a group of four local singers to come to her home at Charity Farm. Grainger found that two of the four, John Collett and William

---

10 Youssef Cassis, *City Bankers, 1890–1914* (Cambridge: Éditions de la Maison des Sciences de l'Homme and Cambridge University Press, 1994), p. 171.

11 Percy Grainger to Karen Holten, 18 November 1907, in Kay Dreyfus, ed., *The Farthest North of Humanness: Letters of Percy Grainger, 1901–14* (Basingstoke: Macmillan, 1985), p. 162.

12 London, Vaughan Williams Memorial Library, Percy Grainger Collection, no. 315 [Full English Digital Archive: PG/5/220].

Newman, were able to provide worthwhile material, and he proceeded to note down several items which he found of considerable interest. He especially commented on John Collett's version of 'Green Bushes' (Roud 1040), saying, 'It is really a remarkable feeling, after one has composed so long around a melody like this (& has ½ come to think of it as one's own) to hear it in the mouth of such an amusing old man!'[13] At the time Collett sang for Grainger he was aged fifty-nine — so he wasn't quite as old as one might think, although he may have well have seemed that way to the 24-year-old Grainger. This appears to have been a successful trip for Grainger, but he probably had no intention of returning to the Cotswolds after he had exhausted the contacts that Wedgwood had thus far been able to supply at short notice.

In December 1907, William Gair Rathbone's daughter Elena, an enthusiastic member of the Folk-Song Society, had attended Grainger's talk on collecting folk songs with the phonograph at the society's AGM.[14] Then, over the New Year, she went to stay with Eliza Wedgwood at Stanton. Elena could write music and so, on New Year's Day, 1908, the two young ladies went to Winchcombe Workhouse to collect some songs. There they met William 'Daddy' Shepherd and Elena Rathbone wrote out the words and music of one of his songs, which she called 'Yonder Sits a Spanish Lady', a version of 'O No John' (Roud 146). Cecil Sharp also collected this song from 'Daddy' Shepherd a little over a year later and his notation has only one note different from that of Elena Rathbone, and only one line of the text differs.[15] Considering that this was Rathbone's first attempt to note a song from an elderly traditional singer, she shows an impressive accuracy.

The following day Rathbone wrote to Percy Grainger, enclosing a copy of the song she had collected and imploring Grainger to visit Gloucestershire again at the earliest possible opportunity. She wrote:

> We had a splendid afternoon at the Winchcombe workhouse yesterday afternoon.
> Several old men sang, one of [whom?] seemed to me promising. He knew a lot of

13 Grainger to Holten, 18 November 1907.

14 Elena Rathbone (1878–1964) was an astonishing young woman, described by Virginia Woolf in a letter to Vanessa Bell of 20 February 1922: 'I think she is quite the nicest human being I have ever met — solid — splendid — sedate — with the body of a matron and the mind of a child and the tastes of a schoolboy; so maternal to me that I fell in love with her at once — Perhaps I always have been in love with her.' She married Bruce Richmond, editor of the *Times Literary Supplement*, and became Lady Richmond. She continued to support Grainger throughout his life, and some of his compositions are dedicated to her. In addition, she was a champion of midwifery and nursing.

15 Cambridge, Clare College Archives, CCPP/SHA, Cecil Sharp Collection of Folk Song Manuscripts, Folk Tunes 2148, Folk Words 2015–2016 [Full English Digital Archive: CJS2/9/2015, CJS2/10/2148].

'Lord Bateman' who to my ignorant ears was the real thing & the words not familiar, but I know nothing about it anyway. I should think he was well worth a try with a phonograph. He sang rather low but said his words very distinctly. Alas! We had to catch a train & began Lord Bateman at the end of our time so we could not have it repeated & I didn't get the words. Before that he sang the enclosed song ['Yonder Sits a Spanish Lady']. I guess the last line will be wrong & you'll laugh at my first effort at recording, & probably everyone but me would know all about it isn't a folk song—??? There is a one-eyed old person with no teeth & a stammer who sang the 'Limerick Races' of which I have what I understand of the words. They also sang Green Bushes and the Draggle Tail Gypsies best [?] of all, they were very keen to sing & had been racking their old brains & trying to remember all they knew. I shall come bothering Mrs Grainger & ask to be shown how to take down for Miss Wedgwood songs I may come again and try. She hopes you'll come whenever you can & that you will just wire 'coming'. A room will be found & the old men collected. We did so wish you'd been here yesterday & we felt so helpless before the beautiful opportunities which we couldn't cope with. They were so nice & dear, I wish we could have stayed much longer & talked with them. There's a delightful old woman too, who sings, but I rather thought the songs she sang yesterday were not v[er]y interesting, but clear & concise was the best & by way of being Scotch. She's v[er]y well educated & writes out the words herself in a fine round hand.

The old men are nearly all shepherds.

Such a gorgeous clean, cold good-to-be-alive day! Isn't this the nicest place in the world to stay?[16]

It may not be a coincidence that, immediately following the suggestion of his patron's daughter that the singers 'may well be worth a try with a phonograph', Grainger purchased such an item and, by early April 1908, was once again visiting Gloucestershire, this time to stay as a guest of Lady Elcho at Stanway House. There is no sign of Grainger feeling that he was being treated as a 'performing monkey' at this weekend—his letters show that he thoroughly enjoyed both the company and the entertainment. There was a glittering social array of other guests, including John Singer Sargent, H. G. Wells and his wife, J. M. Barrie, and Arthur Balfour, whose Rolls-Royce was used to take the party out to visit singers. Grainger loved this: 'Balfour's motor is a dream and he a dear beyond words.' Again, he was able to go

16 Melbourne, Grainger Museum, Elena Rathbone to Percy Grainger, 1 January 1908. Many thanks to the staff at the Grainger Museum for their help in providing me with a copy of this letter. Previously, this letter has been ascribed to 'Stella' Rathbone—Elena's curious signature makes this error perfectly understandable.

folk song hunting during the day, while the evenings were spent encouraging the other guests to sing Bach.

Grainger seems to have been absolutely delighted with the preparatory work and help he received from Wedgwood, and arranged that she should use the phonograph after his departure to continue the collecting work in Gloucestershire. This was at a period when he was constantly using the phonograph to continuously replay some of the cylinders he had recorded in Lincolnshire, in order to make the extremely detailed transcriptions for publication in the *Journal of the Folk-Song Society*. Unless Grainger had been able to borrow the phonograph belonging to the Folk-Song Society, there would have been a fairly small window of opportunity for Wedgwood to use the machine. After he had finished his transcription work, he would have had to deliver the machine to Stanton, and then Wedgwood would have had to send it back to London in time for Grainger to record shanties from Charles Rosher on 5 May 1908.

As it transpired, Wedgwood recorded on only one day, 24 April. However, she obviously put some planning into this session, recording seven cylinders, including the final item, 'Shepherd's Song', from George 'Daddy' Lane which had not been recorded earlier in the month, two cylinders of the Warwickshire morris fiddler and singer Sam Bennett, and important items from two new singers who had recently been admitted to the workhouse. These last were Elizabeth Teale, from whom she recorded 'Lord Lovel', and Mary Anne Roberts, who sang 'Cold Blows the Wind' and 'The Rich Bristol Squire'. Grainger, however, had to put these to one side, for at this time he was nursing his article for the *Journal of the Folk-Song Society* through the publication process, after which other things started to impinge, not least an unexpected and lengthy tour of Australia. For her part, Wedgwood joined up with the Sargents and the De Glehns and travelled with them for a lengthy stay in Corfu.

Grainger made one final visit to Gloucestershire in order to record singers. Wedgwood enticed him back by discovering a singer, Mrs Wixey, who sang a version of 'Bold Bonny Boy', a piece Grainger knew and loved but had never heard 'in the field'. Consequently, he arrived with a number of cylinders dedicated to obtaining this item. Wedgwood, however, had lined up several more singers, as well as jogging the memories of some whom Grainger had already encountered in order to produce new songs. In the event, Grainger spent the lion's share of his time with Mrs Wixey and ran out of recording cylinders, having to make pencil and paper notations of the final songs, from William Newman. He also met Cecil Sharp at Wedgwood's house on 9 August 1909, although no mention remains of what transpired or what they discussed. These were the last songs Grainger recorded in the county. There remain four more songs in the Grainger collection for which Wedgwood had collected the words but no tune: 'The Nightingale Sings' from 'Daddy' Lane, 'The Lost Lady Found' and 'The Spotted Cow' from William Martin, and 'I Lived with my Grandmother' from Mary Ann Roberts.[17]

Grainger's working relationship with Wedgwood was similar to his modus operandi elsewhere. He relied on other people to find singers and organize meetings with them, leaving him to record them and transcribe the results. He described his intentions with regard to Gloucestershire as follows: 'Miss Wedgewood [*sic*] can begin first (fertilising the soil) and mother can come with the phonograph and pluck the flowers.'[18] However, he was scrupulous to give credit where it was due. So, against the first songs he noted in Gloucestershire he records that he collected the tune but specifically mentions that the words were collected by Wedgwood.

Some fifty years after the event, Grainger published a book of anecdotes—a mixture of elucidation, recollection, spite, and invention.[19] His story about having hidden under a bed in order to trick an ailing old man into singing a song he particularly wished to record has been shown to be pure fabrication.[20] It is strange, too, that his recollection of H. G. Wells's comment, that during his folk song collecting trips Grainger was not trying to document the songs 'but to record life itself', was not recorded at the time—and it is worryingly similar to a statement made by the protagonist in Wells's novel *Tono-Bungay* (1909): 'I suppose what I'm really trying to render is nothing more nor less than Life.' Grainger's anecdote concerning Wedgwood is that, following a singer's song performance, she had asked whether she would be interested in selling her chest of drawers, a suggestion the singer politely declined. Grainger says that this showed Wedgwood to be 'fussy, go-getting and greedy'—a complete reversal from his previous comments about her. There is nothing to suggest that Grainger had anything but the highest admiration for Wedgwood before this spiteful anecdote, conveniently recollected when its subject was no longer able to give her side of the story.

Cecil Sharp had also turned his attention to Gloucestershire at the behest of a lady, in his case Mary Neal, where he found the contacts that would lead to him recording the morris

17 Jane O'Brien, *The Grainger English Folk Song Collection*, Nedlands, WA: Department of Music, University of Western Australia, 1983), nos 378, 379, 380, 381, respectively.

18 Grainger to Holten, 18 November 1907.

19 A collection of handwritten autobiographical notes written between 1949 and 1954, located at the Grainger Archives, White Plains, NY, and published in Malcolm Gillies, David Pear, and Mark Carroll, eds, *Self-Portrait of Percy Grainger* (Oxford, Oxford University Press, 2006).

20 C. J. Bearman, 'Percy Grainger, the Phonograph, and the Folk Song Society', *Music & Letters*, 83 (2003), 434–55.

dance traditions at Longborough, Sherborne, and Bledington.[21] However, he also used the services of Eliza Wedgwood to identify potential singers, visiting her from 5 to 7 April 1909, at a time when, as Roy Judge notes, 'The village [Stanton] was preparing for an entertainment consisting of Morris dancing, old English folk songs, and games on 23 April, Shakespeare's birthday, under the guidance of Florrie Warren.'[22] Wedgwood passed him a set of words of the 'Shepherd's Song' from George 'Daddy' Lane, who had died a few months previously. She also introduced him to some of the singers at Winchcombe Workhouse and in the neighbourhood, who provided him with various songs and carols, for which she received thanks in the introduction to Sharp's *English Traditional Carols*. She also appears to have passed on the names of two possible sources for country dances, and sent him to William Swallow and John Cook, at Lower Guiting, who played fiddle tunes and talked to Sharp about the morris dancing at Guiting Power.

A year after his visit, Sharp wrote to Wedgwood in order to try and persuade her to use her contacts in support of his attempts to gain influence at the Stratford-upon-Avon festival, against Mary Neal. In his letter he specifically notes that he had not referred to any of the animosity between himself and Mary Neal when he had visited Eliza previously, but now he felt he had to enlist her help: 'I have never mentioned controversial matters with you because we had so many pleasanter things to talk about and I did not want you to be dragged in.'[23] He then attacks Neal and her work at length, and in vigorous terms: 'It is piteous to see a nice girl like Florrie Warren, a born teacher and girl of remarkable ability wasting and misusing her talents all for the lack of proper instruction. When I met her at your house last year she was most eager that I should put her right and agreed to come and see me on my return to town.' And he accuses Neal of changing the material of the dances: 'These she has altered, changed the steps and — worst of all — altered the traditional tunes. This no doubt she was compelled to do to evade the infringement of copyright, but the fact that she could do such an act of vandalism — and for commercial considerations — shows the real spirit which animates her.' This shows, as Roy Judge notes, Sharp's 'rejection of what he saw as faked, revived and decadent. These judgements would be based on his own idealism and his feeling that anything approved

---

21 Paul Burgess, 'The Mystery of the Whistling Sewermen: How Cecil Sharp Discovered Gloucestershire Morris Dancing', *Folk Music Journal*, 8.2 (2002), 178–94.

22 Roy Judge, 'Cecil Sharp and Morris, 1906–1909', *Folk Music Journal*, 8.2 (2002), 195–228 (p. 211).

23 London, EFDSS Archives, Cecil Sharp Collection, Correspondence, Cecil Sharp to Eliza Wedgwood, 22 August 1910.

by Mary Neal must be wrong.'[24] We have no evidence as to whether Wedgwood did use her influence among her acquaintances at Stratford in Sharp's favour. Indeed, there is no evidence that she had any further contact with folk music or folk music collectors.

Wedgwood remained great friends with the Sargent family and accompanied them on their regular late summer tours abroad for a number of years. Although she appears to have attempted no further folk song collecting in the area, she remained in active contact with Winchcombe Workhouse, taking the inmates out to entertain them, the men at Stanway and the women and children at her own house, providing Christmas cheer, and the like. During the First World War she worked in the local hospital, where she was 'Commandant' and nicknamed 'the Queen of Stanton'. Later, she seems to have settled into village life, taking an active part in village affairs and enjoying the company of friends and neighbours, among whom Mary Anderson, the American tragic actress, was her closest friend.[25]

Even in her seventies, Eliza Wedgwood could be described as 'the finest person I know, a pure delight, with the vitality of youth — with such laughter and wisdom and pity and tolerance and wit all merged — to be with her is like drinking some rich cordial that gives one new life'.[26] William Rothenstein remembered her thus:

> Eliza Wedgwood [. . .] with her lace mantilla about her fine head, and her chiselled conversation, puts me in mind of the great French ladies of the eighteenth century, of Madame du Deffand, of Madame de Sévigné. Her cottage overlooks a landscape Madox Brown might have painted, and to her windows come blackbirds, thrushes and nuthatches each day, to take food from her hand. She had originally put out a glove on a stick on to which the birds hopped; and when, after some weeks, she put out her own hand they fed from it as from the glove. Eliza charmed the birds as she charmed her friends.[27]

She again found herself in the role of carer: earlier she had stayed at home with her widowed mother; now she found herself nursing an older sister. She helped found the North Cotswold group of Women's Institutes, and was fondly remembered for using her car to take

24 Judge, 'Cecil Sharp and Morris', p. 224.
25 Mary Anderson (1859–1940) suffered a breakdown on stage and then retired and moved to Court Farm, Broadway, Worcestershire, where she married Antonio Navarro. She was the model for the heroine of William Black's *The Strange Adventures of a House-Boat* and possibly for Lucia in E. F. Benson's Mapp and Lucia stories.
26 Dorothy Warren, *The World of Ruth Draper; A Portrait of an Actress* (Carbondale: Southern Illinois University Press, 1999), p. 150.
27 William Rothenstein, *Since Fifty* (New York, Macmillan, 1940), p. 186.

poorly villagers to the doctor or dentist, and for paying for the children's treatment. Later in life she was a familiar figure around the streets and lanes, walking with a stick, accompanied by her pug, Boot. Her great friend and confidante, Mary Anderson, died in 1940, which was a grave blow to her.

Eliza Wedgwood died 'full of years' in 1947. Her obituary in *The Times* said she was 'a picturesque figure whose nobility of nature and qualities of heart, mind and spirit had endeared her to three generations'.[28] One of her final acts was typical of her. When a new council estate was to be built at Stanton, she was dismayed and paid out of her own funds for all the new buildings to be provided with traditional Cotswold stone roofs.

28 *The Times*, 11 April 1947.

Old Songs and Sugar Mice:
The Story of the Remarkable Miss Mason — *summary*

MARTIN GRAEBE

Published in full in *Folk Music Journal*, 10.4 (2014), 449–77.

Marianne Harriet Mason (1845–1932) was, by any standards, a remarkable woman. There were many ways in which she excelled. She was the first female inspector in the Civil Service, and thus the first senior female civil servant in Britain; a plant collector and expert on alpine gardening; a knowledgeable collector and restorer of old furniture; a psychical researcher; a fellow of the Royal Geographical Society; and a well-regarded painter of South African wild flowers, whose collection of paintings was presented to the nation. And, in this context, most important, she was the first woman to collect traditional songs anywhere in the world. Her *Nursery Rhymes and Country Songs*, published in 1877, was the first collection of traditional songs obtained orally, and presented with piano arrangements intended for the drawing room, to be made available to the public.[1]

Nursery Rhymes and Country Songs has been described as 'the swallow that ushered in the summer'—i.e. the late Victorian folk song revival.[2] Though she moved on to other activities, she never lost her interest in traditional song. She met a number of the other Victorian collectors and was a friend of Sabine Baring-Gould and Lucy Broadwood. In the article Martin Graebe examines Mason's life and work, describes and analyses the collection of songs that she

---

1   M. H. Mason, *Nursery Rhymes and Country Songs, both tunes and words from tradition* (London: Metzler, 1877). The date is sometimes given as 1878, but the preface is dated October 1877 and it was advertised for sale in December of that year.
2   David Gregory, *Victorian Songhunters: The Recovery and Editing of English Vernacular Ballads and Folk Lyrics, 1820–1883* (Lanham, MD: Scarecrow Press, 2006), p. 359.

made, and considers its importance as a pioneering work of folk song publication. Previously unpublished details of her life have been found in articles written by her and in the autobiographical memoir, *A Pioneer Life*, that she left behind in manuscript.[3] This, she tells us, was based on the personal diaries that she kept from her teenage years and on the extensive records that she kept of her work as a government inspector.

Mason was reluctant to call her songs 'folk songs'. Most of them were sung in her grandfather's family, the Mitfords, and many of the rest came from people close to the Mason family. Contemporary views on who 'the folk' are would exclude such a family because of its social class, though it is increasingly clear that people of this social class played a significant role in the preservation of traditional song—particularly nursery songs, hunting songs, and ballads. Though her achievement is dwarfed by many who collected after her, Marianne Mason's claim to be a pioneer in song collecting, as in the other fields she worked in, deserves to be recognized.

---

3 Nottinghamshire Archive, DD716/51, M. H. Mason, *A Pioneer Life*, typescript autobiography, incompletely paginated and heavily corrected by hand. The date of the typescript is not given, but the sections are marked as having been revised in 1925.

Maud Karpeles and her Folk Song Collecting

DEREK SCHOFIELD

In 2011, in a paper on Maud Karpeles's folk dance collecting following the death of Cecil Sharp, I argued that, far from continuing Sharp's work, she collected dance styles that had been neglected by Sharp.[1] As Simona Pakenham writes about Maud's folk dance collecting: 'She felt both inadequate and melancholy attempting this on her own, but the activity gave her more of a feeling that she was carrying on his work than she obtained from sitting on committees or delivering her lecture-sermons.'[2]

After Sharp's death, any correspondence to the English Folk Dance Society that contained information about traditional dances (and songs, especially after the merger of the song and dance societies in 1932) was seemingly passed on to Karpeles to deal with. With a small private income, she was not constrained by work and had the freedom to travel in order to collect. Among the dances she collected, and which Sharp had neglected, were morris dances from Herefordshire, Worcestershire, and Lancashire, including the dances of the Britannia Coconut Dancers of Bacup, and traditional social dances from Northumberland, the Lake District, and Dorset. She tended to avoid the core of Sharp's collection—south Midlands morris, sword, and interpretations of Playford dances. Karpeles's folk dance collecting extended the existing knowledge of folk dance, and I concluded: 'Her dance collecting confirms

1 Derek Schofield, '"Groping in a Sunless World": Maud Karpeles as Folk Dance Collector and Promoter, 1925–1935', paper presented at the conference As if Possessed: Celebrating the Life and Work of Maud Karpeles, London, Cecil Sharp House, 1 October 2011.

2 Simona Pakenham, *Singing and Dancing Wherever She Goes: A Life of Maud Karpeles* (London: English Folk Dance and Song Society, 2011), pp. 164–66.

Maud Karpeles as an important collector in her own right, and not merely as someone who "carried on Sharp's work".[3]

Does this argument, and that conclusion, apply equally to Maud Karpeles's folk song collecting?

It had been Sharp's intention to visit Newfoundland to see if, as in Appalachia, there was a store of folk songs of English origin there. A lack of funds, coupled with the need to restart the folk dance revival after the First World War, not to mention Sharp's increasingly poor health, prevented such a trip. It fell to Karpeles to fulfil his dream, and in 1929 and 1930 she travelled to Newfoundland to collect folk songs.[4] Those visits have been investigated by David Gregory, Martin Lovelace, and others.[5] In addition, Gregory has written about Maud's limited song collecting in other parts of Canada.[6] It is therefore her collecting in England and Wales on which I want to concentrate.

Not that there is much to concentrate on. Her manuscripts reveal, I think, that songs did not generally come from systematic collecting trips in England and Wales, and that some were noted as the result of chance meetings. The first songs in the manuscripts were noted from Mr and Mrs Miles, of Woodlands, Dorset, in 1927. The words of three songs — 'My Mother Bid Me' ('An Old Man Came Courting Me'), 'Dark Eyed Sailor', and 'Billy Boy' — are given, and she records that Ralph Vaughan Williams had noted the tunes.[7] The tunes have not, however, been located in Vaughan Williams's collection. There is no further information. Were the songs collected in Dorset, and if so why were Karpeles and Vaughan Williams in this remote Dorset village? Or were Mr and Mrs Miles visiting London? Or did Maud memorize the

3 Schofield, 'Groping in a Sunless World'.

4 Maud Karpeles, *Folk Songs from Newfoundland* (London: Faber and Faber, 1971).

5 Carole Henderson Carpenter, 'Forty Years Later: Maud Karpeles in Newfoundland', in *Folklore Studies in Honour of Herbert Halpert: A Festschrift*, ed. Kenneth S. Goldstein and Neil V. Rosenberg (St. John's: Memorial University of Newfoundland, 1980), pp. 111–24; David Gregory, 'Maud Karpeles, Newfoundland, and the Crisis of the Folksong Revival, 1924–1935', *Newfoundland Studies*, 16.2 (2000), 151–65; David Gregory, 'Song Collecting in Newfoundland: Maud Karpeles, 1930', *Canadian Folk Music*, 42.4 (2008), 1–13; Anna Kearney Guigné, *Maud Karpeles (1885–1976): A Retrospective of Her Newfoundland Fieldwork, 1929 and 1930* (St. John's: Memorial University of Newfoundland, 2011); Martin Lovelace, 'Unnatural Selection: Maud Karpeles's Newfoundland Field Diaries', in *Folk Song: Tradition, Revival, and Re-Creation*, ed. Ian Russell and David Atkinson (Aberdeen: Elphinstone Institute, University of Aberdeen, 2004), pp. 284–98; Neil V. Rosenberg, '"She's Like the Swallow": Folksong as Cultural Icon', *Newfoundland and Labrador Studies*, 22.1 (2007) <http://journals.hil.unb.ca/index.php/NFLDS/article/view/10098/10353> [accessed 28 March 2014].

6 David Gregory, 'Before Newfoundland: Maud Karpeles in Canada', *Canadian Folk Music Bulletin*, 37.1 (2003), 1–8.

7 London, EFDSS Archives, Maud Karpeles Collection, MK/1/1/4422, MK/1/14424, MK/1/1/4426.

tunes, which were later notated by Vaughan Williams? But why are the tunes missing? Karpeles does, however, reveal a concern in her unpublished autobiography: 'My fear that I should not be competent to note the tunes deterred me for some time, for I had little musicianship in the sense of being able to see what I heard and hear what I saw. So I endeavoured to train myself by writing down tunes that I already knew.'[8]

In July 1929, in Canada, she collected songs from Ida Ruttle in Peterborough, Ontario, publishing them in the 1930 issue of the *Journal of the Folk-Song Society*, including the comparatively rare song, 'Lady Leroy'.[9] Then she moved on to Newfoundland, where the experience of the intensive collecting trips in 1929 and 1930 no doubt honed her skills in music notation — but there was no resulting increase in her song collecting in England.

The first post-Newfoundland entry in her manuscripts is dated May 1932, when Karpeles collected the tune and first verse of 'Green Broom' from Abraham Young, aged eighty-three, in Kilvedon, Essex.[10] The next entry is almost nine months later: 'Lord Lovel' from Mrs Clara Chapman, aged sixty-nine, of Balham, noted in Hampstead in January 1933.[11] How she came to meet these people is unknown.

A few weeks later, on 8 March 1933, she noted three songs from a phonograph recording of Sir Frank Short. Then aged seventy-five, Short was born in Stourbridge, Worcestershire, and studied at art school, becoming a distinguished engraver and etcher. He had taught at the Royal College of Art and was president of the Royal Society of Painters-Etchers.[12] The songs were 'Farmers Marco and Pedro' (learned from his father and his father before him), 'Joan's Ale', and 'The Twelve Apostles'.[13] In addition to the phonograph recording, Karpeles was able to draw upon Frank Short's daughter's singing of the same songs, and she also provided a fourth song, 'Pigs' Tails', learned from her father.[14]

Only the tunes and first verses are given for these post-Newfoundland songs. Karpeles followed Sharp's practice of putting song words in one notebook (Folk Words) and tunes in another (Folk Tunes). The pages are numbered differently in each notebook. Her Folk Words book ends at 4645, in August 1929, and another book starts at 4904. It is not clear what happened to pages 4646–4903. Perhaps there is a lost 'words' notebook which contained the

8   Karpeles Collection, MK/7/185, Maud Karpeles, unpublished autobiography, p. 157.
9   *Journal of the Folk-Song Society*, 8.4 (no. 34) (1930), 218–30.
10 Karpeles Collection, MK/1/4/5333.
11 Karpeles Collection, MK/1/4/5334.
12 <http://collection.britishcouncil.org/collection/artist/5/17601> [accessed 28 March 2014].
13 Karpeles Collection, MK/1/4/5335–5337.
14 Karpeles Collection, MK/1/4/5338.

words of the songs just mentioned, or perhaps there is no missing book and she just did not bother to note in full the words of well-known songs such as 'Joan's Ale'.

Another Hampstead-collected song was 'The Three Sons' ('King Arthur Had Three Sons'), from Miss Ruth, on 14 May 1934, who had learned it from her mother (who was from Shepton Mallet, Somerset), who in turn had it from her mother. In this case, the words are written into the Folk Tunes notebook.[15] In August 1937, in the Aran Islands, Co. Galway, with her nephew John Kennedy, Karpeles collected three songs.[16] Then in January 1938 she collected a tune and variant and one verse of 'The Nobleman and the Thresherman' from James Turney, of Slapton, Buckinghamshire.[17]

This brings us up to the start of the Second World War, although we need to backtrack slightly to examine Karpeles's collecting in South Wales. Her first collecting trip to Wales was in April 1928. From Mrs Brown, of Southgate, Penmaen, she collected a 'Wassail Song' and 'Young Roger'.[18] A version of the 'Wassail Song' was also noted from Edwin Ace, of Llangennith, and his version was published in the 1930 *Journal of the Folk-Song Society*.[19] Again, there is no clear reason why Karpeles was in South Wales. Penmaen and Llangennith are on the Gower peninsula and Llangennith was the home village of the traditional singer Phil Tanner, who sang the same version of the 'Wassail Song' and also sang 'Young Roger Esquire'. But on this 1928 visit, Karpeles did not come across Phil Tanner—surprisingly, because the accounts of his life suggest that he was well known in the area.

In 1932 Phil Tanner turned up during an evening sing-song at a holiday camp for unemployed workers and their families and sang sentimental songs as well as folk songs. One of the student helpers, F. A. Bracey, recognized the value of his songs and in 1937 arranged for Tanner to visit London.[20] In the meantime, Karpeles must have found out about Tanner and in August 1936 she was back in Gower and noted two songs from him—'Ten Joys of Mary' and 'Henry Martin'.[21] Surprisingly, though, she did not publish either of the songs, and neither does she seem to have noted any of the other songs in Tanner's repertoire—this is in spite of writing in her autobiography, 'One of the best singers I ever heard was Phil Tanner, of Glamorganshire, who was introduced to me by Mr B [presumably 'Bracey']. Happily he

15 Karpeles Collection, MK/1/4/5339.

16 Karpeles Collection, MK/1/4/5349–5352.

17 Karpeles Collection, MK/1/4/5353.

18 Karpeles Collection, MK/1/3/4992c–4993.

19 Karpeles Collection, MK/1/3/4992; *Journal of the Folk Song Society*, 8.4 (no. 34) (1930), 231–32.

20 Doug Fraser and Tony Green, 'Phil Tanner', *Traditional Music*, 7 (mid-1977), 4–9.

21 Karpeles Collection, MK/1/4/5343–5344.

was recorded by the Columbia Gramophone Company. I was present at the recording session and was filled with admiration not only by his singing but by his complete self-possession.'[22]

The Columbia recordings were made on that Bracey-arranged visit to London, when he also sang on the BBC radio programme *In Town Tonight*. The notes to the Veteran CD *The Gower Nightingale* state that the Columbia recordings were 'initiated' by Karpeles.[23] Two records, with four tracks, were issued commercially in 1937. Later that year the BBC recorded two songs from him at Llangennith, and in 1949 the BBC returned to record him once again. All the recordings were later released on the EFDSS LP *Phil Tanner*,[24] and subsequently on the Veteran CD. Between Columbia and the BBC, therefore, only a handful of Tanner's songs were recorded. The puzzle remains—why did Maud Karpeles not note down more of his repertoire? On one occasion, he is reported to have sung eighty-eight songs in a single session.

By the end of the Second World War, Karpeles was on the eve of her sixtieth birthday; but, while many people would be contemplating retirement, she was about to embark on an important period of her life—as honorary secretary of the International Folk Music Council (IFMC). The annual IFMC meetings allowed her to travel, and in 1950 she went back to the Appalachians. Accompanied by Mrs Sidney Robertson Cowell, she returned to communities that she and Sharp had visited more than thirty years before. With a tape recorder borrowed by Cowell from the Library of Congress, they recorded a hundred songs. Karpeles's manuscripts contain the words only of just two of these—though words *and* tunes of these two songs, 'The Cruel Ship's Carpenter' and 'The Gypsy Laddie', are included in her article on the trip in the *Journal of the English Folk Dance and Song Society*.[25] Why just two songs? Perhaps she did not have her own copy of the tape recordings, or she did not have access to a tape recorder back in England, or she was too busy with her IFMC responsibilities, or she felt that the songs would be transcribed back in the US, or she felt that they added nothing to Sharp's collection, or they were not the focus of her interest at the time. Or because having a recording was sufficient. Or perhaps, since they had loaned the tape recorder, the Library of Congress owned the tapes.

22 Karpeles autobiography, pp. 155–56.

23 Phil Tanner, *The Gower Nightingale*, CD (Veteran VT145CD, 2003), notes by Doug Fraser, John Howson, and Roy Palmer.

24 Phil Tanner, *Phil Tanner*, 12-inch LP (EFDSS Folk Classics LP1005, 1969), notes by Tony Wales.

25 Karpeles Collection, MK/1/2/4904–4905; Maud Karpeles, 'A Return Visit to the Appalachian Mountains', *Journal of the English Folk Dance and Song Society*, 6.3 (1951), 77–82.

This trip to the Appalachians was, in an important way, different from her pre-war collecting in that she was accompanied by a colleague, unlike her solo outings in the 1920s and 1930s. The visit must have reminded her vividly of her time there with Cecil Sharp. She had also very much enjoyed a trip to Yugoslavia in 1936 with her nephew, John Kennedy, and his death in the Second World War was a severe blow to her. By 1950, John's brother, Peter, had been enthused by folk music and dance, and her final period of song collecting saw her accompanied by Peter, or Patrick Shuldham-Shaw, or Marie Slocombe.

Marie Slocombe was the first librarian at the BBC Sound Archive and was central to the BBC Folk Music and Dialect Recording Scheme (1952–57).[26] She edited the influential BBC radio programme *As I Roved Out*. She first met Karpeles in 1943 and later became a member, then secretary, of the IFMC Radio Committee (later also covering television and sound and film archives). In April 1952, Karpeles and Slocombe went on a two-day collecting trip for the BBC in Somerset.

Two weeks later, Karpeles returned with Peter Kennedy, then working for the BBC scheme, and spent a further five days there, visiting the same singers and recording them. Karpeles's report on the trip—evidently made because the BBC was funding it—sets out its objective: 'to find out whether the folk song were [*sic*] remembered by any of the descendants of the singers from whom Cecil Sharp noted songs between the years 1903 and 1913'.[27] Karpeles selected thirty-two of Sharp's singers—those with 'large or valuable repertoires'. No surviving descendants could be found for fourteen of the singers, but they traced and visited sons, daughters, or grandchildren of the remaining eighteen, along with some additional people who were said to know some old songs.

By the end of their trip they had recorded songs from four different singers. Sidney Richards, of Curry Rivel, the son of Harry Richards, sang 'The Trees They Grow So High', 'The Green Mossy Banks of the Lee', 'The Sweet Primroses', and 'The Banks of the Nile'.[28] Bill Squires sang 'The Seeds of Love' and 'Poor Old Jeff'. Edwin Thomas, who had responded to

---

26 Madeau Stewart and Craig Fees, 'Obituary: Marie Slocombe 1912–1995', *Folk Music Journal*, 7.2 (1996), 270–73.

27 London, VWML, AL KARPELES/8454, 'Report on Collecting Expedition in Somerset and Devon April 15 to 17 and April 29 to May 4 (inclusive) 1952'.

28 'The Banks of the Nile' was released on *A Soldier's Life For Me*, The Folk Songs of Britain, vol. 8, 12-inch LP (Topic 12T196, 1971). (The Folk Songs of Britain series of LPs were first released by Caedmon in the USA in 1961.) The other three songs, plus some tunes played by Sidney Richards on the melodeon, were released on a tape cassette by Peter Kennedy on his Folktrax label, *Herchard of Taunton Dene: Village Traditions, Somerset*, cassette (Folktrax FTX-405, 1980). Kennedy also released 'The Banks of the Nile' on *The White Cockade: Soldiers and their Sweethearts*, cassette (Folktrax FTX-518, 1979).

a letter from Karpeles in the local press, sang 'Searching for Young Lambs', 'Bold Reynard', 'Barbara Allen', 'Henry the Poacher', 'Three Gypsies' ('The Lost Lady Found'), and 'The Miller's Last Will'. The songs sung by the fourth singer, George Bonston, are not known.[29] None of these songs were transcribed into Karpeles's manuscripts, although the tune of Bill Squires's 'The Seeds of Love' was published in 1959.[30]

In her report, Karpeles wrote, 'practically all the descendants of Cecil Sharp's singers remembered hearing the songs and recognised the titles or some of the words, but very few were able to sing a complete folk song. Nearly always the "old" songs they produced were the popular songs of Victorian times and not folk songs. This bears out Cecil Sharp's statement that the children of the traditional singers usually looked down on their parents' songs. Over and over again those we visited admitted that they had not formerly taken much interest in the old songs, but they now regretted this as they realised that they were much better than the new ones.'

Karpeles's second collecting trip for the BBC was in August 1952, with Patrick Shuldham-Shaw.[31] Pat Shaw was a musician, singer, dancer, composer (of dances and tunes), collector, and writer.[32] Shaw and Karpeles went song collecting in the Forest of Dean and Herefordshire, and although Karpeles wrote in her autobiography that they had 'little result',[33] they did collect 'The Holly and the Ivy' from Peter Jones, of Bromsash, Herefordshire; 'The Bitter Withy' from William Payne, in Gloucester; and 'The Cherry Tree Carol' from John Partridge, of Cinderford, Gloucestershire.[34] They also collected 'Seventeen Come Sunday', 'The Country

29 Bill Squires's 'The Seeds of Love' was released on *The Seeds of Love: A Study of English Folk Song*, cassette (Folktrax FTX-136, 1979). Peter Kennedy also filmed Bill Squires in 1983 and a video was released, *The Seeds of Love*, video cassette (Folktrax FF-2207, 1983). It may be that 'Poor Old Jeff' was only recorded on this later visit. Edwin Thomas's recordings were released on *Herchard of Taunton Dene, A-Beggin' I Will Go: Songs of the Trades*, cassette (Folktrax FTX-021, 1975) and *All Jolly Fellows: Songs of Country Life*, cassette (Folktrax FTX-023, 1975). Since Peter Kennedy's death the Folktrax label has ceased to operate, but details of releases are available on the archived website, <http://www.folktrax-archive.org> [accessed 28 March 2014]. Peter Kennedy's archive of recordings is now held by the British Library.

30 *Journal of the English Folk Dance and Song Society*, 8.4 (1959), 202, gives the tune of 'The Seeds of Love' from Jim Squires, recorded in 1904, with a transcription of the recording of Jim's son, William, made by Peter Kennedy and Maud Karpeles in 1952. It is not clear who submitted the songs or who transcribed the recording.

31 VWML, AL KARPELES/8454, 'Report on Collecting Expedition.

32 Brenda Godrich, ed., *Pat Shaw 1917–1977: His Life through the Memories of his Friends, his Music, Dances and Songs* ([n.p.]: Nicolas Broadbridge, 2010).

33 Karpeles autobiography, p. 230.

34 All three recordings were released on *Songs of Ceremony*, The Folk Songs of Britain, vol. 9, 12-inch LP (Topic 12T197, 1971). They were also released on *The Bitter Withy: Early Folk Carols*, cassette (Folktrax FTX-504, 1978).

Gorby', and perhaps two other songs from Peter Jones, but 'The Holly and the Ivy' is the only item included in Karpeles's manuscripts, where she transcribed both words and the tune.[35]

Of Peter Jones she wrote in her report: 'He knows a great many songs, but they are mostly "comics" and I doubt whether he has many more genuine folk songs.' She also listed all the villages they visited, which included Corve Dale in Shropshire, where, two months later, Peter Kennedy recorded Fred Jordan and others. Maud wrote: 'The songs appear to be almost unknown in these districts.' She felt that the Forest of Dean area was the most likely for further investigation, especially among the Gypsy population, and listed a number of possible contacts.

The third, and final area that Maud Karpeles visited in connection with the BBC scheme was Kent. An initial visit in October 1953 was followed by a second trip in January 1954, with Peter Kennedy.[36] In October she stayed with a school friend, Miss Violet Rumney, who drove her around—they covered about four hundred miles, visiting twenty-seven villages. She found one song, 'John Barleycorn', from Dave Wicken, of Smarden, and six songs from Albert Beale, of Kenardington, who sang 'Blow Away the Morning Dew', 'As I Sat on a Sunny Bank', 'The Moon Shines Bright', 'Undaunted Female', 'Sons of Levi', and 'Frog and the Mouse'.[37] Kennedy later visited Albert Beale again and recorded a further three songs. Again, some of these songs were released on Folktrax cassettes.[38] Albert Beale's father had sung 'The Moon Shines Bright' for Cecil Sharp, and Albert's singing of the same song has recently been issued on CD.[39]

However, the main success of this first trip to Kent was the finding of a family of Gypsies, the Stanleys, at Bettenham. On the second visit, with Peter Kennedy, Karpeles again met Mrs Stanley (whose real name was Bird), who was the sister of Charles and Oliver Scamp, 'both of whom have a big repertory of songs which they learned from their parents. The Scamps are a big Romany clan scattered all over Kent and most of them seem well-to-do.' Karpeles and

35 Karpeles Collection, MK/1/2/4906, MK/1/5/2. There is also a letter from Peter Jones to Maud Karpeles, MK/5/55.

36 Karpeles Collection, MK/1/2/4907–4908, 'Folk Song Collecting Expedition: Kent. October 12th–17th incl., 1953'; VWML, AL KARPELES/8454, 'Report on Collecting Expedition.

37 'Frog and the Mouse' was recorded by Kennedy on the second visit and included on *Songs of Animals and Other Marvels*, The Folk Songs of Britain, 12-inch LP (Topic 12T198, 1971).

38 Some of these were released on *South Downs and The Weald: Songs Recorded in Sussex and Kent*, cassette (Folktrax FTX-428, 1975); *The Baffled Knight: Classic Ballads 2*, cassette (Folktrax FTX-502, 1976).

39 *You Never Heard So Sweet: Songs by Southern English Traditional Singers*, The Voice of the People (Topic TSCD671, 2011).

Kennedy moved on to record the Scamp brothers in Chartham Hatch, Canterbury. Karpeles commented on their singing styles. Of Charlie, she wrote: 'He has a fine voice and his style, though hardly "authentic", is interesting. He has the florid gipsy way of singing, combined with a conscious voice production (self-trained, of course). He has modelled himself on Al Johnson [*sic*—Jolson].'[40] Of Oliver: '[He] has not taken up the new songs and his style of singing is much more straight forward than that of his brother.' The Scamp brothers had a sister, Phoebe Smith, whom Peter Kennedy, Frank Purslow, and others later recorded.[41]

One final song collecting trip, again with Peter Kennedy but not under the auspices of the BBC, came in 1962 when they visited people from the South Atlantic island of Tristan da Cunha who had been evacuated following the volcanic eruption of the island. A handful of folk songs were collected, but not the 'composed songs of the late nineteenth century'.[42]

What, then, can we conclude from all of Maud Karpeles's song collecting activities? My original proposition that, as with the folk dance collecting, she may have diverged from Sharp's policies, seems not to apply to folk song. If it were correct, then she would perhaps have adopted a broader collecting policy in Newfoundland—collecting, for example, the locally composed songs rather than just those of British and Irish origin. Similarly, in England she would have been more willing to collect the 'popular songs of Victorian times', 'composed songs', and 'comics' that she disregarded. In fact, all the songs she collected were, in Sharpian terms, 'genuine folk songs'.

The only song from her three BBC recording trips that made it into her manuscripts was Peter Jones's version of 'The Holly and the Ivy', and perhaps the notes, by Alan Lomax and Peter Kennedy, to the *Songs of Ceremony* LP indicate why: 'Peter Jones's tune does not seem to have been collected before in association with this carol, and it is interesting to find a new variant of such a well-known song still surviving among traditional singers.' The song was published in 1969 and the tune has become the standard one for the carol within the folk revival.[43] The 'Gower Wassail' as noted from Edwin Ace was published in 1930 and, again, this was perhaps because it was a different, localized version of the wassail song. The songs collect-

---

40 Charlie Scamp's songs are included on *Smiths, Fullers and Scamps: Gypsy Families in Sussex and Kent*, cassette (Folktrax FTX-140, [n.d.]); *The Roving Journeyman: Songs of the Travellers*, cassette (Folktrax FTX-031, 1975); *The Voice of the People, I'm a Romany Rai: Songs by Southern English Gypsy Traditional Singers*, The Voice of the People, CD (Topic TSCD672D, 2011).

41 For example, Phoebe Smith, *The Yellow Handkerchief*, CD (Veteran VT136CD, 1998).

42 Maud Karpeles, 'A Report on Visits to the Tristan da Cunha Islanders', *Journal of the English Folk Dance and Song Society*, 9.3 (1962), 162–67.

43 *English Dance & Song*, 31.4 (1969), 133.

ed in Canada that were published were perhaps singled out because they were British songs found in a new location.

The same may apply to the published two songs from the Tristan da Cunha islanders, 'The Little Cabin Boy' ('The Golden Vanity') and 'In London There Lived a Rich Merchant' ('The Highwayman Outwitted'). The tunes were transcribed for by Pat Shaw, so perhaps Karpeles felt there was no reason to write them down in her manuscripts. The two songs, out of one hundred, from the 1950 Appalachian trip that are found in her manuscripts are described by Karpeles as 'not previously [. . .] noted'. 'The Gypsy Laddie' is 'a pure pentatonic scale', and 'The Cruel Ship's Carpenter' has an 'interesting modal quality [. . .] it has the sharpened fourth, which is characteristic of the Lydian mode—very rare in English folk song.'

In other words, songs were likely to be transcribed into her manuscripts and/or published, only if they were from a new geographical location with British connections, or were musically of interest, or were sung to a different tune. The exception, perhaps, lies with the songs of Phil Tanner, of which there are only two in her manuscripts, neither of which was published. In her review of the 1969 *Phil Tanner* LP, Karpeles describes him as 'that prince among traditional folk singers' and calls his singing 'an outstanding example of what is most praiseworthy in the style and technique of the traditional singer's art', and comments on his 'inimitable ornamentation' of 'Henry Martin'.[44] So why not note more of his repertoire?

The most important song collecting period of Maud Karpeles's life was working with Sharp in the Appalachians. Newfoundland was the most important of her own folk song collecting experiences. The collecting in England and Wales was, certainly before the war, unsystematic, but it did include Phil Tanner; post-war recordings were, and continue to be, released commercially by Topic Records; and she did provide the contacts that led Peter Kennedy to the Scamps and to Phoebe Smith.

But beware of assuming that the manuscripts tell the full story of a collector's folk song experiences. Apart from a single letter, there is no mention in Maud Karpeles's manuscripts of the Dorset singer Charlie Wills, yet she wrote sleeve notes to his Leader LP, commenting on the 'immediate bond' they felt between them when they first met, their 'close friendship', and her 'many' visits to his home.[45] Yet there is nothing of his in the manuscripts.

44 *Folk Music Journal*, 2.1 (1970), 67–68.
45 Charlie Wills, *Charlie Wills* (Leader LEA4041, 1972), sleeve notes. Wills visited London in 1953 or 1954 for the BBC television programme *Song Hunter*, produced by David Attenborough ('David Attenborough and the Natural History of Folk', BBC Radio 2, 12 February 2014). Karpeles may have met him on that visit.

Maud Karpeles's contribution can be seen as a symbolic bridging of the two eras of folk song collecting. She started in the pen and paper era. With Sharp, she endured all the hardships of the Appalachian mountains to write down the words of songs while he notated the tunes. Alone, she undertook both tasks, words and tunes, in the only slightly less harsh environment of the Newfoundland outports. Then, with Peter Kennedy and Pat Shaw, she travelled in the relative comfort of the motor car to record the songs on tape—and like many collectors who employed similar techniques, she saw little need to write down the words and transcribe the tunes, either in the field or in the comfort of her home.

A Singer in the Quantocks: Jane Gulliver — Her Times and Songs

ANGELA SHAW

Like legions of others Jane Gulliver would have passed into obscurity were it not for the upsurge of interest in folk music that led to her coming to the attention first, in 1905, of the Hammond brothers (Henry and Robert) and then, in 1908, of Cecil Sharp. (Sharp mistakenly refers to her as Jane Gulliford, which was a local variant of the name). Jane had a large repertoire, learned primarily from her mother and grandmother, and 'other old people', although she also learned one song from someone in Taunton, suggesting a positive interest in adding to her repertoire. Henry Hammond described her in a letter to Lucy Broadwood as 'a wonderful woman',[1] and she clearly collaborated enthusiastically with the folk song project, singing over forty songs for the Hammond brothers and twenty for Cecil Sharp.[2]

The collectors valued traditional folk songs and tunes, and appear to have regarded the singers primarily as channels for the songs. They seem to have had little interest in them in their own right, or in what the songs meant to them. They also had little interest in how the singers saw their traditional songs in relation to other songs they might know. Hammond, for instance, in the letter to Broadwood cited above, describes some of Jane Gulliver's songs as 'abominations', referring specifically to one, 'Won't You Tell Me Why, Robin?', which is a sentimental parlour song from America.[3] So we know almost nothing about what other kinds of song she had in her repertoire, and what relationship she saw between the various genres, or how she valued them. Similarly, we cannot know to what extent she modified or extended the repertoire passed on to her by her mother and grandmother — how much, that is, she se-

---

1   London, EFDSS Archives, Hammond Collection, HAM/5/37/3.
2   Four of the latter were not among those she sang for the Hammonds.
3   'Won't You Tell Me Why, Robin!', words and music by Claribel (1830–69), published by Balmer & Weber, St. Louis, MO <http://dc.lib.unc.edu/cdm/ref/collection/sheetmusic/id/32119>.

lected songs because they meant something specific to her. A century on, this lack of curiosity is frustrating. It is possible, however, to piece together some biographical facts, a consideration of the social context of the singer, and an analysis of the songs, and to draw some tentative conclusions from these data. The size of Jane Gulliver's repertoire makes her a good subject for this exercise.

She was born Jane Lovell, in 1862, in Lydeard St Lawrence, Somerset.[4] She was the eldest child of George and Elizabeth Lovell. George, born in 1832 in the nearby village of Ash Priors, was an agricultural labourer. Elizabeth, born in 1842, came from Lydeard St Lawrence. Jane had four sisters and two brothers. The family moved around, but always within a tight circle of Somerset villages only two or three miles apart.

Jane was born the year the West Somerset Railway was opened, and this had a huge impact on the local community, including improved employment prospects. Once the navvies who built the railway had moved on, there was a continuing need for maintenance workers.[5] By 1881, George Lovell had become a railway packer, part of a team that maintained the tracks. By then, the family was living in Combe Florey and Jane, now aged nineteen, was working as a general domestic servant, possibly at one of the big houses in the village. Unlike her younger sisters, she appears not to have gone away into service in her early teens. At some time in the next decade she moved near Taunton, but in 1891 she moved back to Combe Florey to marry Frederick Gulliver, who, like his father and hers, was a railway packer. Their marriage produced four children.

We know nothing for certain about the material circumstances of Jane and her extended family. George Lovell had initially been an agricultural worker, at a time when agriculture was a depressed industry, and farm labourers in Somerset were particularly badly affected by extremely low wages and dreadful housing.[6] Attempts to organize the labourers went on throughout the 1870s and 1880s, but they were not as successful as elsewhere in the country and petered out in the face of bad winters and intransigent farmers and landowners.[7] There are, however, signs that George Lovell and his family were able and willing to take advantage of what opportunities life offered and, as has been noted, he moved into the better-paid life of

---

4 All dates, occupations, and locations are taken from the relevant censuses and Registers of Births, Marriages and Deaths.

5 Christian Wolmar, *Fire and Steam: A New History of the Railways in Britain* (London: Atlantic Books, 2008).

6 Brendon Owen, *One from the Plough: The Life and Times of George Mitchell (1826–1901)* (Montacute, Somerset: Gazebo Press, 2001).

7 F. E. Green, *A History of the English Agricultural Labourer, 1870–1920* (London: P. S. King and Son, 1920).

a railway worker.[8] Although Cecil, the youngest son, was an agricultural worker at the age of twelve, he eventually ran a grocer's store. In particular, the number of daughters in the family may well have proved a blessing in an age when domestic service was expanding very rapidly.[9] Jane and all her sisters went into domestic service. While this was hard work, and could be demeaning, lonely, and exploitative, it relieved the family of the need to maintain the girls, who, however poorly paid, earned more than they could in the fields.[10] There are indications that the family was well regarded. Emma, the next daughter after Jane, started as a kitchen-maid in the local rectory and rose to become parlour-maid for a canon at Wells Cathedral.

Apart from her brief foray to the 'big town' of nearby Taunton, Jane Gulliver lived an unremarkable life circumscribed by geography, class, and gender, barely moving from a few square miles of Somerset. We only know of her now because of the research that brought the Hammonds and Cecil Sharp into Somerset in the 1900s. We have, therefore, only her extant repertoire of folk songs from which to reconstruct some idea of what singing meant to her.

Her repertoire bears a resemblance to that of other singers in the area. Notably, her songs barely reflect the lived reality of her life. Although the menfolk in her family were deeply involved with the railway, there are no railways songs in her repertoire—although it is highly likely that they would have been of no interest to the Hammonds in any case. Similarly, although being in service was a major feature of the lives of young women during the latter half of the nineteenth century, and figured largely in the lives of Jane and her sisters, her songs hardly reflect it. The one exception is 'The Lady and the Box' (Roud 289),[11] which is a fantasy story in which a serving girl shoots several highwaymen and marries an admiring gentleman in consequence. Neither does her repertoire reflect the agricultural pursuits or the seasons' round, which must have been of huge significance in her life, and of which there is a large

---

8 It is extremely difficult to work out relative wages in this period. They varied between counties and fluctuated considerably throughout the last half of the century. Furthermore, wages were often reckoned to include payments in kind, which may or may not have been received, and which may or may not have had any real worth. However, as a rough guide, a male agricultural worker with a family in Somerset received between nine and eleven shillings per week during this period; a young kitchen-maid in London would have received about the same, with clothing, lodging, and food all found.

9 John Burnett, ed., *The Annals of Labour: Autobiographies of British Working Class People, 1820–1920* (Bloomington: Indiana University Press, 1974).

10 A particular grievance in this period was that farmers expected the wives and children of agricultural labourers to work in the fields, usually for a pittance. See J. Y. Stratton, 'The Life of a Farm Labourer' (1864), in *The English Rural Poor, 1850–1914*, vol. 1: *The Moral and Material Condition of the Mid-Victorian Rural Poor*, ed. Mark Freeman (London: Pickering and Chatto, 2005), pp. 123–31.

11 Hammond Collection, HAM/2/2/14.

folk corpus. There were also 'union' songs, about the struggle of the agricultural workers. We do not know whether Jane and her family supported the union, but she passed on no songs about it. Finally, there are no songs about the daily reality of life for women—housework and childbirth and child rearing—which is unsurprising given the general absence in song of that aspect of a woman's life.

Instead, her songs allowed her to move outside the constraints of her actual life. Like 'The Lady and the Box', many of her songs tell stories of lovers separated and reunited ('A Fair Maid Walking in her Garden', Roud 264), faithfulness rewarded ('The Bonny Blue Handkerchief', Roud 378), and bravery recognized ('Billy Taylor', Roud 158), or of love lost ('The Unquiet Grave', Roud 51) or betrayed ('Catch Me if You Can', Roud 1028), murder ('Polly's Love', Roud 1403), and suicide ('Poor Mary in the Silvery Tide', Roud 561).[12] A large proportion of her songs are about voyaging on the sea. Many feature women in heroic and feisty or even violent roles ('The Banks of the Sweet Dundee', Roud 148), setting off in a rowing boat to find her lost lovers ('Early Early in the Spring/Sweet William', Roud 152), or dressing up as a soldier to go adventuring ('The Female Drummer Boy', Roud 226).[13] While there are documented instances of women joining the army or going to sea, it seems unlikely that she knew of any instances herself. I would argue that the attraction of these songs is not that women did, very occasionally, do such things, but the joyfully transgressive fantasy that they might do such things.

Some of Jane Gulliver's songs have a distinctly antiquarian flavour. She sang two songs ('Billy Taylor' and 'The Banks of the Sweet Dundee') about the press gang, a popular topic. In her grandmother's day, the press gang was a real and present danger, especially in villages close to the sea. Merchant seamen, and even landlubbers, could legitimately be seized to serve in the Royal Navy.[14] However, although the laws were never rescinded, in reality there was no known case of impressment after *c.*1815. So, while her grandmother might possibly have known of actual cases, the appeal for Jane seems more likely to have been one of imaginative empathy.

Thus most of her songs enabled her to enter imaginative worlds that took her away from the hard reality of life in rural England in the late nineteenth century. There was one reality, however, that she did not evade. Like other singers, she sang of amorous, sexual encounters.

---

12 Hammond Collection, HAM/2/1/17, HAM/2/2/13, HAM/2/2/17, HAM/2/2/8, HAM 2/2/15, HAM/2/1/25, HAM/2/2/10.

13 Hammond Collection, HAM2/2/19, HAM 2/1/16, HAM 2/1/14.

14 Impressment: The Press Gang and Naval Recruitment <http://www.royalnavalmuseum.org/info_sheet_impressment.htm>.

At least thirteen of the songs she sang for the Hammonds are about seduction,[15] of which nine end in a pregnancy that is explicitly ruinous for the girl and/or the child. From 1834, a 'reform' of the Poor Law, inspired by Victorian alarm at rising rates of illegitimate births, made the mother alone responsible for maintaining her illegitimate offspring (the father had no legal responsibility), and also made her ineligible for outdoor state relief, so that if they found themselves destitute, both mother and child would be obliged to enter the workhouse. This act led to the deaths of many babies, and the destitution of many women, whether they were willing sexual partners or the victims of seduction or rape.[16]

So, whatever these songs might have meant to Jane Gulliver's grandmother, by her mother's time they referenced a terrifying reality. Jane was ten before the worst effects of the act had been mitigated by further legislation, but the social attitudes engendered by the Poor Law lingered well into the twentieth century.[17] For women in service, these attitudes could be particularly ruinous, as they were liable to be 'turned out' without a reference and therefore without much hope of another job if they became pregnant.[18]

These were not theoretical matters for Jane Gulliver. In 1851, her father's sister, Sarah, was living with her parents at the age of thirty-seven and is described in the census as a 'pauper'—an unusual description for a woman living in her family's home. There is also a small girl, Georgenna (*sic*) Norman Lovell, who is the grandchild of the head of the family—i.e. Sarah's father. It seems likely that Georgenna was in fact Sarah's illegitimate child, taken in by the family along with her mother. In rural areas particularly, this was a frequent solution to the social tragedy of illegitimacy. The child would often take the surname of its maternal grandparents, while an unusual middle name often indicates the actual surname of the father.[19]

Thus Jane might well have grown up with an illegitimate cousin and an aunt reduced to pauperism. Furthermore, Jane herself gave birth to a son, Frederick Archer Gulliver Lovell, in 1883. He was in fact the son of Frederick Gulliver,[20] whom Jane married in 1892. In 1891,

---

15 She also sang several songs of love, and the dividing line between these and songs of seduction is not always clear. 'Sweet Queen of May' (Roud 594), for instance, describes seduction that ends in marriage (Hammond Collection, HAM/2/2/4).

16 Dorothy L. Haller, 'Bastardy and Baby Farming in Victorian England' <http://www.loyno.edu/~history/journal/1989-0/haller.htm>.

17 Tom H. MacKenzie, *Last Foundling* (London: Pan, 2014).

18 Judith R. Walkowitz, *Prostitution and Victorian Society* (Cambridge: Cambridge Universtiy Press, 1980).

19 Ruth Paley, *My Ancestor Was a Bastard: A Family Historian's Guide to Sources for Illegitimacy in England and Wales* (London: Society of Genealogists, 2004).

20 As shown on his birth certificate; in the census he appears as Frederick A. G. Lovell.

Frederick junior was living with his grandparents; Jane was not at home and may have been living in Trull, near Taunton.[21] Even after his parents' marriage, young Frederick remained living with his grandparents, and he took over their home after their deaths. He appears never to have used his father's surname. So in two generations we can see the impact of illegitimacy on family life.[22] This must have deeply coloured Jane's understanding of lines such as:

> Now nine long months being gone and past
> This poor girl had a child at last
> This poor girl had a child at last
> But the child it had no father. ('Catch Me if You Can')

We nearly lost Jane's contribution to folk song. She died of cancer at the age of forty-seven, only two years after Sharp collected from her. The early collectors did us a great service in seeking out and recording a wonderful body of folk song. Inadvertently, they also bequeathed to history traces of the lives of ordinary men and women who would otherwise, like their peers, have disappeared without trace. However, we need to acknowledge that Jane Gulliver and her like were themselves bearers and shapers of tradition—if without the songs we would not know of Jane, then assuredly without Jane and her faithfulness to her heritage we would not have the songs.

21 According to her marriage certificate.
22 Office of National Statistics figures, April 2012

Going Up into the Next Class: Alice Snow, Folk Song Collector

YVETTE STAELENS

Folk song collecting in England in the nineteenth and early twentieth centuries was essentially a middle-class leisure activity. Collectors needed literacy, musical ability, and, most importantly, time and money in order to take part. It was a hobby enjoyed by a self-selected few. The most famous and active collectors include well-known characters such as Cecil Sharp, Sabine Baring-Gould, Frank Kidson, the Hammond brothers, George Gardiner, and Lucy Broadwood, alongside composers such as Ralph Vaughan Williams and Percy Grainger.

The greatest of all collectors of English folk song in terms of volume of songs, tunes, and words collected, plus associated data which include portrait photographs of singers and their families, was Cecil Sharp. Sharp began his song collecting in the county of Somerset in 1903, working initially with his friend and collaborator, the Rev. Charles Marson, who was the vicar at Hambridge. Sharp and Marson disseminated versions of the songs they collected through prompt publication, including in the series of volumes of *Folk Songs from Somerset* issued in 1904, 1905, and 1907, until the two men had a disagreement.[1] Following the split, Sharp continued song collecting in Somerset and published two further volumes of *Folk Songs from Somerset* in 1908 and 1909.

During this later phase Sharp worked with various collaborators and supporters, who were either local clergymen or middle-class enthusiasts. His collaborators took various roles, which included finding singers, providing accommodation and perhaps transport, and, if they were clerics, introducing him to other clergy who could identify singers of folk songs within their parishes. The most notable were the Rev. A. A. Brockington (Taunton), the Rev.

---

1 David Sutcliffe, *The Keys of Heaven: The Life and Work of Revd Charles Marson, Socialist Priest and Folk Song Collector* (Nottingham: Cockasnook Books, 2010), pp. 262–68. Sharp and Marson had their disagreement in November 1906 and never met again. Sharp attended Marson's funeral on 7 March 1914.

Francis Etherington (Minehead), Frances Balfour Kettlewell (Mendips), the Rev. G. Peppin (Marston Magna), the Rev. W. K. Warren (Bridgwater), and Priscilla Wyatt-Edgell and Katherine Sorby, who lived on the Quantock Hills. Mostly, these people introduced Sharp to local singers; however, some were also inspired to engage in the process of collecting. A good example is Katherine Sorby, who collected songs and carols, plus games from local children, and sent them to Sharp.[2] All of these collaborators may be identified as middle-class. However, there was another Somerset collector who was not from this social class. Her name was Alice Catherine Snow (Figure 1).

From 1906, Snow corresponded with Sharp and sent him folk songs that she had taken down from her immediate family and friends, who lived in Somerton. The census re-

Figure 1. *Alice Snow photographed by Cecil Sharp in 1906. Courtesy of EFDSS.*

turns (1841–1901) reveal that she came from a family of agricultural labourers and factory and domestic workers, some of whom were outworkers for the local gloving industry. Various questions arise. What is known about Alice Snow? Why did she collect, what did she collect, and from whom? And, most importantly, how was it possible for a working-class woman to work alone, when most collectors—even Sharp—worked in partnership, with one person notating the tunes and the other the words?[3]

Alice Catherine Snow was born in Somerton in 1881. This was a town of around 1,800 inhabitants, which had some small-scale industry, including a brewery, a gloving and shoe-bindings factory, a cardboard-box factory, and a rope twine-making and bonnet-making enterprise. Both of Alice's parents worked for the biggest employer in the town, a linen shirt-collar busi-

---

2 London, EFDSS Archives, Katherine Sorby to Maud Karpeles, 15 November, [*c*.1931]: 'Mr Sharp came often to stay with us at Enmore and did a good deal of his Somerset collecting from there. I think we first met him in 1905 or /6.' Katherine Sorby collected mostly around Enmore and Nether and Over Stowey.

3 Sabine Baring-Gould, Frank Kidson, and George Gardiner all worked with collaborators whose role was to notate the tunes they found.

ness on Broad Street, which had been established in 1866 by Edward Welsh.[4] Her mother, Ellen (née Culliford), was a machinist and her father, William, a 'gas engine driver'. In the year of Alice's birth, the collar factory provided employment for 125 people: eighty-one women; thirty-four girls; nine men; and a boy.[5] It is interesting to note a connection between work and song at the factory. There was a company rule that no singing was allowed during the period 8 a.m. to 6 p.m. However, 'girls might sing at their work' after 6 p.m.[6] Alice had two younger brothers, William, born in 1884, and Francis (Frank), born in 1887. Her mother was born in Somerton, and her father was from Bridgwater; his father had been a sailor.

A musical family

Alice was born into a musical family. Her mother and father, and her grandmother, Betsy Pike, all knew and sang folk songs. Her brothers were musicians, singers, and performers, and Alice played piano to concert level. The local papers provide a record of the family's performing abilities. In 1901, for example, when she was twenty, Alice played a piano solo titled 'Lucrezia Borgia' at Somerton Wesleyan Chapel bazaar and concert.[7] The following year, on 11 and 12 April 1902, her brothers performed, and evidently excelled, in a 'Minstrel Entertainment' at the Parish Rooms in aid of the cricket club and the town band:

> the troupe had gained great notoriety in the past and on this occasion they were fully up to their standard of excellence, if not more than so, and delighted the audience with a most excellent and mirth provoking programme [. . .] Messrs F. R. Snow and C. W. Hunt were exceedingly good. Their jokes and witticisms were very clever indeed, and caused roars of laughter. Some excellent songs were introduced and the choruses were well taken up.[8]

Frank also sang 'Dinah, She Say Yah!' and William sang 'Will my Darling Come Again?' The brothers then contributed a comic duet, 'Of Course', and Frank played a female role, Angelina Sweet Beltina Chowder, in a farcical play.

4 M. Richardson, *An Archaeological Assessment of Somerton* (Taunton: Somerset County Council, 2003), p. 170.
5 P. Daniel, 'Somerton Town Trail', *Somerset Industrial Archaeological Society Bulletin*, 119 (April 2012).
6 M. J. Taylor, ed., *The Story of Somerton*, compiled by Members of the Somerton Women's Institute (Somerton: Somerton Women's Institute, 1953).
7 *Taunton Courier*, 26 June 1901.
8 *Langport and Somerton Herald*, 13 April 1902.

In 1904, Alice performed as an accompanist and duettist at the Somerton Concord Lodge concert. Frank also performed a sketch, played solo violin, and sang a solo and a duet with his brother. The account in the *Langport and Somerton Herald* gives an indication of the scope of the concert and the contributions of the Snow family:

> the members of Concord Lodge gave another of their interesting entertainments in the Friends' schoolroom on Fri evg. Full attendance, presided over by Mr Gunning. Comic items vigorously encored. Prog: song 'Silence reigned supreme' Mr Taylor; song 'At our threepenny hop' Mr Carey; piano duet the Misses A. C. Snow & Wheeler; Song 'She's the only girl I love' Mr T. Richards; song 'The dear little shamrock' Miss Isherwood; 'The Empress of the wave' Mr T. E. Carey; sketch 'Fat and the lean' Mr Taylor & Mr F. Snow; song 'The gift' Mrs Stephens; vocal duet 'Soldier & Sailor' Mr W. J. Snow & Mr F. Snow; song 'Down the line' Mr James Cox; comic song 'Take your umbrella, John' Mr B. Taylor; violin solo Mr F. Snow; comic song 'Polly Wolly Doodle' Mr Carey; Song 'Let her drown' Mr F. Snow; dialogue 'Advertising for a wife'. Accompanist Miss A. C. Snow.[9]

The Concord Lodge of the International Order of Good Templars, a temperance organization, is reported as having given another programme of popular entertainments in the Friends' Schoolroom in November 1904. William sang 'My Girl', Frank sang 'Bill Bailey', and Alice performed a piano duet with Miss Rowley and was the accompanist for the singers.[10] Their next performance included a piano solo by Alice, a violin duet by Frank and Miss Pike, probably his niece Florence, and a song by Frank.[11] The impression is that the family were interested in the classical and popular music of the day and were keen performers. They also knew folk songs. Exactly when they became aware of the folk song collecting activity of Sharp and Marson is unknown; it is necessary, therefore, to consider the circumstantial evidence.

Why did Alice begin collecting?

It may be significant that in early December 1904, Charles Marson gave a lecture in Langport on 'The Somerset Ballads'.[12] Perhaps Alice was present. We do know that twelve months later Sharp was in Somerton and that he visited Lucy Swain (1842–1926) to collect a version of 'The Old Shannon Side'. Lucy was a widow who lived in North Field and Sharp

9 *Langport and Somerton Herald*, 2 April 1904.
10 *Langport and Somerton Herald*, 5 November 1904.
11 *Langport and Somerton Herald*, 3 December 1904.
12 *Langport and Somerton Herald*, 10 December 1904.

collected from her on 30 December 1905. This was his first visit to Somerton and Lucy was the only singer he met. Interestingly, she was a neighbour of Mary Ann Lawrence, from whom Alice Snow collected songs in March 1906. Both of these women lived just around the corner from Alice, who resided in New Street. It is possible that Alice knew of Sharp's visit to Lucy, and perhaps she even met him on that occasion. If not, then no doubt she would have heard of his visit through her acquaintances.

What is certain is that on Saturday, 6 January 1906, Sharp gave a lecture at Cheddar, supported by the singer Mattie Kay.[13] Did Alice attend his lecture, and was that the stimulus for her to begin recording songs from her maternal grandmother, Betsy Pike, to send to Sharp? The letters and manuscripts that she produced have not survived. However, Sharp meticulously recorded the songs in his notebooks as 'per Miss Snow'.

How was it possible for Alice to collect songs?

How was it possible for a working-class woman to collect songs alone when many other collectors relied upon collaborators to assist them? The answer is that she was musically literate and had the necessary skills to collect both words and tunes. This combination was unusual among folk song collectors. While they might themselves be musical in the sense of being able to play the piano, notation was another skill entirely. In addition, to collect by ear required special skills and confidence. For these reasons, collectors sought out collaborators.

In addition, collectors who were from working-class backgrounds were extremely rare. Alfred Williams, who collected in Wiltshire and the Upper Thames Valley was one, but he was unable to take down tunes.[14] It may be that Alice Snow was the only working-class collector with the ability to take down both words and tunes. We may never discover what motivated her to engage in what was essentially a middle-class pursuit, but we do know what enabled her to do so. First, she was surrounded by a very musical family, including an older generation who knew a wealth of folk songs; and secondly, like Sharp, she was a teacher. In order to understand Alice's life and the role of music within it, it is worth examining her chosen career.

In 1901, Alice was aged twenty and was teaching at a 'private school' in Somerton. The location of this school is not known. Other schools in the town at this time were: Somerton Free School, for boys (built 1840–45); Monteclefe National School, for girls and infants, (built 1851); and West Street Infants Board School (built 1890). The normal career route for a teacher before the establishment of teacher training colleges was the pupil-teacher system.

13 *Weston Mercury*, 13 January 1906.
14 Alfred Williams, *Folk-Songs of the Upper Thames* (London: Duckworth, 1923).

Thus, Alice would have started as a pupil-teacher at eleven years, moving from behind her own desk old to stand before the class along with the assistant mistress. When the mistress felt that she could be left alone, she would be entrusted to take a lesson from time to time. Once she had passed her scholarship exam, at about seventeen to eighteen years of age, she could take a paid job as an Article 68 teacher.

During Alice's lifetime there had been great changes in education policy and delivery, moving from dame schools and education controlled by the church to a broader curriculum governed by a Code of Regulations issued annually by the Board of Education.[15] The Code defined the core curriculum at various levels, and in infant schools it included singing. At Monteclefe School, the infants had singing lessons and the older girls studied singing by 'old notation'.[16]

In 1902, Alice changed schools and began teaching at the elementary (infants) school in Somerton, known as West Street Infants Board School. Having supplied a medical certificate to demonstrate her sound health, she began work on 21 April 1902.[17] The Somerset County Council Education Committee return for that year shows that she was teaching under Article 68 and had achieved first-class blackboard and second-class freehand qualifications. The return document is signed by Alice, who has also added ticks to the section enquiring whether she was formerly a pupil-teacher and if she was trained. However, she gives no dates for the training and no college. The date of her appointment on this document is noted as 26 November 1902. This is confusing. Perhaps that was the date she passed Article 68. The school inspector's comments for that year record, 'The children are under bright kindly teaching and generally speaking the progress is satisfactory. A. C. Snow is recognised under Article 68 of the Code.'

Alice was paid six shillings per week for forty-three weeks, and superannuation was also deducted from her salary. There was an all-female teaching staff: Kate Richards (head teacher); Edith Hiscock (certificated teacher); and Eva Gardiner (monitor). There were seventy-two children on the books and average attendance was 50.4 pupils. The curriculum covered the three Rs, plus object lessons, needlework, drawing, physical exercise, and singing.

15 Derek Gillard, *Education in England: A Brief History* (updated 2011) <www.educationengland.org.uk/history> [accessed 5 May 2014].

16 Education Act 1902, Elementary School Return, Somerton Free School: 'all subjects taken under section b (i) of Article 15'.

17 West Street Infants Rough Minute Book, 3 April 1902, notes: 'Assistant Mistress—matter adjourned until Wed 9th 6.30. Write to Miss Snow—medical certificate as to state of health.' At the Board Meeting on 9 April it was noted that the certificate had been received and passed, and that A. C. Snow should be appointed.

What did Alice collect and from whom?

Alice Snow collected her first songs from her grandmother, the remarkable Betsy, or 'Granny', Pike, who lived at Ivy Cottage, Acre Lane, Somerton. It is seldom possible to create a character portrait of a source singer, but in this case there are plenty of stories, supported by Sharp's photographs.

Elizabeth (Betsy) Culliford was born on 10 February 1832. Her father, Charles, born *c.*1795, was an agricultural labourer, and her mother, Mary Ann, was born in 1799. Betsy worked as a glover and her first daughter, Ellen, was born illegitimately. She remained an unmarried mother until she was forty years of age, when she married James Pike, a labourer from Monkton in Devon, born about 1811, who lived at Old Hill in Somerton. James was more than twenty years older than Betsy and recently widowed. He had three chil-

Figure 2. *Betsy 'Granny' Pike photograph by Cecil Sharp in 1906. Courtesy of EFDSS.*

dren. The stigma of Betsy's illegitimate daughter would doubtless have rendered her unmarriageable after the natural father had abandoned them, and so this late marriage to a widower might have been the best she could hope for. There is no evidence whether this was in any way a love match, although their five children might provide a clue.

By 1871, Betsy had given birth to Elizabeth, Sarah Ann (whose family nickname was 'Tit'), Mary Jane (nicknamed 'Jinnie'), and a boy, Samuel, and girl, Alice, who both died young. William, James Pike's son from his first marriage, was fourteen years old and working as a farm labourer. Betsy's daughter Ellen was now working in the linen-collar factory in Broad Street. Sometime prior to 1881, Ellen married William Snow. During the first years of their marriage they lived in New Street, Somerton, with William's sixty-year-old mother, Ann. She had been widowed by the time she was forty years old, and one can only imagine the hardship she must have endured trying to bring up her three children on a charwoman's wages. By 1891, Ann had died, and William Snow was employed as the gas-engine driver at the collar factory. His family consisted of Alice, born 24 March 1881, William, born in 1884, and Frances (called 'Frank'), born in 1887.

By 1901, Betsy Pike was still living in her three-roomed cottage in Acre Lane, with her granddaughter, Florence, who was eighteen years old and working as a monitress at the National School. Florence was the daughter of William Pike, Betsy's stepson, and his wife, Annie, who lived in West Street. Exactly why Florence was living with her grandmother is unknown. It may simply have been that, as the oldest girl, she was sent to Betsy as a home-help and carer. In addition, the West Street home, where there was a family of six children, would have been rather crowded.

In the Vaughan Williams Memorial Library file on Betsy Pike there is correspondence containing a quantity of anecdotal evidence which reveals a woman of considerable gifts and ingenuity, someone who might be referred to as a 'character'. Several stories survive that illustrate her mischievous personality. Her neighbour Arthur Café recalled:

> I knew Mrs Betsy Pike of Acre lane, Somerton very well indeed. I was ten years of age at that time (1906) when Mrs Pike lived there. It was news to me that she was a Folk singer but Betsy was no fool and no doubt would have warbled a song or two to Mr Cecil Sharp. She was a respected widow woman who did laundry work for some for the local landed gentry. She also made concoctions of herbal remedies. I myself tried some for an aching tooth. I well remember the few seconds of intense pain as I applied some around the tooth but the cure was certain and the pain soon passed. I think the nerve was destroyed outright. Quite a few locals got help from Betsy's herbs etc.[18]

Café also recalls:

> Betsy was a wily old lady. There is the true story about Betsy attending a meeting of the 'Mothers Union' here in Somerton. They were given tea, cakes, etc. and Betsy was seen dropping cakes into her umbrella. The Vicar the Rev. G. T. Steacy had also spotted this and (he enjoyed a joke) so on leaving the meeting he saw Betsy to the door, a

18 London, Vaughan Williams Memorial Library (VWML), letter from Arthur Café (aged 76) to David Bland, 31 August 1973.

spot of rain descending, he opened her umbrella for her, and the cascade of food etc. 'manna from heaven'd descended'.[19]

Betsy's granddaughter Alice, daughter of Sarah Ann, had memories of Cecil Sharp visiting her aunt Ellen Snow and also recalled some wonderful details about Betsy's appearance—how she attended the Methodist church on a Sunday night, very smartly dressed in a lovely silk cape trimmed with rows of black lace and sequins, and a bonnet trimmed with either a rose, lilacs, or violets:

> She walked very upright and used to tell us children off if they slouched whilst listening to her reciting poetry or telling 'weird' tales. She taught her cat how to unlatch the door and to draw down the blind. She was very particular that potatoes were planted early on a Good Friday morning.[20]

These and other anecdotes can be found in a collection of correspondence from the 1970s between former EFDSS librarian David Bland and those who knew Betsy Pike. Perhaps one of the most amusing, however, is a story recorded by Sharp in his field notebook. Betsy told him, 'I'm a teetotaller, but I drinks cider for cider don't count.'[21] Francis Pattemore recalls, 'She was short of stature, she knew her own mind and was not backwards in coming forward to make her point.'[22]

Alice also collected songs from her mother, Ellen, and one song from her father, William. She also performed children's games with her mother for Sharp to collect, and collected them from friends and neighbours. Table 1 shows the songs that Alice and Sharp collected in Somerton. It appears that Sharp first visited Alice's family on 18 January 1906 and that on that occasion he recorded songs from Betsy, with Alice giving him songs that she had already taken down from Betsy and her father, William. There is evidence that she obtained further verses of songs after Sharp had left and sent them on to him. For example, in his notes he records: 'Additional verse for The Seeds of Love given me by Miss Snow at Somerton 11 April 1906.' It must have been a jolly occasion when Alice and her mother played and performed children's games for him to record on that day! This was their last recorded meeting.

19 VWML, letter from Arthur Café to David Bland, 21 January 1974.

20 VWML, letter from Alice Sandford (Betsy Pike's granddaughter) to David Bland, November 1973.

21 London, EFDSS Archives, Cecil Sharp Collection, CJS1/9/11/1, Cecil Sharp Field Notebook 11 (Words), 2–28 August 1906, [part 1], p. 3.

22 VWML, Francis L. C. Pattemore, 'The History of Betsy Pike' (handwritten).

Table 1. Songs collected in Somerton by Alice Snow and Cecil Sharp

Singer	Song	Roud no.	Collector	Date
Lucy Swain	The Old Shannon Side	1453	Cecil Sharp	30 December 1905
Betsy Pike	The Outlandish Knight	21	Alice Snow	5 January 1906
Betsy Pike	Lord Rendal	10	Alice Snow	5 January 1906
Betsy Pike	Jealousy	218	Alice Snow	5 January 1906
Betsy Pike	A Farmer's Son So Sweet	1431	Alice Snow	5 January 1906
Betsy Pike	As I Walked Out One Summer Morning/I'm a Day Too Young	1003	Alice Snow	5 January 1906
Betsy Pike	Flanders	2636	Alice Snow	18 January 1906
Betsy Pike	William Taylor	158	Alice Snow	18 January 1906
Betsy Pike	The Cruel Ship's Carpenter	15	Cecil Sharp	18 January 1906
Betsy Pike	Forty Long Miles	608	Cecil Sharp	18 January 1906
Betsy Pike	The Black Pudding	12721	Cecil Sharp	18 January 1906
Betsy Pike	Waly Waly/The Prickly Bush	144	Cecil Sharp	18 January 1906
Betsy Pike	I Am A Sailor By My Right	568	Cecil Sharp	18 January 1906
William Snow	Golden Vanity	122	Alice Snow	18 January 1906
Betsy Pike	Cupid's Garden	297	Alice Snow	7 February 1906
Betsy Pike	William O'Reilly	714	Alice Snow	7 February 1906
Betsy Pike	Bold Fisherman	291	Alice Snow	7 February 1906
Betsy Pike	Cupid	4688	Alice Snow	March 1906
Betsy Pike	Sheffield Apprentice	399	Alice Snow	March 1906
Betsy Pike	William O'Reilly/Mantle of Green	714	Alice Snow	March 1906
Betsy Pike	It's a Cold Winter's Evening	4688	Alice Snow	March 1906
Mary Ann Lawrence	The Spotted Cow	956	Alice Snow	March 1906
Mary Ann Lawrence	The Basket of Eggs	377	Alice Snow	March 1906 Sharp notes: 'additional verses sent to me later by Miss Snow'
Mary Ann Lawrence	The Gipsy Girl/Lass	229	Alice Snow	March 1906
Mary Ann Lawrence	The Militia Captain	12726	Alice Snow	March 1906
Mary Ann Lawrence	Young Barnswell	955	Alice Snow	March 1906
Mary Ann Lawrence	Long Look For Come at Last/Courtship	1643	Alice Snow	March 1906

Betsy Pike	Hush A Bye Baby	2768	Alice Snow	6 April 1906
Betsy Pike	Thomas A Lynn	294	Cecil Sharp	11 April 1906
Betsy Pike	The Mallard/Berkshire Tragedy/ Miller's Apprentice	263	Cecil Sharp	11 April 1906
Ellen Snow and Alice Snow	London Bridge	502	Alice Snow/ Cecil Sharp	11 April 1906
Ellen Snow and Alice Snow	Lady of the Land	12729	Alice Snow/ Cecil Sharp	11 April 1906
Ellen Snow and Alice Snow	Wallflower	6307	Alice Snow/ Cecil Sharp	11 April 1906
Ellen Snow and Alice Snow	Mother May I Go Out To Play	12730	Alice Snow/ Cecil Sharp	11 April 1906
Ellen Snow and Alice Snow	Sally Water	4509	Alice Snow/ Cecil Sharp	11 April 1906
Ellen Snow	Verse of Seeds of Love	3	Alice Snow	11 April 1906
Mary Ann Lawrence	Barbara Ellen	54	Cecil Sharp	11 April 1906
Eliza Sweet	Searching for Lambs	576	Cecil Sharp	2 August 1906
Eliza Sweet	The Death of Queen Jane	77	Cecil Sharp	2 August 1906
Eliza Sweet	Robin-A-Rood/Jan's Courtship	575	Alice Snow	30 August 1906
Betsy Pike	Bold Robinson	2411	Cecil Sharp	October 1906
Betsy Pike	The Summer is Very Wet	12743	tune Alice Snow words Cecil Sharp	19 October 1906
Eliza Sweet	Robin-A-Rood/Jan's Courtship	575	Cecil Sharp	16 August 1907
Eliza Sweet	Ploughboy's Courtship/As I walked thro' the Meadow	594	Cecil Sharp	16 August 1907
Ellen Snow	Mummers Song	12747	Cecil Sharp	16 August 1907
Ellen Snow	Brisk Young Lover/Bessie Watson/Roses in Her Apron/ Down In The Meadows	18829	Cecil Sharp	16 August 1907
Betsy Pike	Arise and Pick a Posy	2445	Cecil Sharp	16 August 1907
Ella Gooding	Ruggleton's Daughter of Iero'	117	Cecil Sharp	16 August 1907
Betsy Pike	Tom Boleyn/Brian A Lynn/ Thomas A Lynn	294	Cecil Sharp	16 August 1907
Ella Gooding	Green Gravel (no tune)	1368	Cecil Sharp	13 August 1908
Ella Gooding	Draw a bucket of Water	11635	Cecil Sharp	13 August 1908

Why did Alice stop collecting?

The *Langport and Somerton Herald* of 30 March 1907 includes the following paragraph: 'Infants Council School—on Wednesday, Miss Snow, upon resigning her appointment as assistant mistress was the recipient of a chaste Wedgwood biscuit box, the gift of the children and the school mistress. It was accompanied with every good wish for her future happiness.' A few days later, on 3 April 1907, Alice was married to John Lock at the parish church in Somerton. This was the end of her working life and of her association with the town. Her teaching career had coincided with a time of great change in education which opened up opportunities for young women. However, this came at a cost, for the marriage bar meant that only single women could have a career for life. Any female teacher seeking marriage and a family would have to resign. It is likely that this was the situation for Alice.

Her husband, John, was born in Somerton and was two years younger than she was. His family lived in West Street, and his father James was a shoe- and boot-maker. Although he was the eldest son, John chose not to follow his father's profession and was instead apprenticed as a carpenter. He came from a large family and had seven siblings recorded in the 1901 census. His home was in the centre of this busy market town and his neighbours included the local police constable, shirt-collar factory workers, a dressmaker, a laundress, an outfitter's apprentice, a groom, a butcher, and a tailor.

It appears that John had secured employment that necessitated his moving to Bedwellty, in the Rhymney Valley, near Bargoed, in South Wales. So Alice left Somerton for her new life in the summer of 1907. There is evidence that she continued with her musical life in Bedwellty: for example, in correspondence between her mother, Ellen, and Cecil Sharp. In a letter of 31 December 1909, Ellen notes: 'My daughter is still doing a little in the musical way chiefly church music as she takes their little [?] Choir week evenings as their organist lives three miles over the mountain ... her little girl is very fond of music and will bang down the piano keys and sing "G" it's funny to see her.'[23]

Here we find Alice leading a choir, and her daughter is demonstrating some musicality, too. In the same letter, Ellen states: 'I sometimes get an old Line or refrain come into my head and think that's one of Granny's [i.e. her mother, Betsy, who was called "Granny" Pike] old songs and wonder if Mr Sharp has that, but it goes so quickly and as I have no one now to jot it down I forget these again, I often feel thankful that you were led Sir to save some of the

---

23 London, EFDSS Archives, Cecil Sharp Collection, Correspondence, Ellen Snow to Cecil Sharp, 31 December 1909.

dear old dittys.' This is a rare example of a folk singer's appreciation of Cecil Sharp's work, plus evidence of four generations of musical women.

Conclusion

Alice Snow was a remarkable working-class woman who had special musical abilities and skills that enabled her to collect from within the tradition and to engage in what was essentially a middle-class leisure pursuit. A further observation on social class and leisure may be made in respect of her two brothers, who distinguished themselves on the football field,[24] as well as through music, such accomplishments being more middle- than working-class in the context of the time. This also extends to Alice's cousin, Florence Pike, who played violin to performance level, while her father worked as a carter for the brewery in Somerton. Overall, the impression is of an aspiring, upwardly mobile family, whose progress (for Alice's immediate family) was brought to a sudden halt when her father, William Snow, lost his job as a result of illness, c.1910. Her mother, Ellen, died only two years later.

As regards folk song collecting, what marks out Alice is that she was a musically literate collaborator who came from humble origins, someone within the tradition who could send tunes to Sharp, and, importantly, she can be viewed as having contributed directly to *Folk Songs from Somerset* because Cecil Sharp came down to tread in her footsteps.

24 Somerton AFC team list, in *Somerton and Langport Herald*, 22 October 1904.

What's in a name? Alfred Williams and his Singers

CHRIS WILDRIDGE

It is my intention here to demonstrate that Alfred Williams matters more as a song collector than has generally been accepted. I will also suggest that, on occasion, he discreetly misrepresented some of the singers from whom he collected in respect both of name and, sometimes, place. Having worked in Wiltshire libraries since 1972, I was only too aware of Williams's *Folk-Songs of the Upper Thames* of 1923,[1] and of the existence of the Alfred Williams archive held now at the Wiltshire and Swindon History Centre—formerly the Wiltshire and Swindon Record Office (WSRO).[2] Of course, I was not the first to follow the Williams trail. A biography of Williams had appeared in 1945.[3] A special issue of *Folk Music Journal* dedicated to Alfred Williams appeared in 1969.[4] At some point in the 1960s, Colin Bathe and Ivor Clissold compiled their Bathe/Clissold Index.[5] In 2006, Andrew Bathe submitted his thesis on Williams, 'Pedalling in the dark', to the University of Sheffield.[6] I owe a debt to all those upon whose work I have been able to draw.

My last project for the library service was to coordinate, along with two colleagues, the launch of a local studies initiative, Wiltshire Community History.[7] This was devised as a series of interlinked databases reflecting different aspects of local studies. It is, in the jargon of these

1 Alfred Williams, *Folk-Songs of the Upper Thames* (London: Duckworth, 1923).
2 Chippenham, Wiltshire and Swindon Archives, 2598, Alfred Williams Literary Manuscripts.
3 Leonard Clark, *Alfred Williams: His Life and Work* (Bristol: William George's Sons 1945; rpt. Newton Abbot: David & Charles, 1969).
4 *Folk Music Journal*, 1.5 (1969).
5 Swindon Public Library, Colin Bathe and Ivor Clissold, 'Bathe/Clissold Index' (unpublished).
6 Andrew Lee Bathe, 'Pedalling in the Dark: The Folk Song Collecting of Alfred Williams in the Upper Thames Valley, 1914–1916 (unpublished doctoral thesis, University of Sheffield, National Centre for English Cultural Tradition, 2006). I am grateful to Andrew Bathe for supplying me with a copy.
7 <history.wiltshire.gov.uk/community/>.

things, content-rich. The website was launched with full data on three parishes in 2002. Table 1 shows a simple example of the type of information provided by the website — it looks almost banal, but it requires access to rare material only held in one or two places in the county.

Year	Population – South Marston	Population – Wiltshire
1801	252	185,107
1811	288	193,828
1821	299	222,157
1901	348	271,394
1911	387	286,822
1921	363	292,208
1931	396	303,373

Table 1. Wiltshire Community History (extract): Population of South Marston from 1801 (there are no data for 1871, 1881, 1891)

Two hundred and sixty-one parishes in Wiltshire are covered in all. There is also some material, such as population data, for parishes in the Swindon area. Although I did not plan it this way, it became apparent that traditional song, dance, and drama would fit easily within its scope — South Marston is Alfred Williams's home village.

My initial idea was only to transcribe all the 'Wiltshire' songs in the Alfred Williams archive. Briefly, the song part of the archive consists of six packets.[8] Five of these, containing the majority of the songs, are arranged largely by county: Berkshire (Bk.); Gloucestershire (Gl.); Oxfordshire (Ox.); Wiltshire (Wt.); with a Miscellaneous (Mi.) packet containing un-attributed material. Had the Full English Digital Archive project been even a straw in the wind in 2004, I probably would not have started on my own project. However, anyone with any awareness of traditional song collecting in southern England will know that Wiltshire has been seen as a largely blank space on the map. At that time, under those circumstances, I had every reason to proceed.

To begin at the beginning, I started transcribing from the manuscript the first 'Wiltshire' song, 'Old True Blue' collected from Sam Bennett (Wt. 309):

8 Wiltshire and Swindon Archives, 2598/36, Alfred Williams Folk Song Collection, <http://history.wiltshire. gov.uk/community/folkintro.php> now also accessible via the Full English Digital Archive <www.vwml.org. uk/>.

What's in a name? Alfred Williams and his Singers

69

Song title: Old True Blue
Collected from: Bennett, Samuel
Location: Ashton Keynes
County: Wiltshire
Secondary source: Unpublished
Primary source: WSRO: 2598/36 Packet 4 - Wiltshire: Williams, A: MS collection No Wt. 309
Roud number: 21214

Verse 1
I come of a free and jovial race,
With a name that has never yet known disgrace,
And I'll tell you the reason why;
I'm the chip of the block, of ancient stock,
And I'm loyal, brave and true,
I'm one of the race that can go the pace,
Although I'm seventy two.

It all seemed easy: the Wt. numbers run from 309 to 521, meaning that there are only 212 of them in total, so the task could be achieved in a very short time. But this was where the thread began to unravel. Bathe and Clissold appear to have based their geographical attributions on Williams's notes to the songs. For example: the note to 'Old True Blue' reads: 'Although I had often heard of this, I had some difficulty in obtaining a copy. I eventually found one to sing it however, at Ashton Keynes, where the piece is still popular. Obtained of Mr Sam Bennett.' This is interesting in itself—Williams records the song only in Ashton Keynes, but he 'had often heard of it'.

As I progressed through the file, it became apparent that things were not quite as they seemed. In the notes to 'The Gamekeeper' (Wt. 317), Williams writes:

By chance I stumbled upon the piece at Blunsdon, where it was still remembered by an old woman named Hancock, who told me she learnt it of her father, when a girl. I was quite six months in getting the song as my informant was very forgetful and could only tell me two or three lines at a time. In the end I obtained it complete with the exception of the first two lines of the 'warning'. I had decided that I should not get them, but by and by I called to see another dear old woman also considerably over eighty, named Dickson, of Brinkworth and the first thing she told me was the warning verse of the 'Gamekeeper'—she had forgotten everything else. The Brinkworth version had in the fourth verse, 'With her baby sprawling in her arms'.

This note reveals two aspects of Williams's collecting. First, this is what I term a 'compound text': that is, the fair copy that eventually appeared in *Folk-Songs of the Upper Thames* is a collation of two sources, Hancock in Blunsdon and Dickson in Brinkworth. Secondly, it is one of the few instances where Williams identifies such differences in the sources of the published texts. The question of compound texts became even more problematic when I came across 'Canada-i-o' collected from David Sawyer (Wt. 437)—of whom more later. The note to the song reveals yet another aspect of Williams's compound songs:

> This song has also given me the same trouble, I had the first part of it at Stratton St Margaret, and a little at Latton, and had almost given up hopes of completing the piece when I happened to stumble upon the remainder at Eynesham, near Oxford. The two halves suggest a slight difference of versions. The piece is as I received it. Obtained of David Sawyer, Ogbourne and Henry Leach, Eynesham, Oxfordshire.

Having realized that Williams's compound songs could straddle different counties, I felt I had no option but to work on the packets for the other three counties. Then, having transcribed those, I turned to the songs in the Miscellaneous packet. The point I wish to make here is not a criticism of Bathe and Clissold, who were not archivists or librarians and who were working within the limitations of the technology of the 1960s. Rather, it is that by accepting the constraints imposed by the Bathe/Clissold Index running from Bk. 1 to Mi. 755, the true scale of Williams's collecting is missed. By my calculation, Alfred Williams collected over one thousand songs or versions of songs. This number is based on: my transcriptions of the manuscripts; Williams's own attributions; the material published in *Folk-Songs of the Upper Thames* and also in Williams's *Round About the Upper Thames* of 1922;[9] material published in a series of articles in the *Wilts and Gloucestershire Standard* in 1915 and 1916, which predated both books;[10] and other references in the archive and articles by Williams in other newspapers.

For example, there are references to 'Barbara Allan' attributed to Elijah Iles, Inglesham, Wiltshire; James Mills, Latton, Wiltshire/South Cerney, Gloucestershire (these parishes lie

9 Alfred Williams, *Round About the Upper Thames* (London: Duckworth, 1922).
10 Alfred Williams, 'Round about the Upper Thames', *Wilts and Gloucestershire Standard*, January–August 1915 [33 parts]; Alfred Williams, 'Folk-Songs of the Upper Thames', *Wilts and Gloucestershire Standard*, October 1915–September 1916 [44 parts].

either side of the county border and he lived in both); and Charles Tanner, Bampton, Ox-fordshire—but there is only one text (Wt. 388). My assumption is that Williams's lost field notes might well have revealed any differences, but there are few instances in which this can be proved.

When transcribing the songs from the articles in the *Wilts and Gloucestershire Standard*, I assigned numbers to the songs in each published part. For example, 'A-begging buttermilk I will go' was published in *Folk-Songs of the Upper Thames* (p. 40), but also in the *Wilts and Gloucestershire Standard*, 30 October 1915 (p. 2, part 5, no. 8—being the eighth song from the top left of the article). In this way, I was able to source some material missing from the archive, identifying singers and locations, and thus enhancing the Bathe/Clissold Index data. For example, a fragment comprising verse 1 and the chorus of 'Wiltshire Labourers' appears in the manuscript (Wt. 521). But in the *Wilts and Gloucestershire Standard*, 26 February 1916 (p. 3, part 20, no. 9), all eight verses appear, as does the attribution, to Alfred Howse of Latton, Wiltshire.

Similarly, the song 'Captain Brooks and his Gallant Crew' is attributed to Edwin Roberts of Liddington, Gloucestershire (Gl. 138). However, in an article in the *Wiltshire Times*, 28 August 1926 (p. 9), there is another reference, without attribution: 'while at Cricklade another sang of valiant Captain Brooks, and the fight between the Chesapeake and the Shannon off Boston twenty years earlier'.[11] In fact, Williams collected twenty-eight other songs in Crick-lade, all but one of them from Henry ('Wassail') Harvey, so I feel some confidence that the source for 'Captain Brooks' was also Harvey. Williams wrote:

> The old man, who was ninety years old at the time I knew him, as well as being a wassailer—he was known to the locality as 'Wassail' Harvey—was a rare singer of folk songs. In my collection of Upper Thames Folk Songs, there were many good pieces of his rendering; he knew several hundreds of folk songs, besides a large mass of folklore. (*Wiltshire Gazette*, 2 December 1926, p. 3)

By bringing the sources together in this way, it is possible to identify the song with a Wiltshire singer.

---

11 Williams, Alfred: Random Papers series, Folk song and locality, Wiltshire Times [Captain Brooks and his gallant crew]

Another example of how a close comparison of the various Williams sources can assist in identifying songs is 'Farmer's Boy' (Mi. 565). In his book *A Wiltshire Village*, in which Williams writes about his home village of South Marston, he records:

> Jemmy stood up with half shut eyes, and after some little hemming and hawing, provided the treat of the evening,
>
> > The sun was settin' be'ind the 'ills,
> > Across yon stormy moor.[12]

In his thesis, Andrew Bathe suggests that 'Jemmy' is Jemmy Boulton, though he does not explain how he reaches this conclusion.[13] If he is right, then the only readily traceable Boulton within the likely demographic is John James Boulton, *c*.1839–1903. So, I claim this song from the Miscellaneous packet justifies a Wiltshire attribution too.

To return for a moment to the Wiltshire Community History website, I persuaded my former colleagues that adding traditional song texts would be feasible. It was agreed that I would undertake the transcriptions on a voluntary basis and that the material could be included in the website. My aim was to bring the archive on to the world stage. The integration of the data on the Wiltshire Community History website with the Full English Digital Archive will take that objective further, with links being developed to connect the digital images of the manuscripts with my transcriptions.

In addition, with the assistance of Malcolm Taylor and the staff of the Vaughan Williams Memorial Library I was able to obtain copies of all songs collected in Wiltshire by other collectors. A total of 1,113 songs, from all sources, is currently listed on the Wiltshire Community History website. Titles are still being added, either from my own continuing researches or as a result of contributions from users of the website. The latest is a version of 'Buttercup Joe' with the second line 'Me father comes from Sarum', sent in by James Hatch.[14] James now lives in Canada, but was formerly from Cookham, in Berkshire. His father sang the song. It was also collected in this form by A. G. Street and can be found, with this wording, in the typescript of

---

12 Alfred Williams, *A Wiltshire Village* (London: Duckworth, 1912), p. 122.
13 Bathe, 'Pedalling in the Dark', p. 387.
14 <history.wiltshire.gov.uk/community/getfolk.php?id=1251>.

What's in a name? Alfred Williams and his Singers

73

his *Farmer's Glory* (which differs from the published text).[15] I should also mention as an example of fruitful cooperation the 'Sherston Wassail' kindly forwarded to me by Gwylm Davies.[16]

As well as the songs, the website also contains fifty-five play texts, or references to their existence. These are mainly mumming plays, but there are also one or two 'rural' plays. The latest play acquisition is a version of the Shrewton Mummers' Play from a shorthand typescript by A. E. Howlett, commissioned in 1936 by Gerard Bonham-Carter, who was at that time resident in Shrewton House, and kindly supplied by Ron Shuttleworth of the Morris Ring Folk Play Archive.[17] This is the earliest known text of the play.

Following the lead of Andrew Bathe's thesis, I was prompted to extend my project yet again, into the realm of the singers and their identities. The thesis includes a number of biographies, some illustrated with photographs, of key singers such as Elijah Iles, David Sawyer, 'Wassail' Harvey, and Shadrach Haydon. (At this point I must pay tribute to Andrew's work, most of it probably undertaken before the advent of sophisticated online genealogical sources.) Lacking any prior interest in genealogy, I had to start from scratch to develop a structure to record census, birth, marriage, and death data on singers that would be easy to follow. My view is that I am offering evidence-based suggestions as to the identities of singers. More importantly, by providing a published audit trail, I am allowing others the opportunity to agree or disagree with me. Here is an example:[18]

> Name: Boucher, Thomas
> Listed by Alfred Williams as T. Bowker.
> Birth/baptism: Faringdon, Berkshire, *c.*1836 [Census 1841]
> Marriage 1: to Naomi Lavender, Hanover Square, London, 1866 [SA]. Widowed, Oct, Nov, Dec, 1880, Naomi died aged 33 [Berkshire, Faringdon, vol. 2c, p. 176].
> Marriage 2: Two candidates: Berkshire, Faringdon, Jul, Aug, Sep, 1881, vol. 2c, p. 501, Berkshire, Gloucestershire, Oxfordshire, Wiltshire, Faringdon, vol. 2a, or vol. 2c.
> Death / burial: Berkshire, Gloucestershire, Oxfordshire, Wiltshire, 1915, Apr, May, Jun, age, 78, vol. 2c, p. 290. June 1915 [SA].
> Census information: Census 1911: Listed as Thomas Boucher. Place of birth, Faringdon, Berkshire, *c.*1838; age, 73; address, Star Inn, London Street, Faringdon; occupation, inn keeper and carrier; widower.

15 Wiltshire and Swindon Archives, 3219, Pamela Street Archive, A. G. Street, *Farmer's Glory* unpublished manuscript, pp. 38, 39.

16 <history.wiltshire.gov.uk/community/getfolk.php?id=1229>.

17 <history.wiltshire.gov.uk/community/getplay.php?id=1219>.

18 <history.wiltshire.gov.uk/community/getfolkbio.php?id=163>.

Thomas Boucher is a useful example. One of his descendants, Simon Aldsworth (SA in the audit trail given above), contacted me by email and provided much additional information. This also happened with the family of Elijah Iles.

This is where the title for my presentation evolved. It became apparent that simply by using the names recorded by Williams it was not possible, in many instances, to trace singers. An earlier researcher perpetuated Williams's use of names, which, initially, was quite misleading. Here are some examples of misheard names (and there are many more):

Listed by Williams as:	Actual name:
Baughan, Thomas	Baughn, Thomas
Bowker, T.	Boucher, Thomas
Falconer, William	Faulkner, William [also Frederick, James, and John]
Hambridge, Charles	Hambidge, Charles
Leech, Henry	Leach, Henry
Merritt, W.	Merrett, William
Parrot, [Mrs]	Parrott, Mrs Mary Hannah
Pitt, [Mrs]	Pitts, Mrs Esther
Price, Jasper	Price, Eli Jasper
Zillard, Gabriel	Selwood, Gabriel

(At this point I must make clear that my identifications of these singers may be seen as contentious. It has been claimed that the biographical entries in the Wiltshire Community History website are in some cases inaccurate. That is entirely possible. If any individual is able to offer corrections, I will be happy to incorporate them, with full acknowledgement.)

Anyone familiar with *Folk-Songs of the Upper Thames* will recognize that there is one name listed above from whom Williams clearly stated he did not collect anything. In his introduction, Williams says of 'Gabriel Zillard': 'Of Zillard it is said that he could unbutton his shirt collar at six in the morning and sing for twelve or even eighteen hours, if necessary, with the perspiration running down his cheeks.'[19] Using the terms 'Gabriel' and 'Hannington' in ancestry.co.uk you can find two Gabriels in Hannington—probably father and son. My view is that Williams is referring to Gabriel Selwood (1832–93). This Gabriel Selwood worked in the Great Western Railway works in Swindon from at least 1881. I believe that Williams knew

19 Williams, *Folk-Songs of the Upper Thames*, p. 15.

of Selwood by reputation within the railway works, and the absence of any songs is explained by the date of his death.[20]

The census data can suggest other things, too. For example, Williams refers to 'Tibby' Barrett as a mat-maker. A search of the censuses reveals that Alfred Barrett was the son of a blacksmith, and in the 1881 census his recorded occupation was 'blacksmith'. But in 1891 he had moved from Sevenhampton, his place of birth and was then a lodger in Highworth, his occupation listed as 'working in a mat factory.' In 1901, listed as Alfred Darrett, still residing in Highworth, his occupation is mat-maker. He is still at the same address in 1911.[21] At some point between 1881 and 1891, I suggest that he probably suffered a serious industrial injury and went from a high-status occupation to a much lower one.

This brings me to an aspect of Williams's collecting which, until it was possible to access the 1911 census data, was impossible to determine. Williams, aware of the mainstream view of his day that only people living in a rural environment could be true representatives of the 'folk tradition', had to find a way of getting round this. He did so by means of a sleight of hand in noting the locations of his singers. Thus David Sawyer was always, more or less, 'of Ogbourne'. Here are some examples:

Name:	Location as given by Williams:
Bridgeman, William	Wanborough, Wiltshire
Couling, George	Kempsford, Gloucestershire
Herbert, George	Poulton, Gloucestershire
Hinder, Sam	Crudwell, Wiltshire
Poole, Walter	Minety, Wiltshire
Sawyer, David	Ogbourne St Andrew, Wiltshire

What all these individuals had in common is that they were all living in Swindon when Williams was collecting from them. Many of them were working in the same railway factory as Williams, some of them since at least 1881. I cannot, for example, accept that Williams would have cycled out to Kempsford to meet George Couling when he was in fact living in Beatrice Street, Swindon—and, in my view, this also applies to the other singers resident in Swindon:

20 <history.wiltshire.gov.uk/community/getfolkbio.php?id=269>.
21 <history.wiltshire.gov.uk/community/getfolkbio.php?id=13>.

William Bridgeman worked on the GWR coal wharf from at least 1881 and lived at the same address, 40 Exeter Street, Swindon, in 1901 and 1911.

George Couling left Kempsford some time between 1881 and 1891, and lived at various addresses in Swindon, where he was working for the GWR. In 1911 he was living at109 Beatrice Street, Swindon; occupation, railway wagon builder.

Herbert George hailed from Poulton in Gloucestershire, but had been resident in Swindon since 1891, living at 47 and 48 Morris Street, New Town. In 1911 he lived at 109 Linslade Street, Swindon; occupation, old-age pensioner, retired blacksmith; widower; living in the household of son-in-law, Albert Harbour; age, 27; place of birth, Long Crendon, Buckinghamshire; occupation, GWR loco worker drilling.

Sam Hinder's family moved to Swindon between 1871 and 1881 when they lived at 34 Haydon Street. Sam Hinder is not listed in the 1881 census but he was at this address between 1891 and 1911, when his occupation was general labourer, railway company.

Walter Poole left Crudwell some time between 1871 and 1881, when he lived at 1 Queens Road, New Swindon. He lived at other addresses in the town and in 1911was living at 204 Ferndale Road; occupation, railway wagon builder.

Of all Williams's singers, David Sawyer is the most intriguing. Williams collected fifty songs from Sawyer. The location to Ogbourne is unusual because it is nearly nine miles south of Swindon. It is only when you trace Sawyer's movements through the census that it is possible to identify Williams's sleight of hand. Sawyer was born in Ogbourne St Andrew c.1832 and lived in the village until at least 1861. In 1871 he is residing in Bishopstone, on the eastern edge of Swindon; in 1881 he is living close to the centre of Bath; in 1891 he is living on the eastern outskirts of Bath; in 1901 he is living at 39 Winifred Street, Swindon; and in 1911 he is aged 78 and living in Stratton St Margaret. Williams often refers to Sawyer as a shepherd or shearer, yet his occupations as listed in the various census returns are agricultural labourer, general dealer, labourer, and gardener.

Another oddity is Shadrach Haydon. Williams links him to Hatford five times, Lyford twice, and Bampton four times. But he must have collected from him in Bampton because he was living there from at least 1891.

Does this analysis of Williams's disguising of the locations of his singers at the time the songs were collected diminish his contribution to the recording of traditional songs in England? I would argue that it does not. Some of his attributions were made in order, I believe, simply to sustain the credibility of his sources. This reflects an aspect of his approach to collecting. In the introduction to *Folk-Songs of the Upper Thames* he writes:

> And from the beginning I laid down this rule—never by any means to admit a piece into my collection unless I had definite and personal proofs that it was actually sung in the neighbourhood and within the area I have mapped out. My pieces may have been sung in Somersetshire, Cornwall, Surrey, Warwickshire, Lancashire, Yorkshire, or Aberdeenshire, if you will. But as long as I have proof that they were also popular in the Thames Valley I am satisfied. That fact alone answers my purpose. And though infinitely better songs and ballads may belong to the counties I have mentioned, unless I have certain proofs of their having been here, I shall not admit them to a place in my collection.[22]

He sums up his approach to the songs he heard as follows:

> I make no apologies for the musical tastes of the people; I cannot help what they liked. That is no business of mine. I want to show not what they might have sung, nor what they ought to have sung, but what, in fact, they did sing. And what right have I, or anyone else, to condemn the taste exhibited in, or the imperfections of the old songs, and mutilate, patch, polish, or correct them in deference to the wishes of those trained exclusively according to the modern ideas of poetry and music, and who are unable to appreciate simpler measures?[23]

And he had a view, too, about the appropriation of songs to one county in particular:

> I am led to the conclusion that there is either inertia or downright neglect in the attribution of folk songs, and that some collectors, having become interested in a certain locality, and certain individuals, and having obtained a good number of songs, were unwilling to take further pains to ascertain to what extent the pieces were popular elsewhere, but wrote them down as belonging to a district or county when, as a matter of fact, they were equally popular and as firmly established all over the country.[24]

22 Williams, *Folk-Songs of the Upper Thames*, p. 13.
23 Williams, *Folk-Songs of the Upper Thames*, pp. 28–29.
24 Alfred Williams, 'Local Distribution of the Folk Song and Folk Music', *Wiltshire Gazette*, 6 August 1925, p. 3.

He is referring here, I think, to Cecil Sharp and his attribution of songs to Somerset.

In conclusion, here are a few observations about Alfred Williams. Born in 1877 into a working-class household, the fifth of eight children, he grew up in a single-parent household. He ended full-time education at the age of eight, started work in the GWR railway works at fifteen, where his health was broken by the working conditions. Later, he joined the army, serving in Ireland and India. He died almost certainly in poverty in 1930, aged 53. He was a largely self-educated man, who published volumes of poetry and prose that were feted in both Britain and the USA. His first collection of poetry, *Songs in Wiltshire*, appeared in 1909.[25] Here is one of the poems from that book, 'The Reaper':

> The tufted lark is over the plain
> The southern breezes blow
> The dew-balm's wet on the bending grain,
> Cheerily, merrily O!
> The panting horses of the day
> Leap into the eastern sky,
> Now 'tis time to be up and away
> My nut-brown lass and I.

'The Reaper' has been set to music and was recorded by Alex Atterson on his LP *Pushing the Business On* (1977)—but attributed to the Wiltshire vernacular poet Will Mead. This false attribution has been corrected by my former colleague Mervyn Grist of the Wiltshire History Centre, who correctly identified the piece as being by Williams. As his biographer says, he was regarded as one of the finest poets of the early twentieth century.

To my mind, it is his background that marks Williams out. Other collectors—Cecil Sharp, Baring-Gould, Lucy Broadwood, Ralph Vaughan Williams, and the rest—belonged to various levels of the middle class. Williams is the only serious collector of his era to have come from within the working class. He may not have collected as many songs as Sharp. He may not have noted any fine tunes. But he overcame his background in this as in many other facets of his life, to leave a working-class man's perspective of the songs performed in his community.

---

25 Alfred Williams, *Songs in Wiltshire* (London: Erskine MacDonald, 1909).

Phyllis Marshall and the Bathpool Singers

GEOFF WOOLFE

In 1916 and 1917 Phyllis Marshall, an Oxford graduate, collected a clutch of songs from her home parish of West Monkton in Somerset. This paper examines her life and interest in traditional song, as well as the lives of the singers from the area. I will refer to the songs and make some observations about Marshall's collecting methods and her place in the early twentieth-century folk revival.

West Monkton was, and remains, a rather sprawling parish, a few miles to the north-east of Taunton.[1] Its two village centres are Monkton Heathfield and, to the south, Bathpool, which is where most of the singers lived. The area was primarily centred on agriculture, but a few associated small industries developed alongside the Bridgwater to Taunton canal and a branch of the Great Western Railway. Chief among these was a paper mill in the next village, Creech St Michael. Today, Bathpool is virtually a suburb of Taunton; a new housing development will link the town to the village (Figure 1).

From 1917 to 1920 Phyllis Marshall sent her manuscripts to the folk song collector Janet Blunt, of Adderbury, Oxfordshire. After her death, Blunt's collection was sent to the Vaughan Williams Memorial Library.[2] Michael Pickering wrote about three of the songs from Bathpool sent by Marshall in his *Folk Music Journal* article on Janet Blunt.[3] Tony Foxworthy also

---

1   Archival and other sources used in the preparation of this paper include parish and census records at Somerset Heritage Centre and at <www.findmypast.co.uk>; *Kelly's Directory for Somerset* (1914); J. Reeves and R. Gardner, eds, *West Monkton Then and Now* (West Monkton: West Monkton Parish Council, 2001); Rev. Maurice E. Roynon, *The Church of St Augustine of Canterbury, West Monkton* (1968); St Augustine's parish magazines 1930–1960.

2   London, EFDSS Archives, Janet Blunt Collection <www.vwml.org/>.

3   Michael Pickering, 'Janet Blunt: Folk Song Collector and Lady of the Manor', *Folk Music Journal*, 3.2 (1976), 114–57.

Figure 1. *Bathpool today. Photo by Geoff Woolfe.*

published two of the Bathpool songs in *Forty Long Miles*, a selection from the Janet Blunt archive.[4] In addition, Bob Patten has discovered another copy of Phyllis Marshall's manuscript (Figure 2).[5] This includes a few songs that are not in the Blunt collection, and it was prepared earlier than the fair copies of music and texts sent to Blunt. There are twenty-five separate songs across the two versions of the manuscript, the majority from one singer, Elizabeth Nation.

The songs and singers are discussed below, but firstly here is what is known about Phyllis Marshall's life and her interest in the early twentieth-century folk revival. Phyllis Mary Marshall was born into a middle-class family in 1889 in Witley, Surrey. Her father, Ed-

---

4   Tony Foxworthy, *Forty Long Miles: Twenty-Three English Folk Songs from the Collection of Janet Heatley Blunt* (London: Galliard-EFDSS, 1976).

5   Bob and Jacqueline Patten, *Somerset Scrap Book: Songs, Stories and Music from the County of Somerset* ([Priddy]: Ina Books, 1987); Bob and Jacqueline Patten, *A Somerset Scrapbook: Songs, Stories and Music from the County of Somerset* CD-ROM (Musical Traditions MTCD252, 2013).

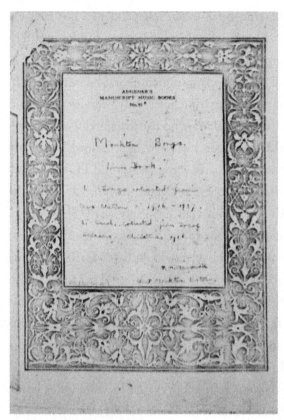

Figure 2. *Phyllis Marshall manuscript book. Photo courtesy of Bob Patten.*

ward Shearburn Marshall, was a scholar of Brasenose College, Oxford, and an Anglican minister.[6] He held two rectorships, in Sussex and Wiltshire, before taking up the same office in West Monkton in 1904. Phyllis followed her father and her brother, Edward junior, to Oxford University, in 1909, reading English at Lady Margaret Hall and graduating in 1912. She then worked at the Bodleian Library until 1916, and from 1917 to 1925 she worked for the Girls' Friendly Society as head of the members' department for three separate dioceses, Bath and Wells, Monmouth, and Llandaff.

In 1919 her father was taken ill and retired. This was a difficult time for Phyllis. In that year, her mother, uncle, and then her father, all died within a few weeks of each other. Her father had already bought a small estate at Tidenham in the Forest of Dean, where he had intended to devote most of his time to his great interest in botany. He wrote several works and articles on flora of the West Country.[7] The estate was named Offa's Dyke, close to the long distance path of that name. Phyllis moved there with her parents in 1919, and later devoted her life to the local church at Tidenham and Tutshill, close to Chepstow. She played the organ and taught at the local Sunday school for many years, until late in her life. She had been left a substantial legacy, part of which was the benefice of the West Monkton parish. In 1968 this income reverted back to the diocese of Bath and Wells. In the 1920s she went into partnership with Walter Bounds in a share in Mapleford Colliery, near Coleford. Her brother, Edward junior, moved to Ceylon (Sri Lanka) in the 1920s where he ran a tea plantation. His wife, Agnes, gave birth to a son, another Edward, in Ceylon in 1923.

6　Personal communication (emails from Oliver Maloney, archivist, Lady Margaret Hall, University of Oxford).

7　James Britten, obituary of Edward Shearburn Marshall (1858–1919), Journal *of Botany, British and Foreign*, 58 (1920), 1–11.

Edward briefly returned to live at Offa's Dyke after Sri Lankan independence, but later returned to a tea plantation in Sri Lanka. Phyllis Marshall lived at Tidenham until her death in May 1979, aged eighty-nine, at Mount Pleasant Hospital, Chepstow.

While she was at Oxford, Phyllis Marshall became active in the folk revival in the city. In 1912, she lodged at 11 Woodstock Road, a short distance from both Lady Margaret Hall and Somerville College, where a fellow lodger was Daisy Daking who had attended Cecil Sharp's dance classes at Chelsea College in London. Roy Judge's history of the Oxford University Morris Men,[8] his article on Mary Neal and the Espérance movement,[9] and Hilary Clare's book on Daisy Daking, provide useful information about the Oxford revival.[10] In 1911 the first meeting of the Oxford branch of the English Folk Dance Society (EFDS) was held, with Cecil Sharp and William Kimber in attendance. One of the founders of the branch was Charlotte Sidgwick, who lived at 64 Woodstock Road. I have no doubt that Marshall became a dance enthusiast at this time, and that her friendship with Daisy Daking led her to help with Janet Blunt's dance collecting in Oxfordshire. The Blunt archive lists Phyllis Marshall as one of the collectors of several morris dances in the Adderbury area in February 1914. The previous year she had sent Cecil Sharp a dance and tune, 'The Breast Knot', collected from Mrs Wyatt, a farmer's widow in West Monkton. In June 1914 Sharp went to West Monkton and collected the same dance again, along with two more, from Mrs Wyatt. He wrote in his notes: 'Mrs W is a farmer's wife between 50 & 60(?) who came from Buckland S[t]. Mary. She says they are too close to Taunton (about 3 miles) for dances, because the townspeople come out & spoil them. People from towns are so stiff & formal, and not graceful & gay as we like to be.'[11]

It is possible that Marshall met Sharp—we cannot tell from his notes. It seems certain, however, that she knew of his published Somerset song collections. A letter to Janet Blunt in June 1917 shows that she was aware of traditional song sources, including broadsides:

8 Roy Judge, ed., 'The Ancient Men: The OUMM and its Background', rev. Ian Hall and Gerard Robinson (1993) <http://www.yetaco.plus.com/am39/oummhist.pdf>. Summary at <www.yetaco.plus.com/am39/history.html>.

9 Roy Judge, 'Mary Neal and the Espérance Morris', *Folk Music Journal*, 5.5 (1989), 545–91.

10 Hilary Clare, *The Fine Companion: The Journal of a Caravan Trip from Oxford to Stratford-upon-Avon in the Summer of 1914* (Romsey: Elsie Jeanette Oxenham Society/Abbey Chronicle, 2011)

11 Cambridge, Clare College Archives, CCPP/SHA, Cecil Sharp Collection of Folk Song Manuscripts, Folk Tunes 2964 [Full English Digital Archive: CJS2/10/2964].

West Monkton Rectory
Taunton
5 June 1917

Dear Miss Blunt,

I send herewith the songs I have got so far — there is half a verse of 'the constant farmer's son' which is pure nonsense[:] 'But mark returning home again and said his wife was won for by my mistake his life did take of her constant farmer's son'.

I believe the song is extant in a broadside pr[inted] by Such but hitherto I have not met it. I have had to omit one verse in 'One night as I lay' as it was imperfect & not quite proper & the same with 'When first to London'. [O]therwise they are to all intents as taken down.[12]

The 'unbowdlerized' versions of these two songs, apparently sent some years later, are in the Janet Blunt collection.[13]

The Bathpool Singers

Elizabeth Nation was born Florence Elizabeth Gunningham in February 1864, in Kingston St Michael, a village a few miles north of Taunton. She told Phyllis Marshall that she had learned her songs from her mother Mary (née Martin). All her family were farm workers. She worked in service in Taunton before she married Fred Nation, a groom from Bishops Lydeard. In 1901 they lived at Bawdrip, near Bridgwater, where Fred was a farm labourer. They had two children, Clifford and Lily, and by 1911 had moved to Bathpool, first to Laurel Cottage and then to Baytree Cottage. As a widow, Elizabeth Nation moved to the local Spital Almhouses in the 1930s, and remained there until her death in 1954 (Figure 3). Her descendants still live in Somerset. Her grandson, Fred junior, and his son Victor both sang in the Bathpool church choir (Figure 4). Elizabeth Nation gave Marshall fifteen songs:

'Cupid's Garden' (Roud 297)
'Spotted Cow' (Roud 956)
'British Man of War' (Roud 372)
'Dabbling in the Dew' (Roud 298)
'One night as I lay on my bed' (Roud 672)
'Blow ye winds I O' ('Steal Away the Morning Dew') (Roud 11)

12 Blunt Collection, JHB/10/5A.
13 Blunt Collection, JHB/10/11.

Figure 3. *Spital Almshouses residents, including Mrs Nation and Mrs Thomas, 1930s. Photo courtesy of John Reeves and West Monkton Parish Council.*

'Pretty Ploughboy' (Roud 186)
'Constant Farmer's Son' (Roud 675)
'Lord Bateman' (Roud 40)
'Oh If I was but a butterfly' (aka 'Irish Girl') (Roud 308)
'Seeds of Love' (Roud 3)
'(When First to) London Town' (Roud 914)
'Johnny Collishaw' (Roud 920)
'Horn Fair' (Roud 2482)
'Midsummer's Evening' (Roud 2512) (a version of 'Shady Green Grove')

'(When First to) London Town' is notated in 9/4 time and Marshall clearly had difficulty settling on this time signature. In fact, it is similar to a version from Jane Gulliver of Combe Florey (about fifteen miles away) collected by the Hammond brothers and notated in 5/4. 'Johnny Collishaw' is a press-gang song with Irish roots. Lucy Broadwood collected a version, under the title 'Captain Galligan', from Mrs Joiner of Chiswell Green in 1914.

Figure 4. *Mrs Nation and her grandson Victor. Photo courtesy of John Reeves and West Monkton Parish Council.*

Ellen Millington was a teacher at Monkton Heathfield village school, where her husband, John, was the head teacher. He was a churchwarden, and they were both stalwarts of the village and church community, and therefore close to Marshall and her family. Mrs Millington was born Ellen Rogers in Taunton in 1866. Her father was a cooper, and she married John Millington, who was originally from Worcestershire, in 1891. Like Phyllis Marshall, she was an organizer with the Girls' Friendly Society. Her daughter, Edith, wrote a short history of the parish.[14] She gave Marshall four songs: 'The Dilly Song' ('What is your one O') (Roud 133); 'The Old Couple' (Roud 491); 'King Alfred's Three Sons' ('King Arthur's Sons') (Roud 130); and a fragment of 'The Trees They Do Grow High' (Roud 31). None of these songs are among the Phyllis Marshall songs in the Blunt collection. There is no obvious reason for this. Perhaps 'The Trees They Do Grow High' was considered too well known, and in any event it was only a fragment; the others may have been thought of as 'just' children's songs.

Mrs Thomas lived at the Spital Almhouses in 1916–17 (see Figure 3). She sang 'Twelve Bulls', a version of 'The Twelve Days of Christmas' (Roud 21939). She was still living at the almshouses at the same time as Mrs Nation in the 1930s.

The White family sang a version of 'The Hog Tub' (Roud 1273). Marshall's notes do not indicate where the family lived. There are two Whites listed nearby in the 1911 census. One ran Leacroft Farm, and the other was George White, a farm bailiff who lived in Bathpool.

Mrs Murphy was noted as the singer of 'Love and Liberty', also known as 'Sweet Swansea' (Roud 300/1612). Marshall's manuscript notes that Mrs Murphy 'learnt it from a Welsh girl in Cardiff'.[15] Mrs Murphy's biography has proved elusive; she may have been a temporary domestic worker.

14 Edith Mary Millington, *Our Parish of West Monkton* ([c.1970]) [copy at Taunton, Somerset Heritage Centre].
15 Blunt Collection, JHB/10/18.

Mrs Rosa Duke lived at Creech St Michael. Many of her family worked at the paper mill there. She sang a version of 'The Female Soldier' (Roud 226). She was born Rosa Horrill in 1875, in West Monkton. At the age of sixteen she worked as a paper sorter at the mill. In 1896 she married William Duke, a labourer, who in 1911 was working at the mill as a stationery stoker.

Mrs Thirza Burge sang 'The Banks of the Sweet Dundee' (Roud 148). She was born in West Monkton in 1865. In 1891 she was working at the paper mill as a sorter. In 1911 she was living in Bathpool with her husband William, a carter and coal merchant. She died in 1919 and was buried at West Monkton on 2 December. In Marshall's manuscript in the Blunt archive Mrs Burge is named as the singer of another version of 'The Female Soldier', but it is possible that this is an error. The manuscript note reads 'sung by Mrs Burge, now dead', indicating that Phyllis Marshall sent this copy of the manuscript to Janet Blunt in 1919 or later.[16]

Three of Thirza Burge's eight children were working at the Creech St Michael paper mill in 1911. The mill was a major employer in the area, owned by the Somerville family.[17] It used raw materials such as rags, wood pulp, and imported esparto grass and bamboo, brought in by rail. There was a ready supply of spring water and the north Somerset coal fields supplied fuel for the boilers. The paper produced there was used by Bristol printers. Working conditions were sometimes difficult, as hazardous dyes and dirty rag flock were used. The company was probably a typical family-run business. There was an annual seaside outing by train (but there is no record of any songs that might have been sung on the journey home). There was no history of labour disputes, although there was a controversy about alleged low wages which led to a question in the House of Commons in 1914. The mill continued operating until the early 1990s, having at one time been owned by Robert Maxwell's British Printing Corporation.

The Marshall manuscript contains two further songs. One is a version of 'The Dark Eyed Sailor' (Roud 265). It is unattributed, but may have been sung by Mrs Millington. The other song is a Dutch/Flemish Christmas carol noted from Josef Sciaens, a Belgian visitor to the rectory in 1916.

Phyllis Mary Marshall was a dance and song enthusiast, who was a collector for just a few years of her life. She was a 'feeder' collector, sending material to Janet Blunt in the same way as others who sent material to Sharp and the Hammonds. She had been inspired by the folk

---

16 Blunt Collection, JHB/9/10.

17 Taunton, Somerset Heritage Centre, A/CKN/7/6 M/3810, Gwyneth Bryant, 'The Somervilles and the Early Days: A Draft Research Paper on Creech St Michael and the Paper Mill' (1990); Gwyneth Leighton, article on Creech St Michael Paper Mill (2005) <www.creechstmichael.net/about/paper-mill>.

revival in Oxford in the early twentieth century, and she was clearly motivated to help Janet Blunt with her collection, but there is little evidence that she wanted to perform the songs or to campaign like Cecil Sharp. Like many of her time, Marshall came from an educated, middle-class background. She was evidently committed to her family's background in the Church of England, devoting her later working life to the Girls' Friendly Society, an Anglican organization. She does not appear to have been influenced by the more radical ideas current at the time, such as women's suffrage, the Fabian Society, or Christian socialism.

Like Janet Blunt, Marshall was essentially an amateur enthusiast for traditional dance and song. She played the organ, and her musical experience may have been mainly centred on church activities. Her later life has similarities with Janet Blunt's, whom Pickering describes as a 'Lady of the Manor'. The Offa's Dyke estate at Tidenham was a small farm with estate workers and a domestic staff. Apart from Mrs Millington, all of Marshall's singers were from the rural working class. Most of the Bathpool singers were mature women, but Marshall's notes tell us little about their lives. The songs mainly fit the model of folk song advocated by Sharp and other early twentieth-century collectors. Most of them can be found in other Somerset versions, collected by the likes of Sharp and the Hammond brothers. There is no contemporary or music hall material and it is possible that Marshall 'filtered out' such songs. She was minded to bowdlerize at least two of the songs, but later relented.

Thanks to Bob Patten's eye for song archives, and to Janet Blunt's housekeeper who sent her collection of songs to the Vaughan Williams Memorial Library, we have a record of songs sung in West Monkton in 1916–17. Phyllis Marshall deserves to be remembered especially for the songs from Elizabeth Nation — a few of which are included in the *New Penguin Book of English Folk Songs*.[18]

Acknowledgements

Thanks to Steve Roud, Bob Patten, Keith Burgum of Tidenham Historical Group, Mrs Nation's descendants, John Reeves of West Monkton, Lady Margaret Hall archivist Oliver Maloney, the archivists at Somerset Heritage Centre, and fellow members of folk song group the Hotwells Howlers, John and Angela Shaw, Dave Byrne, Olga Shotton. Four songs from Bathpool can be found on *Love and Liberty,* a Hotwells Howlers double CD <www.thehot-wellshowlers.com>.

18 Steve Roud and Julia Bishop, *The New Penguin Book of English Folk Songs* (London: Penguin/EFDSS, 2012).

II. Songs

II. Songs

'No father, no mother, nor no friend at all': 'The Poor Murdered Woman' as Local Composition and Subversive Crime Ballad

CLARE BUTTON

The long and healthy trade in gruesome broadside ballads reveals much about the public's insatiable zeal for crime songs. Songs describing true crimes in particular possessed the extra frisson of reality, and the 'last goodnights' of criminals were hawked near the gallows even before the noose had been tied. In Leatherhead, Surrey, however, there was to be one song about a real crime that would not only evade the broadside trade, but entirely confound its placement within the genre of crime balladry.

'The Poor Murdered Woman Laid on the Cold Ground' (Roud 1064) narrates the discovery of a woman's body on Leatherhead Common by the Surrey Union Fox Hounds on 11 January 1834. Composed by local brick-maker James Fairs, the song was collected only once, in Milford, Surrey, in 1897, by the Rev. Charles John Shebbeare (1865–1945) from a Mr Foster, a 'young labourer'.[1] The song was first published in the *Journal of the Folk-Song Society*, under the title 'The Poor Murdered Woman Laid on the Cold Ground', and subsequently in Lucy Broadwood's *English Traditional Songs and Carols* with some slight textual variations and the shortened title 'The Poor Murdered Woman'.[2] Broadwood did not have much to say about the song's poetic qualities, deeming the words 'doggerel'. However, I shall argue that the song's composer displayed far more creative dexterity than Broadwood supposed.

Although strikingly factual in its language and structure, the song does not resemble a simple piece of versified reportage. Neither does it conform to the 'crime ballad' type, refusing many common generic motifs while still seeming to display an awareness of them. This paper

1 Lucy Broadwood, ed., *English Traditional Songs and Carols* (London: Boosey & Co., 1908), p. 121.
2 *Journal of the Folk-Song Society*, 1.4 (1902), 186–87; Broadwood, *English Traditional Songs and Carols*, pp. 70–71.

will argue not only that the song subverts the crime ballad genre, but also that it is a highly unusual example of a locally composed response to violence, not widely found in collected form, which has much to tell us about the function of such songs both within their immediate, contemporary communities and for a wider, modern audience.

Given that 'The Poor Murdered Woman' is one of the most starkly factual songs in the English collected tradition, it is sensible to begin by examining the real event that underpins it. In the interests of clarity, the song text is given below as it appears in the *Journal of the Folk-Song Society*:

> It was Yankee, the squièr, as I have heard say,
> Who rode out a-hunting on one Saturday.
> They hunted all day, but nothing they found
> But a poor murdered woman laid on the cold ground.
>
> About eight o' clock, boys, our dogs they throwed off,
> On Leatherhead Common, and that was the spot;
> They tried all the bushes, but nothing they found
> But a poor murdered woman laid on the cold ground.
>
> They whipped their dogs off, and kept them away,
> For I do think it proper he should have fair play;
> They tried all the bushes, but nothing they found,
> But a poor murdered woman laid on the cold ground.
>
> They mounted their horses and rode off the ground,
> They rode to the village, and alarmed it all round:
> 'It is late in the evening I am sorry to say,
> She cannot be removèd until the next day.'
>
> The next Sunday morning, about eight o' clock,
> Some hundreds of people to the spot they did flock;
> For to see that poor creature it would make your hearts bleed,
> Some [c]old and some violence came into their heads.

She was took off the Common down to some inn,
And the man that has kept it, his name is Jonson
The Coroner was sent for, the jury they joined,
And soon they concluded, and settled their mind.

Her coffin was brought, in it she was laid,
And took to the churchyard that was called Leatherhead,
No father, no mother, nor no friend at all,
Come to see that poor creature put under the mould.

So now I'll conclude and finish my song,
And those that have done it will find themselves wrong,
For the last day of judgement the trumpet will sound,
And their souls not in heaven I am afraid won't be found.

The Times newspaper report, printed only three days after the discovery of the body, re-counts that on 11 January 1834 the Surrey Union Fox Hounds found the remains of a woman under some bushes on Leatherhead Common, that the state of the body prevented its being removed until the following day, when it was taken to the Royal Oak inn, that the doctor's examination concluded that the cause of death was a head injury, and that rumours abounded that the victim was 'the wife of a travelling tinker.'[3] A Travelling man was arrested soon after-wards, on the verbal evidence of a young girl, but the lack of any written record of an ensuing trial suggests that investigations reached an impasse.[4] Exactly how soon after the event the song was composed is unknown, but it bears out the main circumstances as reported, from the finding of the body by the hounds, through the transportation of the body to a public house, to the coroner's inquest.

On this basis, it would be justifiable to classify 'The Poor Murdered Woman' as a crime ballad, in that it tells the story of a crime (or, more exactly, the aftermath of a crime). Yet closer analysis reveals much that is inconsistent with this definition. 'The Poor Murdered Wom-

3 'Supposed Murder', *The Times*, 14 January 1834, p. 5.
4 See the article 'The Tale of the Poor Murdered Woman, Featuring Shirley Collins', with historical background information by Alun Roberts, posted to accompany a documentary broadcast on Folk Radio UK in April 2013, at <www.folkradio.co.uk/2013/04/new-programme-the-tale-of-the-poor-murdered-woman-an-interview-with-shirley-collins/> [accessed 20 February 2014]. At the same time, a special exhibition on the subject was mounted at Leatherhead Museum of Local History, opened by Shirley Collins <www.leatherheadlocalhistory.org.uk/goto_museum.html>.

an' lacks many of the common elements of earlier crime ballads, which Joy Wiltenburg summarizes as 'revulsion and sorrow at violent crime, remorse for one's sins, pity for the repentant sinner, grief for one's own death or that of others, and fear of execution, victimization or God's judgment.'[5] Using Wiltenburg's criteria as a useful framework, a closer comparison of 'The Poor Murdered Woman' with other crime ballads based on supposedly true events will highlight the ways in which the song both denies and systematically subverts these typical features.

The most immediately striking feature of 'The Poor Murdered Woman' is its straightforward tone: there is none of the gore-stained melodrama and heightened language characteristic of many crime ballads. Such matter-of-factness precludes any trace of what Wiltenburg calls 'revulsion and sorrow at violent crime'. The discovery of the body is reported with no overt sense of 'revulsion', and without the more explicit details present in the newspaper report. The song does not convey the sense of a strong emotional reaction on the part of the local populace, except perhaps a morbid fascination with the spectacle: 'Some hundreds of people to the spot they did flock'. The only sense of 'sorrow' is implied in the repeated use of the word 'poor' to describe the woman, while empathy, when it occurs, is confined to the conditional tense: 'For to see that poor creature it *would* make your hearts bleed' (my emphasis). Murderers' own hearts frequently 'bleed' as part of the emotional patterning of remorse in crime ballads, as in the opening lines of a broadside based on the execution of Thomas Randall for the murder of Roger Levins in 1696:

> With melting Eyes and bleeding Heart,
> of Grief and Heaviness,
> Before this Life I do depart,
> my Sins I here confess.[6]

In 'The Poor Murdered Woman', however, it is the hearts of the listeners—of people outside of the song—that would bleed upon seeing the victim.

The absence of a perpetrator precludes outright the possibility of two of Wiltenburg's motifs, 'remorse for one's sins' and 'pity for the repentant sinner'. If there is no criminal, there can be no punishment and no sense of closure. The audience is not invited to 'condole with

---

5   Joy Wiltenburg, 'Ballads and the Emotional Life of Crime', in *Ballads and Broadsides in Britain, 1500–1800*, ed. Patricia Fumerton and Anita Guerrini (Farnham and Burlington, VT: Ashgate, 2010), pp.173–86 (pp. 183–84).

6   *The Mournful Murtherer; or, The Last Dying Lamentation of Thomas Randall* (London: J. Blare, [1696]) [ESTC R234349; Pepys Ballads 2.161].

victims and abhor the crime',[7] or to participate in the stylized repentance of the criminal. The murder of Maria Marten by William Corder in 1827 became the subject of several ballads, with the justice meted out to Corder in reality (he was hanged the following year) finding its fictionalized counterpart in a broadside text as his character declaims:

> Now at the age of twenty-four you see,
> From friends and acquaintances I cut off must be,
> A desolate [*sic*] life I have led on this earth,
> The vilest of mortals that ever drew breath.[8]

Crime ballads like this allow words to be placed satisfyingly into the mouths of real-life victims and criminals, in contrast to the stark wordlessness offered by 'The Poor Murdered Woman'.

There is no perpetrator to grieve for his own death in the song, but even Wiltenburg's fourth motif, which is concerned with grief for the victim, is problematic. Surrounded upon her discovery, the victim is alone at her burial: she categorically has 'No father, no mother, nor no friend at all' to mourn her, a subversion of the characteristic catalogue of a crime's grievous effects upon the families of victim and criminal. A broadside based on the shooting of the Earl of Ripon's gamekeeper by a poacher in 1848, for example, depicts the widow and children of the murdered man weeping over his grave and decrying:

> Oh! murderous man, what hast thou done?
> Reflect upon thy awful crime!
> What peace of mind to thee can come,
> Oh wretch repent while thou hast time![9]

This florid scene of bereavement mixed with reproach is in stark contrast to the deserted graveside in 'The Poor Murdered Woman'. Even 'Six Dukes Went a-Fishing' (Roud 78), a song not ostensibly in the crime genre but which shares in common with 'The Poor Murdered Woman' its factual tone, stark narrative detail, and subject matter (the discovery and subsequent treatment of a dead body), allows the drowned protagonist an elaborate and well-at-

---

7   Wiltenburg, 'Ballads and the Emotional Life of Crime', p. 173.

8   *The Red Barn Tragedy* (Glasgow: James Lindsay, [1851–1910]) [Oxford, Bodleian Library, 2806c.13(96)].

9   'The Widow's Lament', in C. J. Davison Ingledew, *Ballads and Songs of Yorkshire* (London: Bell and Daldy, 1860), pp. 282–86 (p. 283).

tended funeral.[10] In 'The Poor Murdered Woman', 'no friend at all' attends the funeral and the nameless victim is literally outside society—no more identifiable in the song than was the real-life victim. Just as we are never presented with the figure of the woman alive, the song depicts the crime *post-mortem*, with no attempt to reshape it into something more dramatic, palatable, or satisfying for an audience.

Wiltenburg's final motif, 'fear of execution, victimization or God's judgment', depends upon either an identified criminal or else an omniscient narrator who can step in to provide authority and comfort, as in a broadside based around the execution of George Sands, 'after many enormous crimes by him committed', in 1626:

> Loe here you see a fearfull end,
> of Sir George Sands his sonne,
> Let euery one a warning take,
> and better courses runne:
> Which to effect let us all pray
> to him that gaue vs breath,
> That of his mercy he'll vs keepe
> from such vntimely death.[11]

The narrative voice of 'The Poor Murdered Woman', in contrast, knows as much—which is to say, as little—as we do. Eternal judgement is implied, but only in the last stanza: 'And those that have done it will find themselves wrong, / For the last day of judgement the trumpet will sound, / And their souls not in heaven I am afraid won't be found.' But even this rings a little hollow: 'will' hints at certainty, but the relegation of punishment to the afterlife lacks confidence, while 'I am afraid won't be found' is too meek to evoke a sense of condemnatory brimstone. Such lack of resolution acts as a deeply unsettling force within the song.

The 'true crime' ballads mentioned above are found in broadside form, with a currency and purpose distinct from songs composed within a local community which describe true events in a more nuanced, vernacular style. 'The Poor Murdered Woman' may be reconceptualized in the context of such local pieces. James Fairs' composition does not merely summarize a small piece of text in a national newspaper, nor does it construct a dramatic literary piece around the crime. Rather, it reclaims the event into the fabric of Leatherhead's immediate experience and

---

10 *Journal of the Folk-Song Society*, 3.3 (no. 12) (1908), 170–79.
11 *The Life and Death of M. Geo: Sands* (London: F. Couls, [1626]) [ESTC S126172; Pepys Ballads 1.128–129].

history. Rooted in its geographical environs, the song more exactly resembles a local chronicle. This 'chronicling' effect is frequently achieved in localized songs through the verisimilitude of nomenclature, most usually that of personages and geographical locations. Hunting songs in particular are often characterized by their profuse naming, seeming to run a breathless race to enshrine local lives and events. A brief scan through the text of 'Swarthfell Rocks' (Roud 1578), for example, quickly garners the names of the sportsmen Henry Wilkinson, Richard Mounsey, Joe Clarke, and, of course, the dogs Countess, Blossom, and Fury.[12] This urge to name is shared by 'The Poor Murdered Woman', which, considering the song begins with a hunting scene, is fitting. George James Barnard Hankey, master of the Surrey Union Fox Hounds, and John Simms, licensee of the Royal Oak inn at Leatherhead, were real individuals, alive at the time of the crime.[13] Yet while naming in hunting songs such as 'Swarthfell Rocks' is frequently congratulatory and laudatory, the names in 'The Poor Murdered Woman' are used sparsely, to heighten the awful reality of the crime.

This mix of careful factuality and specific locality is at odds with the earlier crime ballads. This remains true even when a localized song is directly about a crime. 'The Death of Bill Brown' (Roud 609), which, like 'The Poor Murdered Woman', deals directly with the after-math of a murder, is one of two distinct songs about the shooting of the poacher Bill Brown in 1769 and the revenge subsequently taken against his killer. As in James Fairs' song, direct language is employed, with little moralizing or emotive fuss. Yet the song not only names Bill Brown's killer (although the name alters from George Miller to Tom Green between the two different songs), it even goes so far as to describe the clothes he was wearing at the time of the shooting: 'Black jacket he had, and red waistcoat on.'[14] Ultimately, the song's narrator takes revenge and achieves closure on Bill's behalf, as he declares: 'I've crowned his hopes and his memory.' But there is no one in Leatherhead to do the same for the murdered woman.

In view of the dearth of songs with which it can easily be compared, it may be surmised that 'The Poor Murdered Woman' is a song apart, composed and maintained within a localized district and fulfilling particular functions therein. Of course, one cannot conduct retrospective fieldwork to ascertain exactly what those functions might have been, but the evidence of the song's existence in a local singing tradition can be examined. It is known that the song was collected over sixty years after the discovery of the murdered woman, in Milford, a village

---

12 *Journal of the Folk-Song Society*, 2.4 (no. 9) (1906), 267–69.

13 'Tale of the Poor Murdered Woman'.

14 Frank Kidson, *Traditional Tunes: A Collection of Ballad Airs* (Oxford: Chas. Taphouse & Son, 1891), pp. 131–33 (p. 132).

twenty miles away from Leatherhead, and it has not been collected anywhere else. Even in 1908, both the actual events and the song were remembered sufficiently well that a local Milford man, Mr Lisney, could corroborate the facts and name the author of the ballad as James Fairs, a Leatherhead brick-maker.[15] James Fairs' dwelling is said to have been near to the scene of the victim's discovery, so he may have witnessed the events at first hand.[16] Evidently, the song retained sufficient resonance to have migrated the twenty miles to Milford, where it became a 'favourite song' of the 'young labourer', Mr Foster, who sang it in 1897. It is not known whether Mr Foster learned the song orally (he wrote out the words for the Rev. Shebbeare), although the occurrence of a few aurally close mis-namings in the text—'Johnson' for John Simm, 'Yankee' for Hankey—suggests that he might have done so. If that were the case, then the song must have remained in oral currency for at least sixty years after the crime was committed, and both the murder and the song remained in local knowledge up until at least 1908.

It is not difficult to imagine the disturbance to Leatherhead's social equilibrium caused by the discovery of a murder victim, and something of that disturbance can be detected in the text of the song itself. The repeated line 'But a poor murdered woman laid on the cold ground' that concludes the first three verses has the ominous chiming effect of a bell, the brutality of the word 'murdered' disrupting the quietness of the scene in the song just as it must have done in real life. Martin Carthy has described 'The Poor Murdered Woman' as a song about 'a non-event',[17] but it cannot have been so to its composer or its singers. Without first-hand testimony, what the song meant to those who first knew it must remain largely speculative. However, parallels can be drawn with work that has sought to examine songs in their local community contexts and to interrogate why they are sung.

In fact, songs can help people 'make sense' of the world and come to terms with difficult events and emotions. Herbert Halpert offers an example of this sense-making function of a locally composed crime song in 'The Murder of Jim Wainwright', written by Big Bill Estel (or Estelle) about a murder that occurred in New Jersey in 1884. Halpert writes:

> Most human beings gain a great part of their experience of such exciting things as murder, not from direct experience but at second hand [. . .] The folk singers in New Jersey got it from this song. They could refer stories of new crimes to this song.

15 Broadwood, ed., *English Traditional Songs and Carols*, p. 121.
16 'Tale of the Poor Murdered Woman'.
17 Martin Carthy and Dave Swarbrick, *But Two Came By*, 12-inch LP (Fontana, STL5477, 1968), sleeve notes.

Crimes were assimilated in their experience because the song explained that such things did happen.[18]

Unfortunately, Halpert does not quote from the song, and few other references to it appear to exist, aside from a reference in the *New Jersey Courier* in 1929.[19] Halpert claims the song was very popular in New Jersey, but it has not surfaced in any collections consulted for this paper. For Halpert, songs can instruct communities about the existence of crime without moralizing, protesting, or imposing an artificial resolution. When considered against the common features of crime balladry outlined by Wiltenburg, Halpert's example denotes a wholly different type of crime song: one that depends upon the belief of the singers not just in the historicity of the events that are related, but in a sense of emotional truth.

This element of 'truth' is important when examining songs based on real events. Commemorating a true occurrence through the medium of song can engender a sense of occasion and legacy, which in turn helps to ensure repeated performance. A participant in Fay Hield's Sheffield-based fieldwork avers: 'If the song tells a story about something that actually happened [. . .] I do feel that I am keeping that memory alive and that enhances my enjoyment of the song.'[20] A song can therefore operate as a 'tool for remembering',[21] which is particularly important in the context of smaller communities, such as Leatherhead and Milford. The remembrance of local events forms part of the aesthetic choices a singer makes in repertoire selection.

That such a sophisticated degree of choice-making does indeed occur within surrounding social and cultural matrices is highlighted by Ginette Dunn's fieldwork in the villages of Snape and Blaxhall, in east Suffolk: 'because many of his [the singer's] experiences and many of his songs are shared with many of his contemporaries, his repertoire constitutes a reaching out to them whereby his individuality can likewise be brought into consonance with that of the others'.[22] This symbiosis of song function and audience is crucial for a song's survival in local repertoire. Dunn is also emphatic about the need for veracity, in both historical and emotional terms:

18 Herbert Halpert, 'Vitality of Tradition and Local Songs', *Journal of the International Folk Music Council*, 3 (1951), 35–50 (p. 39).

19 'The Murder of Jim Wainwright', *New Jersey Courier*, 29 November 1929, p. 3.

20 Fay Hield, 'English Folk Singing and the Construction of Community' (unpublished doctoral thesis, University of Sheffield, 2010), p. 62.

21 Hield, 'English Folk Singing', p. 55.

22 Ginette Dunn, *The Fellowship of Song* (London: Croom Helm, 1980), p. 220.

a song's proximity to real life could ensure its popularity [...] Besides a belief in the historicity of song events [...] there is a belief in the truth of song emotion. This trust in the emotions of a song is necessary before the song is accepted into the local repertoire. Trust is the root of all feelings of nostalgia that singers and audience have for the communal singing of the past: the proliferation of singing then strengthened the social ties through the communicative act of performance and the adoption of songs of emotional truth.[23]

When a song such as 'The Poor Murdered Woman' is written from within a particular community, it may be felt to possess 'emotional truth' in addition to historical veracity, and therefore to inspire 'trust in the emotions of [the] song'. 'The Poor Murdered Woman' could exist both as a form of local historical commemoration and as a pattern for understanding future experiences of crime, injustice, and non-resolution.

Singers within a community have been shown to be discerning in repertoire selection, judging the 'truth' and meaning of a song based on their experience and knowledge of other songs. The composer, coming also from within the community, is both a participant and active generator of new potential additions to the local repertoire. This conceptualization of the local composer as a creative re-fashioner of immediate experience makes sense if we agree with Michael Pickering that 'men and women in the village were not so much the passive witnesses of history but were much more active participants in the social and cultural process'.[24] 'The Poor Murdered Woman' can be interpreted as a gesture towards positive community participation in the face of senseless violence—a stand against being 'passive witnesses'.

It seems likely that James Fairs and his neighbours would have known other songs in the vernacular tradition, no less than broadside writers were 'well-acquainted with traditional patterns of phraseology and structure'.[25] Shirley Collins imagines Fairs as 'a poor labouring man who wouldn't have had much education [...] he'd had songs from the past, ballads that he'd probably sung—he knew how they were written'.[26] This assumed knowledge is important to the supposition that James Fairs both utilized and subverted popular crime ballad motifs and characteristics of localized songs. A song may have an immediate appeal if it exploits familiar

---

23 Dunn, *Fellowship of Song*, pp. 224–25.
24 Michael Pickering, *Village Song and Culture* (London: Croom Helm, 1982), p. 179.
25 Roy Palmer, *The Sound of History* (Oxford: Oxford University Press, 1988), p. 144.
26 'Tale of the Poor Murdered Woman'.

forms and patterns, but this appeal will become acutely personal if it subverts those patterns in a way to which a community can relate.

In her study of newly composed folk music in former Yugoslavia, Ljerka Rasmussen writes that modern folk songs 'are not just symbolic expressions of in-group values, but also, a principal medium of social announcements [. . .] song messages are not meant to reach out beyond the audience; instead they are intended to reaffirm the genre's own discourse each time it accommodates new social themes'.[27] As opposed to Lucy Broadwood's belief that songs were made by 'local, untaught bards',[28] it makes more sense to envisage locally composed songs as 'wilfully compiled by knowledgeable individuals'.[29] For its immediate audience, 'The Poor Murdered Woman' did not merely recount the discovery of a body, it crafted an orderly, un-hysterical narrative from the event. The subverted borrowings from crime balladry may well have been recognized, perhaps as comforting motifs that placed the real event at one remove while simultaneously arousing a sense of community-specific 'ownership'. In this way, James Fairs can be seen as an innovator, someone who navigated established song genres to create something with longevity, 'truth', and enduring efficacy. This may go some way to explaining why songs that operate in similar ways to 'The Poor Murdered Woman' are not easily found in collected form: while this form of response to crime might have been common among locally composed songs, like Big Bill Estel's New Jersey composition, they did not travel far beyond the communities that fashioned them.

Yet there is a community that has not yet been examined, that of the song's modern performers and audiences. 'The Poor Murdered Woman' may not have been known at all outside of Surrey before it was collected by the Rev. Shebbeare, but it has proved comparatively—one might even say, disproportionately—popular in revival repertoires, appearing on a number of commercially available recordings over the last four decades.[30] Those who, like Shirley Collins, have performed the song often report deeply personal reactions: 'It's a song I never forget. It's one of my favourite songs and it goes through my head [. . .] very frequently. It's a song I don't lose track of at all and I think of it often.'[31] The strong emotional connection expressed

27 Ljerka V. Rasmussen, *Newly Composed Folk Music of Yugoslavia* (London: Routledge, 2002), p. 186.
28 Broadwood, ed., *English Traditional Songs and Carols*, p. 121.
29 Henry Glassie, 'Tradition', *Journal of American Folklore*, 108 (1995), 395–412 (p. 398).
30 Carthy and Swarbrick, *But Two Came By*; Shirley Collins and the Albion Country Band, *No Roses*, 12-inch LP (Pegasus PEG7, 1971); Shirley & Dolly Collins, *Snapshots*, CD (Fledg'ling FLED3057, 2006); Jackie Oates, *Saturnine*, CD (ECC ECC004, 2011); The Woodbine & Ivy Band, *The Woodbine & Ivy Band*, CD (Folk Police Records FPR004, 2012).
31 'Tale of the Poor Murdered Woman'.

through such comments speaks eloquently about our own needs and sensibilities. Writing of 'the problem of why art outlives its origins', Michael Pickering declares that 'we need to understand that response to songs of the past involves a dialectical relationship between contemporary consciousness, conditioned by specific circumstances and processes, and the historical representation and detail supplied by the song texts in question'.[32] The song has moved from its role as a sense-making 'tool for remembering' within a local community to fulfilling the needs of a diverse modern audience overly familiar with news reports of missing persons, the discovery of anonymous bodies, and the emotional landscape of unsolved crime. For all our saturation with news reportage, we are perhaps lacking a sense of regionalized, communal grief. Whatever the myriad causes for the song's continuing popularity, 'The Poor Murdered Woman' reminds us that songs still remain emotionally relevant within communities, even though the construction and operation of those communities have drastically altered from the time that Mr Foster sang the song to the Rev. Shebbeare.

While the emotional truth of 'The Poor Murdered Woman' is still in evidence, the song's historical roots have recently come to the fore with a radio documentary and an exhibition at Leatherhead Museum of Local History (noted above). By 'coming home' in this way, the song has proved its continuing efficacy, being both geographically localized and universally 'local'. While it would be overly simplistic to rely wholly on functionalism, 'The Poor Murdered Woman' does encourage a consideration of how songs composed for and within a community can become part of a dynamically changing but continuous tradition. There is a hinterland of 'true event' songs, fashioned within communities knowledgeable about traditional song forms, whose functions, both past and ongoing, have not yet been fully explored. As Pickering and Green express it, what a song 'signifies and stands for is as much a product of the process of engagement in particular periods and places as of its own inherent expressive properties and qualities'.[33] 'The Poor Murdered Woman' may be one such case. If so, its time is now—we may have never needed it so much.

32 Michael Pickering, 'The Past as a Source of Aspiration: Popular Song and Social Change', in *Everyday Culture: Popular Song and the Vernacular Milieu*, ed. Michael Pickering and Tony Green (Milton Keynes: Open University Press, 1987), pp. 39–69 (pp. 40, 44–45).
33 Michael Pickering and Tony Green, 'Towards a Cartography of the Vernacular Milieu', in *Everyday Culture: Popular Song and the Vernacular Milieu*, ed. Michael Pickering and Tony Green (Milton Keynes: Open University Press, 1987), pp. 1–38 (p. 4).

Infanticide in Folk Song:
An Examination of the Post-Medieval Historical Context

ALASTAIR VANNAN

Infanticide occurs as a theme in numerous traditional ballads from Britain, Ireland, and Europe. Two prominent song traditions that feature infanticide are those of 'The Cruel Mother', which is also known as 'Fine Flowers in the Valley', 'Lady Ann', 'The Duke's Daughter's Cruelty', and 'The Minister's Daughter of Newark' (Child 20), and 'The Well below the Valley', which is also known as 'The Maid and the Palmer' and 'The Maid of Coldingham' (Child 21). Both of these songs relate narratives of mothers who have killed their newborn infants and who subsequently face the consequences of that act, either because their crime is discovered and they are accused of murder, or because they are confronted with the ghosts of the children they have killed. Both of these song traditions are associated with warnings of divine retribution and the mothers are often told of the punishment they will face in hell as a result of their actions.

A comprehensive analysis of the many and varied themes and examples of symbolism that occur within these song traditions is beyond the scope of this paper, as is a comprehensive examination of all relevant historical and sociological aspects of infanticide, but a preliminary examination of the historical context provides an opportunity to begin to understand what they may have been the factors in response to which they were created and sung. The topic is multifaceted and has the potential to sustain numerous avenues of detailed investigation. Therefore, in order to define and, necessarily, limit the direction and scope of this initial investigation, five broad research questions were devised:

1. What message is conveyed by the songs?
2. Did the songs record or remember rare instances of horrific crimes or, conversely, did they describe a social phenomenon that was more common in the recent past than it is at the present day?
3. Are there any contributing factors that help to explain why such crimes might have been more common in the post-medieval period than at the present?
4. Did public perception in the past consider infanticide to be more common than it actually was?
5. What role did these songs fulfil?

These questions will be approached with reference to selected aspects of social, legal, and medical history that may help us to understand why songs of infanticide carried such resonance during the post-medieval period (1540–1914).

Key Themes

'The Cruel Mother' and 'The Well below the Valley' have been the subject of previous research, much of which has focused primarily on comparing differing versions of the songs and analysing their format and content in order to identify key and recurring themes. Although these themes will be briefly summarized, they are not discussed in detail here. 'The Cruel Mother' and 'The Well below the Valley' and their European analogues are considered in detail by F. J. Child.[1] There is a very close relationship between the two ballads, in terms both of the general subject matter and also of the blending of content between the two song traditions. This is perhaps unsurprising, given the similarity of the key themes of illegitimacy, infanticide, and punishment for sin. The frequent occurrence of shared elements may also indicate that 'The Cruel Mother' had a wider spatial distribution than is represented by the versions discussed by Child. It appears to be possible to determine which of the ballad traditions provided the source for each of the key themes and, rather than the transmission of elements being in just a single direction, elements of each song seem to have passed to the other.

---

1   Francis James Child, ed., *The English and Scottish Popular Ballads*, 5 vols (Boston: Houghton, Mifflin, 1882–98), I, 218–227 [hereafter *ESPB*]. Other discussions are in David Atkinson, 'History, Symbol, and Meaning in The Cruel Mother', *Folk Music Journal*, 6.3 (1992), 359–80; Steve Roud and Julia Bishop, eds, *The New Penguin Book of English Folk Songs* (London: Penguin, 2012), pp. 479–81; Vic Gammon, *Desire, Drink and Death in English Folk and Vernacular Song, 1600–1900* (Aldershot and Burlington, VT: Ashgate), pp. 207–29.

'The Cruel Mother'

The earliest known version of 'The Cruel Mother' is a broadside of *c*.1690 titled *The Duke's Daughter's Cruelty*.[2] The central narrative of the numerous recorded versions of 'The Cruel Mother' comprises a pregnant woman going alone into the wilds and enduring a difficult labour before giving birth to a child or, more commonly, twins. The songs often make it clear that the children are illegitimate, and they are often described as the result of a secret affair between the woman and her father's clerk who, in some versions, has abandoned her. The songs relate that the mother then kills the children and returns to her father's hall, sometimes without her pregnancy being known at all. The woman then meets with between one and three children, but most commonly two, and tells them that if they were hers she would cherish them and provide them with comforts such as wine and silk. But the children retort that she is, in fact, their mother, and that she killed them. In some versions, they also tell their mother that they are in heaven but that she will go to hell.

Some versions of the song list penances, such as spending seven years each as the clapper of a church bell, as a bird, and as a fish. These punishments are directly borrowed from 'The Well below the Valley'.[3] Many of the songs also state that she will go to hell, and some of them specify that this will also last for seven years, and the mother often says that she would gladly endure the penances if she could avoid the torments of hell. In some versions she dies and, in at least one, she takes her own life.

> 'Yes, cruel mother, we'll tell to thee,
> What sort of death for us you must die.
>
> 'Seven years a fowl in the woods,
> Seven years a fish in the floods.
>
> 'Seven years to be a church bell,
> Seven years a porter in hell.'
>
> 'Welcome, welcome, fowl in the wood[s],
> Welcome, welcome, fish in the flood[s].
>
> 'Welcome, welcome, to be a church bell,
> But heavens keep me out of hell.' (Child 20 I)

---

2   Roud and Bishop, p. 480; *The Duke's Daughter's Cruelty; or, The Wonderful Apparition of Two Infants whom She Murther'd and Buried in a Forrest, for to Hide her Shame* (London: J. Deacon, [1692?]) [Pepys Ballads 5.4].
3   *ESPB*, I, 218–27.

Trees often feature in the description of her labour, with the mother leaning her back against an oak and, in some versions, her head against a thorn. It is likely that these trees were symbolic, with the oak representing strength and perhaps demonstrating the difficulty of the mother's task, particularly as in some versions her exertions nearly cause the tree to break. A thorn tree also often features, and this might be symbolic of both the pain of labour and the mother's predicament.[4] Her head against the thorn might also have reminded listeners of the Fall, when God tells Adam that the earth will bring forth thorns and thistles (Genesis 3:18), thus introducing the themes of sin and punishment in a Christian context. It is also a reminder of the crown of thorns that Christ bore to atone for the sins of humanity. The themes of sin and penance for sin are central to these ballads.

'The Cruel Mother' fits within the category of ballads and folk tales that are revenant stories, telling of meetings between the living and the returning dead.

> There was a lady, she lived in Lurk,
> *Sing hey alone and alonie o,*
> She fell in love with her father's clerk.
> *Down by yon greenwood sidie o.*
>
> She loved him seven years and a day,
> Till her big belly did her betray.
>
> She leaned her back unto a tree,
> And there began her sad misery.
>
> She set her foot unto a thorn,
> And there she got her two babes born.
>
> She took out her wee pen-knife,
> She twind them both of their sweet life.
>
> She took the sattins was on her head,
> She rolled them in both when they were dead.
>
> She howkit a grave forenent the sun,
> And there she buried her twa babes in.

---

4 Gammon, *Desire, Drink and Death*, p. 211.

As she was walking thro her father's ha,
She spied twa boys playing at the ha.

'O pretty boys, if ye were mine,
I would dress ye both in the silks so fine.'

'O mother dear, when we were thine,
Thou neer dressed us in silks so fine.

'For thou was a lady, thou livd in Lurk,
And thou fell in love with thy father's clerk.

'Thou loved him seven years and a day,
Till thy big belly did thee betray.

'Thou leaned thy back unto a tree,
And there began thy sad misery.

'Thou set thy foot unto a thorn,
And there thou got thy two babes born.

'Thou took out thy wee pen-knife,
And twind us both of our sweet life.

'Thou took the sattins was on thy head,
Thou rolled us both in when we were dead.

'Thou howkit a grave forenent the sun,
And there thou buried thy twa babes in.

'But now we're both in [the] heavens hie,
There is pardon for us, but none for thee.'

'My pretty boys, beg pardon for me!'
'There is pardon for us, but none for thee.' (Child 20 E)

'The Well below the Valley'

'The Well below the Valley' ('The Maid and the Palmer') blends the biblical story of the Woman of Samaria, who meets Jesus at Jacob's Well, with characteristics associated with medieval traditions concerning Mary Magdalene, Mary and Martha, the sisters of Lazarus, and elements of the story of 'The Cruel Mother'.[5] The murder of the children and, in one Wendish example, the revenant meeting between the mother and children are both elements that derive from 'The Cruel Mother'. The power of this narrative and the resonance of the theme are demonstrated by its widespread distribution across much of Europe. Child recorded only one complete version Britain, an English version from the Percy folio manuscript (*c.*1650), though the song is likely to be older than this.[6] However, a Scottish version is found in the Glenbuchat ballad manuscript, called 'The Maid of Coldingham';[7] and a version called 'The Well below the Valley' was collected from the Irish Traveller John Reilly by Tom Munnelly in 1967,[8] with a more complete version recorded in 1969.[9]

> A gentleman was passing by.
> He axed a drink as he got dry
> At the well below the valley O
> Green grows the lily O
> > Right among the bushes O.
>
> My cup it is an (in? on?) overflow
> And if I do stoop I may fall in
> At the well below the valley O
> Green grows the lily O
> > Right among the bushes O.
>
> Well if your true love was passing by
> You'd fill him a drink if he got dry
> At the well below the valley O
> Green grows the lily O
> > Right among the bushes O.
>
> She swore by grass and swore by corn
> That her true love was never born

5   *ESPB*, i, pp. 228–33.

6   Gammon, *Desire, Drink and Death*, p. 214.

7   *The Glenbuchat Ballads*, ed. David Buchan and James Moreira ([Jackson]: University Press of Mississippi, 2007), pp. 89–90, 234–35.

8   *The Bonny Green Tree: Songs of an Irish Traveller, John Reilly (1926–1969)*, 12-inch LP (Topic 12T359, 1977).

9   Bertrand Harris Bronson, *The Traditional Tunes of the Child Ballads*, 4 vols (Princeton: Princeton University Press, 1959–72), iv, 458–59.

At the well below the valley O
Green grows the lily O
    Right among the bushes O.

    Well if you're a man of that noble fame
You'll tell to me the father o' them
At the well below the valley O
Green grows the lily O
    Right among the bushes O.

    Two o' them by your father dear
At the well below the valley O
Green grows the lily O
    Right among the bushes O.

    Two more o' them came by your uncle Dan
At the well below the valley O
Green grows the lily O
    Right among the bushes O.

    Another one by your brother John
At the well below the valley O
Green grows the lily O
    Right among the bushes O.

    Well if you're a man of the noble fame
You'll tell to me what happened then
At the well below the valley O
Green grows the lily O
    Right among the bushes O.

    There was two o' them buried by the kitchen fire
At the well below the valley O
Green grows the lily O
    Right among the bushes O.

    Two more o' them buried by the stable door
At the well below the valley O
Green grows the lily O
    Right among the bushes O.

The other was buried by the well
At the well below the valley O
Green grows the lily O.

Well if you're a man of the noble fame
You'll tell to me what'll happen mysel'
At the well below the valley O
Green grows the lily O
    Right among the bushes O.

Well if you're a man of the noble fame
You'll tell to me what'll happen mysel'
At the well below the valley O
Green grows the lily O
    Right among the bushes O.

You'll be seven long years a-ringin' a bell
At the well below the valley O
Green grows the lily O
    Right among the bushes O.

You'll be seven more a-portin' in Hell
At the well below the valley O
Green grows the lily O
    Right among the bushes O.

I'll be seven long years a-ringin' the bell
But the Lord above might save my soul
From portin' in Hell
At the well below the valley O
Green grows the lily O
    Right among the bushes O.

In some of the ballads, the role of Christ is replaced by a mysterious man, a seer or palmer, whom the woman meets at a well. He asks her for a drink and she refuses, whereupon he says that she would be willing to provide her leman, or lover, with a drink, and she denies that she has any such lover. Although they have never met before, he reveals that he knows about her killing of her illegitimate children. He also describes her pregnancies as the result of incestuous and other taboo relationships, and her father, brother, uncle, and priest are each named as fathers of her children. He then lists the penances she will undergo and states that she will go to hell and, as in many versions of 'The Cruel Mother', she says she could endure the penances but could not bear going to hell.

What message is conveyed by these songs?

Both of these song traditions reflect the patriarchal and Christian society in which they were composed and sung. There is only passing reference to the role of the children's fathers and certainly no judgement of their behaviour or suggestions of any punishment they might face. The songs are quite different from those warn girls to be wary of false-hearted men, such as 'Let No Man Steal your Thyme'. The possibility, or suggestion, of sexual abuse is explicit in some versions of 'The Well below the Valley', but, again, is not the subject of criticism or examination, and little sympathy is extended to the mother.

These songs are stark warnings about peril to the immortal soul and are not explicitly concerned with the physical or emotional health of women. Many of them suggest not that punishment is a penance that will enable sin to be forgiven, but rather that the punishments described are only a prelude to a sojourn in hell. However, the punishments in some of the Scandinavian ballads of 'The Well below the Valley', which appear to correspond with those endured by Martha, the sister of Lazarus, are followed by the declaration that she will now be permitted to enter into heaven.[10]

Slight differences between the narratives in different versions of the songs show that it is not valid to assign an inflexible meaning to song traditions that have developed over long periods and across wide geographical areas. Such traditions will have been influenced by numerous individual perceptions, in addition to accidental modifications as the result of misremembering, or mishearing, parts of songs. Even without changes to the narrative, different listeners or singers may draw different meanings from exactly the same song, depending upon their personal experiences and beliefs. We can, therefore, only attempt to interpret a selection of meanings that the songs may have carried, and we cannot suggest that their meanings are limited to the interpretations presented here — or that all possible past meanings will be accessible to us as we attempt to reconstruct them from fragmentary artefacts of songs, melodies, rhythms, personal anecdotes, and social, religious, legal, and medical history. Indeed, it is pos-

10 *ESPB*, I, 228–33.

sible that these song traditions might possess seemingly contradictory meanings for different people. They might present a harsh, even misogynistic, attitude towards women on the one hand, and yet fulfil a cathartic function for women on the other—which may to some extent be reflected in the high numbers of women from whom the song has been collected.[11]

One example of the potential for variety of understanding and expression comes from two different versions of 'The Cruel Mother' sung by Cecilia Costello. One was recorded on 16 January 1954 by Marie Slocombe and Patrick Shuldham-Shaw for the BBC and was released on an LP in 1975.[12] This appears to have been an example of her own style of performance, and is mid-paced and lilting, and, subjectively, creates an atmosphere that is serious and yet has warmth. Her second performance formed part of Ewan MacColl's 1964 radio series *The Song Carriers* and apparently represents Cecilia Costello's demonstration of that way her father used to sing the song.[13] It is slightly slower than the other version, although the melody and words are the same, albeit with fewer verses. The voice is harder in this version, and more staccato and severe, creating a very sombre and melancholy atmosphere. Indeed, in her introduction to the version recorded in 1954, Cecilia Costello related how her father had presented the song to her as a true story and a warning not to behave in the way that the cruel mother did but to be a kind mother. She also told Marie Slocombe that her father would sing the song 'with his eyes closed, hands clasped, bending over, with great emphasis and drama, very slow. He used to frighten us children with it.'[14] This is a direct example of the song used as a moral lesson by a father, who is described as having been very strict and restrictive, to his daughter.

Did the songs record rare instances of horrific crimes, or did they describe a phenomenon that was more common in the past?

Records of infanticide in England prior to 1624 are extremely rare. This does not necessarily mean that it did not occur, but that it was not recorded by the secular courts or is not easily identified in their records. This is in part due to the fact that it was not until 1624 that infanticide was treated legally as murder, punishable by death.[15] Prior to that date, most cases

---

11 Atkinson, 'History, Symbol, and Meaning', pp. 375–76.

12 Cecilia Costello, *Cecilia Costello: Recordings from the Sound Archives of the BBC*, 12-inch LP (Leader LEE 4054, 1975).

13 Fred McCormick, personal communication. Thanks are due to Fred McCormick for providing recordings of Cecilia Costello singing 'The Cruel Mother'.

14 Roud and Bishop, *New Penguin Book of English Folk Songs*, p. 481.

15 Alan Macfarlane, 'The History of Infanticide in England', in Unpublished Appendices to *The Savage Wars of Peace* (2002) <http://www.alanmacfarlane.com/savage/savageappdx.html> [accessed 26 March 2014].

of mothers killing their infants were tried in the ecclesiastical courts, and there was an aware-ness of various different ways in which such deaths could be caused, including overlaying (a child smothered by its mother's body, giving the appearance of accidental death) and refusal to nurse, as well as death by the mother's hand.[16] There appears to have been a degree of tolerance, or understanding, of infanticide in medieval England, and punishments were often limited to public penance.[17] Although this situation seems anathema to modern Western sensibilities, the anthropological record suggests that infanticide has been an accepted cultural phenom-enon in numerous societies worldwide at different times, associated with a wide variety of motivations and justifications, and even practised as a form of birth control similar to abortion in some cultures, with young infants sometimes considered not to have reached full status as people.[18]

The act of 1624 suggests that the frequency, or the perceived frequency, of such crimes during the early seventeenth century was sufficient to warrant a change in the law. Recorded cases of infanticide did indeed rise following the act, although the levels of indictment were still not particularly high, with between approximately four and ten cases in each decade in counties such as Essex and Surrey during the seventeenth and eighteenth centuries. These figures do appear to be higher than the current figure of eighteen instances over the course of five years for England and Wales,[19] and we might also assume that modern detection rates are higher.

In addition to the song traditions treating of a subject that was generally relevant, there are also instances of songs composed with reference to specific cases of infanticide. Martin Park-er composed a broadside ballad in 1634 called *No Natural Mother, but a Monster*, describing an execution for infanticide at Tyburn. A woman called Jannet Riddle, who was executed in Edinburgh in 1702, was the subject of another such ballad, and Mary Voce from Nottingham was the subject of at least three broadsides.[20]

16 Macfarlane, 'History of Infanticide'.

17 Macfarlane, 'History of Infanticide'.

18 Alan Macfarlane, 'Attitudes to and Incidences of Infanticide', in Unpublished Appendices to *The Savage Wars of Peace* (2002) <http://www.alanmacfarlane.com/savage/savageappdx.html> [accessed 26 March 2014].

19 NSPCC, 'Statistics on Children under One' <http://www.nspcc.org.uk/Inform/resourcesforprofessionals/chil-dren_under_one_statistics_wda79305.html> [accessed 26 March 2014].

20 Gammon, *Desire, Drink and Death*, pp. 211, 214–15.

Are there any contributing factors that help explain why such crimes might have been more common in the post-medieval period?

The character of the act of 1624 is revealing in terms of the types of cases of infanticide that were considered to be common in the early seventeenth century:

> Where as many lewd women that have been delivered of bastard children, to avoid their shame, and to escape punishment, do secretly bury or conceal the death of their children, and often, if the child is found dead, the said women do allege, that the said child was born dead [...] Be it enacted [...] in every such case the mother so offending, shall suffer death as in the case of murther, except such mother can make proof by one witness at the last that the child [...] was born dead.[21]

The act was, therefore, primarily a response to the murder of illegitimate children by their mothers. Although giving birth to illegitimate children was not actually illegal during the post-medieval period, the production of an illegitimate child that would become a financial burden to the parish was illegal and was severely punished. An act of 1576 had ordered that bastards should be financially supported by their putative fathers, and a subsequent act of 1610 had obliged justices of the peace to punish women who gave birth to bastards that would be chargeable to the parish.[22]

In addition to being sent to the house of correction and set to work for a year, which was provided for in law as a sentence from at least as early as 1610,[23] court records show that women were subjected to violent and humiliating punishments. Court rolls from the sixteenth and seventeenth centuries in Lancashire,[24] for example, describe sentences such as:

> Alice Bradshawe to be flogged and set in the stocks in Manchester
> Elizabeth Atkinson to be set in the stocks naked from the waist upwards
> Anne Barton of Chorley to have five stripes of the whip
> Isabel Lathome to be flogged at Ormskirke, 12 strokes
> Joan Pendleton to be whipped in Manchester on three days [this probably means three consecutive market days].

21 Reproduced in Macfarlane, 'History of Infanticide'.
22 Alan Macfarlane, 'Illegitimacy and Illegitimates in English History', in *Bastardy and its Comparative History: Studies in the History of Illegitimacy and Marital Nonconformism*, ed. Peter Laslett, Karla Oosterveen, and Richard M. Smith, (Cambridge, MA: Harvard University Press, 1980), pp. 71–85.
23 7 James, cap. 4, reproduced in Macfarlane, 'Illegitimacy and Illegitimates'.
24 J. Tait, ed., *Lancashire Quarter Sessions Records*, vol. 1: *Quarter Sessions Rolls, 1590–1606*, Chetham Society, n.s. vol. 77 (Manchester: Chetham Society, 1917).

Bastardy, without the means to support the child, was also illegal and the father was generally charged with responsibility for the upkeep of the child.[25] However, fathers could not necessarily be punished if they fled or denied responsibility. The unfortunate quirk of biology meant that women were almost always accountable, whereas men were not, following the Latin motto *Mater semper certa est* ('The mother is always certain').[26] It was not until the introduction of the bastardy clause in the Poor Law act of 1834 that parents of illegitimate children who could not afford to support them no longer faced punishment by imprisonment.[27] However, this legal change was accompanied by modifications that placed greater responsibility for the support of the child on the mother, made it more difficult for the mother to seek affiliation orders for child support, and required corroboration 'in some material particular' for paternity claims.

In addition to punishment for bastardy under the secular law, even if the child was not a financial burden on the parish, the ecclesiastical courts could rule that a woman should stand in public in church to acknowledge her fault.[28] There was, therefore, great pressure on unmarried mothers from the law, church, and wider society, and the consequences of giving birth to an illegitimate child would attract considerable social stigma. Many women in this position who did not have the support of family or of the father of the child could find themselves facing impoverishment. Indeed, in general, public and legal concern focused overwhelmingly on unmarried mothers from poor backgrounds, many of whom were servants.[29] In fact, a majority of women convicted of infanticide during the eighteenth century whose occupation is known were employed in service.[30] A pregnant servant would most usually be immediately dismissed without a reference and would be unlikely to work in service again. The broadside ballad *No Natural Mother, but a Monster* was entered in the Stationers' Register on 16 July 1634, only ten years after the passing of the infanticide act. This ballad presents the confessional 'goodnight', or last farewell, of a domestic servant who was reportedly hanged for murder at Tyburn on 11 December 1633, after secretly giving birth to her illegitimate child on her own and concealing it among straw, where it either died or was deliberately killed.[31]

25 Macfarlane, 'Illegitimacy and Illegitimates'.

26 Harry D. Krause, 'Creation of Relationships of Kinship', in *International Encyclopedia of Comparative Law*, vol. 4, ed. Aleck Choloros (Tubingen: J. C. B. Mohr, 1976).

27 4/5 William IV, cap. 76 (14 August 1834).

28 Macfarlane, 'Illegitimacy and Illegitimates'.

29 Macfarlane, 'History of Infanticide'.

30 Bridget Hill, *Women, Work & Sexual Politics in Eighteenth-Century England* (Oxford: Blackwell, 1994).

31 Hyder E. Rollins, ed., *A Pepysian Garland: Black-Letter Broadside Ballads of the Years 1595–1639* (Cambridge: Cambridge University Press, 1922), pp. 425–30.

For unmarried mothers in the post-medieval period, there was a high likelihood of imprisonment, public humiliation, social stigma, and financial impoverishment. These pressures may also have been accompanied by other factors relating to stress, trauma, and postnatal depression. There is also the likelihood that some pregnancies outside of marriage resulted from incest and rape, and sexual harassment is certainly known to have been committed against domestic servants by members of the employer's household.[32] Intuitively, it is not difficult to imagine that there could have been circumstances where a woman giving birth outside of marriage would have experienced severe levels of emotional and psychological stress, and may have committed a terrible act in desperation.

A paper written by the physician William Hunter in 1783, called 'On the uncertainty of the signs of murder in the case of bastard children' approaches this issue and is free from the possibility of modern commentators projecting anachronistic sensibilities on to past cultures.[33] Hunter writes:

> In making up a just estimate of any human action, much will depend on the state of the agent's mind at the time [. . .] I have seen the private as well as the more public frailties of women in all ranks of life [. . .]
>
> women who are pregnant without daring to avow their situation, are commonly objects of the greatest compassion; and generally are less criminal than the world imagine. In most of these cases the father of the child is really criminal, often cruelly so; the mother is weak, credulous, and deluded. Having obtained gratification, he thinks no more of his promises; she finds herself abused, disappointed of his affection, attention, and support, and left to struggle as she can, with sickness, pains, poverty, infamy; in short, with complete ruin for life!
>
> What is commonly understood to be the murder of a bastard child by the mother, if the real circumstances were fully known, would be allowed to be a very different crime in different circumstances. The most charitable construction that could be put upon so savage an action, and it is to be hoped the fairest often, would be to reckon it the work of phrenzy, or temporary insanity.

Hunter also states that there are numerous cases of which he was aware where women had accidentally caused or allowed the death of a newborn baby, either because they were alone

---

32 Hill, *Women, Work & Sexual Politics*.

33 William Hunter, *On the Uncertainty of the Signs of Murder in the Case of Bastard Children by the Late William Hunter, MD, FRS, Physician Extraordinary to the Queen and Member of the Royal Academy of Sciences at Paris*, read to the Members of the Medical Society, July 14, 1783 (London: J Callow, 1818).

during labour and had no idea what to do, or were exhausted and collapsed and could not tend to the child, or they did irrational things that might have caused injury to the child because they were in a hysterical state. In many of these cases, fear then led them to conceal the child's body, and they were later accused of murder, when the death had in fact been accidental. The broadside ballad *No Natural Mother, but a Monster* presents a contradiction, with one verse stating that the baby was hidden amongst the hay 'where it was smother'd' and a later verse referring to her 'strangled infant'. It is possible that the ballad may record the case of a woman who had concealed her newborn baby immediately after birth, when it may have been either dead or alive, and when the body was subsequently discovered, claimed it had been smothered in the straw — but was convicted of murder.

There does appear to have been some sympathy for women who were accused of infanticide, and fewer women were found guilty by juries after the later seventeenth century.[34] In some cases, even when found guilty, they were not sentenced to death.

Was infanticide in the past perceived to be more common than it actually was?

From 1624 until the early nineteenth century, a woman found guilty of concealing the birth of a child born outside of wedlock, and concealing the body, would automatically be tried for infanticide.[35] There was a presumption of guilt, and the obligation was on the woman to provide a witness to prove that the child had not been born alive.[36] Thus many women who had delivered stillborn babies, or whose babies had died soon after birth, could have quite falsely been branded as murderers. However, in the late eighteenth century William Blackstone recorded that most English trials did require positive evidence that a child had been born alive, although concealment was still presumed to indicate guilt.[37] During the early nineteenth century, several papers were written by physicians who were concerned to prove conclusively whether or not a baby had died of natural causes, and to provide evidence that could be used in a legal context.[38]

---

34 Macfarlane, 'History of Infanticide'.

35 William Cyrus Sprague, ed., *Abridgement of Blackstone's Commentaries* (Detroit: Sprague Correspondence School of Law, 1892), p. 478.

36 Sprague, ed., *Abridgement of Blackstone*, p. 478.

37 Sprague, ed., *Abridgement of Blackstone*, p. 478.

38 Besides Hunter, see William Cummin, *The Proofs of Infanticide Considered, including Dr. Hunter's tract on child murder, with illustrative notes, and a summary of the present state of medico-legal knowledge on that subject* (London: Longman, 1836); William Hutchinson, *A Dissertation on Infanticide, in its Relations to Physiology and Jurisprudence*, 2nd edn (London: J. and C. Adlard, 1821).

There was also a general increase in public perception of the frequency of infanticide from the late seventeenth century in connection with a rise in child abandonment in London and continental cities. In 1690, a Mrs Cellier warned of a great number of children being wilfully murdered, and over the following fifty years there was a public outcry, with numerous writers claiming huge numbers of shocking child murders.[39] It is interesting to note that *The Duke's Daughter's Cruelty* was printed c.1690—the popularity of the ballad could have been directly associated with this rise in public awareness of infanticide.

What role did these songs fulfil?

One key role of these songs appears to have been as a vehicle for Christian ideas in relation to infanticide in connection with pregnancy outside of marriage. The songs represent a harsh version of Christian thought which was not concerned with the social, legal, and emotional wellbeing of women, but primarily with warning that sin would be punished. Broadsides such as of *The Duke's Daughter's Cruelty*, *No Natural Mother, but a Monster*, and *The Last Speech and Confession of Jannet Riddle* can be related to the class of songs known as 'last goodnights', which were specifically intended to provide a warning by describing the fate of a condemned criminal. It has been suggested that, complementing infanticide legislation, such broadsides may have been used as devices to reinforce establishment controls over sexual morality, illegitimacy, and infanticide.[40] Given the chargeable status of illegitimate children to the parish, there was a significant economic motivation for this interpretation.

From the available records, it appears that these songs were often sung by women, and they may also have had a cathartic role, helping examine and come to terms with frightening or disturbing events and ideas,[41] although there is little indication of comfort or support in their message. There are, however, some indications of sympathy for the female protagonist in versions of 'The Cruel Mother' that describe her struggle during labour, with her exertions sufficient to break the oak tree that she is leaning against, as well as a sense of her solitude expressed through the repeated refrain. The songs might also have simply provided a kind of popular entertainment, exploiting themes that were widely and sensationally expressed in other forms such as plays and novels.[42]

---

39 Macfarlane, 'History of Infanticide'.
40 Atkinson, 'History, Symbol, and Meaning', pp. 361–62.
41 Atkinson, 'History, Symbol, and Meaning', p. 375.
42 Gammon, *Desire, Drink and Death*, p. 215.

It can be tempting to think of songs as relatively benign, perhaps as passive records of cultural ideas from the past, or else having been used as positive forces for change. However, we have seen that there were social, economic, religious, and legal pressures on unmarried mothers, which will have been spread through sermons, legal proceedings, public punishments, social and familial reactions to unmarried pregnancies, and written sources—and also through the singing of ballads. So we might consider that these songs not only recorded instances of infanticide, but actually have formed one of the mediums for the transmission of ideas that contributed to the pressures that led to infanticide.

Napoleonic Songs—An Overview

PETER WOOD

The 'French Wars' lasted from 1793 when France declared war on Britain to 1815 when Napoleon was finally defeated. Alternatively, the period can be divided into the 'Revolutionary Wars' and the 'Napoleonic Wars', separated by the Peace of Amiens of 1802, which lasted less than a year. It has been said many times that Napoleon was, and is, far more popular than Wellington, and this is certainly true as judged by the relative number of songs about the two men. This paper looks at the themes of songs that mention Napoleon in a historical context.

The 1790s

Napoleon rose to power in France during the 1790s, but very few folk songs or broadsides from that time mention him. The British were not engaged in the expansion of the French state in Europe. Even when General Napoleon Bonaparte sailed his army to Egypt with the object of blocking British access to India and the Far East, the dramatic annihilation of the French fleet at Aboukir Bay in 1798 gave rise to little celebration in British song and broadside. The later land battle of the same name in 1801, when the British under General Abercrombie defeated Napoleon, seems to have been a little more popular, the most notable song being 'The Banks of the Nile' (Roud 950). This is a song about the cruelty of lovers being parted by war, but it is difficult to date since all surviving broadside versions date from well after the event. Another song, 'Napoleon in Egypt' (Roud 12823) , collected in southern England in the early 1900s, is very similar to 'The Banks of the Nile'. These songs mark the end of the French Wars, after which the Treaty of Amiens, signed in 1802, brought about a brief peace.

The invasion scare (1803)

If there was very little in song up until March 1803, when the British once more declared war on France, the following nine months more than made up for it. Napoleon, now First Consul, started making preparations for an invasion of England, with large numbers of troops at Boulogne and a fleet of barges ready to cross the channel. This brought forth a rush of anti-Bonaparte songs which either insulted him, belittled him, and made patriotic calls to 'put the tyrant down', or else showed signs of panic. The songs, sold in the street, were the equivalent of newspapers, helping people keep up with events. As many as seventy different songs—about half of all the extant songs about Napoleon—have survived, all but four of them as just a single broadside copy. This suggests the songs enjoyed a certain 'news' value, but that they did not stand the test of time. About half of them might be described as high-flown or jingoistic, aimed at the educated classes, with multiple references to classical and British history. Examples are *Freedom or Slavery* and *Unite and Conquer!*[1]

Most of these seventy invasion songs have no tune indication, which was normal for the period, but where a tune is named it is often that of a popular patriotic song, such as 'Rule Britannia' or 'Hearts of Oak'. One song, *The Genius of Britain*, specifies 'The Marseilles Hymn'—'La Marseillaise'—even while it shares a sheet with another song, *The French in a Fog*, which goes to the tune of 'Hearts of Oak'.[2] It has been claimed that some of these broadsides were produced as propaganda, either by the government itself or by other concerned individuals in high places.[3] Support from this idea comes from the fact that many of these items were printed for bookseller/publishers such as James Asperne, John Ginger, and J. Hatchard, who are hardly known as broadside publishers outside of this period and could well have been acting as government agents who paid jobbing printers to produce the songs. Asperne's imprint to *The French in a Fog* declares:

> Noblemen, Magistrates, and gentlemen, would do well by ordering a few Dozen of
> the above Tracts of their different Booksellers, and causing them to be stuck up in

---

1 *Freedom or Slavery, A New Song* (London: J. Wallis, [1803]) [Bodleian Library, Curzon b.10(105)]; *Unite and Conquer!*, by A. Highmore (London: J. Asperne, printed by R. Wilks, [1803]) [Bodleian Library, Curzon b.10(118)].

2 *The Genius of Britain* (London: J. Asperne, [1803]) [Bodleian Library, 2376 a.1(4), Curzon b.10(117)]—which shares a sheet with *The French in a Fog*, to the tune of 'Hearts of Oak'.

3 Vic Gammon, 'The Grand Conversation: Napoleon and British Popular Balladry', Musical Traditions, Article MT033 <http://www.mustrad.org.uk/articles/boney.htm>.

the respective villages where they reside, that the Inhabitants may be convinced of the Cruelty of the Corsican Usurper.

Another large group of invasion broadsides, in contrast, are more salty, earthy, and mocking, and presumably more likely to have been picked up by the man in the street. Examples include *Bonaparte in the Dumps!*, *A Rope's End for Bonaparte*, *New Bellman's Verses for Christmas 1803!*, and *Harlequin's Invasion*.[4] The first two stanzas of the first of these songs, which goes to the popular tune 'Derry Down', are as follows:

> Ye gay dashing Sparks, who delight in the Whip,
> In Bond-Street who lounge, or in Ball Rooms who trip;
> Attend to my Ditty, and you'll understand
> How the Consul of France strove to drive Four in Hand.
>
> > Derry down.

> Said the Consul 'Ive got all the World in a String,
> 'I'm as prous as a Pope, and as great as a King;
> 'I've lash'd the poor Swiss, and I've well-flogg'd the Dutch,
> 'But see, Johnny Bull, I must give him a Touch.'
>
> > Derry down.

A further group of broadsides were designed to encourage recruitment to the local militias, such as *The Buckinghamshire Militia Ballad*, which was printed locally and has a refrain of '*And a-fighting we will go, will go, will go, / And a-fighting we will go*'.[5] A number of the ballads carry woodcuts that look as if they could have been designed for the occasion, or at least were chosen with a view to their appropriateness. *The Buckinghamshire Militia Ballad* is headed with a figure of Britannia; while *Old England's Volunteers* depicts a group of three soldiers who can be easily imagined as the militiamen described in the text, ready to repel the French threat.[6] *John Bull & Bonaparte!* has a stout John Bull squaring up to a thin and stern-looking Bona-

---

4   *How Are the Mighty Fallen!; or, Bonaparte in the Dumps* ([London]: H. Reynell, [1803]) [Bodleian Library, 2376 a.1(12)]; *A Rope's End for Bonaparte* ([London]: J. Pitts, [1802–19]) [Bodleian Library, Johnson Ballads fol. 139]; *A Rope's End for Buonaparte* ([Lincoln: Smith, [1803]) [Bodleian Library, Harding B 22(253)]; *New Bellman's Verses for Christmas 1803!* ([London]: W. Holland, December 1803) [Bodleian Library, Curzon b.22(54)]; *Harlequin's Invasion* ([London]: William Holland, 16 August 1803) [Bodleian Library, Curzon b.12(9)].

5   *The Buckinghamshire Militia Ballad* (Buckingham: B. Seeley, [1803?]) [Bodleian Library, Johnson Ballads 1527].

6   *Old England's Volunteers* (n.p., [1803?]) [Bodleian Library, Harding B 28(135)].

parte, who is nevertheless considerably disadvantaged by having to support an enormous hat.[7] *Crocodile's Tears; or, Bonaparte's Lamentation* shows a weeping Napoleon, squatting on a rock and looking out over what is presumably the Channel, while ominous-looking birds and bats circle around his head.[8]

Napoleon on the run (1812–14)

Napoleon's military successes in Europe after 1805 were perhaps not so well known to the ordinary British people. Certainly, there seem to be hardly any songs from this period. However, a second wave of anti-Bonaparte songs was inspired by his disastrous Russian campaign of 1812, in which he lost half a million men; his organizing of yet another army after he had left his men to die from starvation, cold, and Cossack attacks during the long retreat from Russia; his banishment to Elba in 1814; and his escape in the spring of 1815. These, of course, glory in the Emperor's fall from grace. *Bonaparte's Mistake at Germany* celebrates Napoleon's first major defeat at the Battle of Leipzig (Battle of the Nations) in 1813.[9] *The Devil's Own Darling* and *Bonaparte's Lamentation; or, His Banishment to Elba Island* share a sheet.[10] *The Corsican Tyrant*, which gives a brief summary of Bonaparte's career, emphasizing his rapaciousness and his defeats in Russia and at Leipzig, likewise finishes with his exile on Elba.[11] *John Bull in Alarm; or, Boney's Escape, and a Second Deliverance of Europe* combines alarm at the blunder that allowed Napoleon to return from Elba, with confidence that Britain, supported by its Prussian ally, will defeat him again and deliver Europe once more.[12] Several of these songs associate Bonaparte with the devil, through both text and woodcut images.

Once Napoleon had been exiled to Elba, many well-heeled British flooded into to the once-more fashionable city of Paris, only to be thrown into panic on learning of his escape from Elba and return to the capital. *Boney's Return to Paris* encapsulates the terror induced amongst these ex-pats.[13] The woodcut image shows French soldiers commandeering a (presumably English) coach and horses into the service of the Emperor, who is waving a weapon

7 *John Bull & Bonaparte!* ([London]: Shury, [1803]) [Bodleian Library, Curzon b.22(80)].

8 *Crocodile's Tears; or, Bonaparte's Lamentation, A New Song* (London: J. Wallis, [1803?]) [Bodleian Library, Curzon b.12(62)].

9 *Bonaparte's Mistake at Germany* (Liverpool: Wood, [c.1813]) [Bodleian Library, Harding B 25(248)].

10 *The Devil's Own Darling* and *Bonaparte's Lamentation; or, His Banishment to Elba Island* (Birmingham: S. Taylor, [1815]) [Bodleian Library, Johnson Ballads fol. 198].

11 *The Corsican Tyrant*, by C. X. F. ([London]: Molineux, [1815]) [Bodleian Library, Johnson Ballads 1307].

12 *John Bull in Alarm; or, Boney's Escape, and a Second Deliverance of Europe* ([n.p.: [1815]) [Bodleian Library, Curzon b.5(208)].

13 *Boney's Return to Paris* (London: T. Batchelar, [1815]) [Bodleian Library, Curzon b.32 (64)].

and a tricolour and leading his army into the city. A guillotine is depicted atop the Arc de Triomphe.

Waterloo (1815)

No sooner had Napoleon entered Paris in the spring of 1815 than he organized a new *Grand Armée*, headed by his old generals Grouchy and Ney. The allies found themselves obliged to fight once more, with two armies in southern Belgium, the Prussians under Field Marshal Blücher, and an army of British, Dutch, and Belgians under the command of the Duke of Wellington. The Waterloo campaign comprised a series of battles over three days, starting on Friday, 16 June, when the French tried to drive a wedge between the two allied armies. Grouchy took on the Prussians at Ligny, and Ney attacked the British at Quatre Bras, a farm at a crossroads on the road from Charleroi to Brussels. The French were victorious on both fronts, driving both armies further north. Wellington claimed his was a strategic retreat, as he wished to fight the French from a more advantageous position close to the village of Waterloo. All sides drew breath on 17th, waiting for the main business on Sunday the 18th.

Songs to do with Waterloo can be divided into those describing the battle on the one hand, and 'romantic' songs on the other. About thirty of the 'battle songs' have been identified, but only four have been recovered from oral tradition, the remainder being found only in broadside form and therefore presumed to have been short-lived. The titles 'The Battle of Waterloo', and 'The Plains of Waterloo' are used so widely for a whole range of different songs that they are of no use in identifying individual items, and therefore it is necessary to give them other designations. Notable among 'The Plains of Waterloo' titles is a fourteen-stanza broadside song (Roud 1106), the earliest known printing of which is by Marshall of Newcastle on a broadside probably dating from 1816.[14] An interesting point about this piece, along with other 'battle' songs, is that it is said to have been composed almost immediately after the battle by a soldier who fought at Waterloo — in this instance, one Sergeant Grant of the 92nd Highland Regiment.[15]

The 'romantic' songs are all about lovers parting, the man going to fight at Waterloo. The 'happy' ones are where he returns, the best known of which is 'Her Mantle So Green' (Roud 714). The earliest collected version comes from the log of a New England whaler, dated 1859.[16]

14 *The Battle of Waterloo* (Newcastle upon Tyne: Marshall, [1816]) [Bodleian Library, Johnson Ballads 1953; Cambridge University Library, Madden Collection, vol. 16 (Country Printers, vol. 1), no. 409].

15 Frank Kidson, *Traditional Tunes* (Oxford: Chas. Taphouse & Son, 1891) pp. 120–23 (p. 121).

16 Gale Huntington, *Songs the Whalemen Sang* (Barre, MA: Barre Publishers, 1964), pp.122–23.

The 'sad' ones, where the man fails to return, are fewer and more obscure. 'The Bonny Light Horseman' (Roud 1185), often associated with Waterloo, was in fact written well before the battle and only a few versions mention Napoleon.

The 'Napoleonic ballads'

The next group of songs have been found much more frequently in oral tradition and can be described generically as the 'Napoleonic ballads'. These songs use grandiloquent, inspirational — indeed, epic — language. They often go to memorable tunes, and are sometimes said to be Irish in origin. They laud Napoleon as an exceptional general, to be compared with Alexander, Caesar, and the like, but with poignant references to his defeat in Russia and at Waterloo, and his final exile on Saint Helena. There are eight songs that fit this category, and all appear to have been significantly more popular than the other songs about Bonaparte:

> The Bonny Bunch of Roses (Roud 664)
> The Grand Conversation on Napoleon (Roud 1189)
> The Grand Conversation under the Rose (Roud 21272)
> The Dream of Napoleon (Roud 1538)
> Napoleon's Farewell to Paris (Roud 1626)
> The Deeds of Napoleon (Roud 2419)
> The Isle of St Helena (Roud 349)
> The Green Linnet (Roud 1619)

The most popular of these songs arose some twenty or so years after Waterloo and no doubt reflect a general view of the man as a heroic figure, formed at a considerable historical distance. The Waterloo songs and the 'Napoleonic ballads' are well worthy of detailed analysis, far beyond the scope of this 'overview'.

Aftermath

Not everyone was happy to see the end of the wars and of Bonaparte. The Napoleonic wars had 'made the money to fly about', and several songs testify to this. *Boney's Releasement*, an Irish song, expresses joy at his escape from Elba and return to Paris, but some of the words express the commercial sentiment very well.[17]

---

17 *Boney's Releasement* ([n.p.: 1815?]) [Dublin, Royal Irish Academy, Ian Neilands Collection 0173, 3c37 5].

The shop-keepers too, may now live in hopes,
For the freedom of Boney will their interests promote
As he was the man, all nations must allow,
That made the cash fly, and well he knew how.

John Marshall, the prolific Newcastle printer of both broadsides and chapbooks, issued two songs on this theme. *Forestalling Done Over* is critical of tradesmen who, in times of plenty, squirreled away produce, particularly grain, rather than selling it, in the hope of profiting from a better price later on.[18] The poor suffered greatly from this practice. Here is an extract from the song:

Come, all you poor people, I pray you lend an ear,
And of the roguish Badgers* you quickly shall hear
It's their daily study, and long they've contrived
To raise our provisions, and starve us alive.
So you Farmers, and Badgers, and Millers, I'm sure
You all deserve hanging for starving the poor.

There's the farmers and badgers and forestalling crew
They all stand considering to know what to do.
In raising the grain they will all play their part,
But the D—l will take them in his packet-cart.

[...]

If into the market you chance for to walk,
You'll hear the forestaller and badger to talk
Of buying the butter, eggs, cheese, fowls, and all,
The poor has no chance to buy them at all.

[...]

* A trader who buys produce in order to sell it elsewhere; more generally, a trader or dealer (*OED*).

18 *Forestalling Done Over, A New Song* (Newcastle: Marshall, [1810–31]) [Bodleian Library, Harding B 11(1242)].

Marshall's other song, *The Tradesman's Complaint*, was a local version of a more widespread song.[19] Here is the final stanza, which relates to the economic slump following the end of the wars:

> Poor journeymen tradesmen have cause to mourn,
> They are paid but one-fourth of what they could earn.
> The masters you see have got a fresh trick,
> They will lock you all out three days in the week.

The Napoleonic wars, and in particular their central figure, cast a long shadow over the nineteenth century.

Napoleon died in 1821 on St Helena, and his son, Napoleon II, King of Rome and the subject of 'The Bonny Bunch of Roses', died in 1832. Shortly afterwards, in the later 1830s, the 'Napoleonic ballads' were composed, though the reason for this is not clear. In 1841, Napoleon's ashes were returned to Paris, and this set off another rush of songs—for example, *Ashes of Napoleon*.[20] In the early 1850s, Napoleon's nephew Louis-Napoléon Bonaparte, already elected French president, was crowned as Emperor Napoleon III. This gave rise to a mild reprise of the invasion panic of 1803, at least in a number of broadsides—*Napoleon Talks of War, Boys*,[21] for example, or *Napoleon Is Coming*.[22]

There can be no doubt that the production of songs, notably by the broadside trade, represented a response to perceived emergencies or significant battles, rather than to political events that did not involve Britain directly. It can be assumed that the more rapid the production of broadsides, the less likely they would be to spread among the population at large—and this assumption appears to be borne out by the invasion songs. Even the songs about the Battle of Waterloo itself do not seem to have lingered in the mouths of nineteenth-century singers as much as the 'romantic' songs and the reflective 'Napoleonic ballads'.

Note: The majority of the broadsides discussed here are held at Oxford, Bodleian Library, and are available at <ballads.bodleian.ox.ac.uk/>.

19 *The Tradesman's Complaint, A New Song* (Newcastle: Marshall, [1810–31]) [Bodleian Library, Harding B 11(1242)].

20 *Ashes of Napoleon* (Manchester: [J. O. Bebbington or T. Pearson, *c*.1841]) [Bodleian Library, Firth c.16 (102)].

21 *Napoleon Talks of War, Boys* (London: H. Such, [1849–62]) [Bodleian Library, Harding B 15(213b)].

22 *Napoleon Is Coming* (Northampton: Henson, [1855]) [Bodleian Library, Firth c.16 (107)].

III. Tunes

The Tunes of the Brazil Gypsy Family from Gloucestershire

GWILYM DAVIES

The aim of this paper is to look at the song repertoire of one English Gypsy family with a view to the modality of the tunes they used. I will use the term 'modal' here as shorthand to denote any tune not in the Ionian (major) mode. The generation of the Brazil (pronounced 'Brazzle') family of Gloucestershire Gypsies that I knew consisted of fifteen siblings, born around the turn of the nineteenth/twentieth century. The family considered themselves as English, but spent time in Ireland during the First World War, and several of the siblings were born there. On their return to England, they spent time in Devon before finally settling in Gloucestershire. From the 1960s onwards, their songs were remembered rather than sung regularly, with one exception — namely, that during the 1970s, Harry Brazil would regularly sing in the Pelican public house in the centre of Gloucester, while his wife went to play bingo. At least seven of the family were singers and were recorded by collectors, and in all probability the other siblings also knew the songs. There are few Brazils living in Gloucestershire today and to my knowledge they have not continued singing the songs of the previous generation, so while folklorists and folk singers may enthuse about the value of the songs, the family itself clearly does not see the need to retain them.

The Brazil family and their songs are worthy of study for two particular reasons. The first is that they were a very musical family with a large repertoire of songs; and the second is that they were widely recorded, by several collectors (including myself), from the 1950s onwards, so there is a large body of songs to work on. This is a family repertoire that was performed in public right up until the 1970s, and one can suppose that up to and after the Second World War the songs would have been sung regularly by family members in various social settings.

Often, the same song was noted from several different singers, with variations in tune and words.

A total of more than a hundred songs have been noted from the family. They include typical traditional English folk songs, music hall songs and parodies, and sentimental Irish and Victorian songs. However, the Brazil repertoire includes very few country and western songs, such as Jimmy Rodgers songs, which so many of today's English Gypsies perform. Danny Brazil once told me that he favoured the old songs over the country and western songs. There is evidence of Irish influence—not surprisingly, considering the time the family spent in Ireland—with songs such as 'Dear Old Erin's Shore', 'Sing Me a Song of Ireland', 'I'll Take You Home Again, Kathleen', and 'the Irish Sweep' (i.e. sweepstake) present in the repertoire. However, of what we might call the folk songs in the repertoire, all are more common in England than in Ireland. Indeed, many, such as 'Once a Bold Fisherman Courted Me', 'The Game of All Fours', and 'The Farmer of Leicester', are typical of the English Gypsy repertoire, so very possibly the songs were already part of the family repertoire in England before their sojourn in Ireland. We are therefore looking at a stable repertoire held by one family over many years.

Setting aside the songs that can be labelled as music hall, parody, or Irish/Victorian sentimental, all of which are almost invariably in the major (Ionian) mode, the remainder amounts to a total of about eighty songs, collected between 1954 and 1997, from seven different singers. Of these, the proportions in the various modes are as follows:

Ionian	69%	(47 songs)
Dorian	17%	(12 songs)
Mixolydian	10%	(7 songs)
Aeolian	3%	(2 songs)

This can be compared with the results reported for songs collected by George Butterworth, from non-Gypsies, prior to 1914:[1]

Ionian	51%
Dorian	30%
Mixolydian	11%
Aeolian	8%

---

1   Lewis Jones, 'Modal Scales in English Folk Song: An Analysis with Reference to the Butterworth MSS', paper presented at the English Folk Dance and Song Society's Folk Song Conference, October 2013.

Then, consider a much larger sample—namely, the Cecil Sharp collection. In 1907, by which time Sharp had only completed a portion of his collecting work, he claimed, based on his collection of 1,500 songs, mainly from Somerset, that two thirds of English folk tunes are in the Ionian mode, with the remainder spread evenly among the Mixolydian, Dorian, and Aeolian modes, with a preponderance of Mixolydian.[2] So, we might say:

Ionian	66%
Dorian	11%
Mixolydian	12%
Aeolian	11%

Percy Grainger's collecting in Gloucestershire and Lincolnshire from 1904 to 1909 includes a large number of modal songs, but detailed counting and analysis has yet to be carried out.

It is instructive to compare these results with my own experience of collecting several hundred songs from *c.*1970 onwards. If we take away the music hall songs, Victoriana, and Tin Pan Alley songs, the songs recorded from Gypsies, and the songs recorded in America, then the total number of modal songs I have noted has been a mere handful—and most of those are from one particular singer. So, the statistics from my non-Gypsy English collecting, 1970–2013, are:

Ionian	99+%
Non-Ionian	<1%

On the other hand, the Gypsies I have met and recorded in Gloucestershire and Devon have a significant proportion of modal songs. These include not just the Brazil family but also the Smith family of Gloucestershire and the Orchard family of Devon.

Detailed analyses for other recent song collections are not available, but a glance at, for example, the vast number of songs collected in East Anglia over the last forty or fifty years indicates that those, too, are nearly all in the major key or Ionian mode. The same holds true for recordings made by Peter Kennedy and Mike Yates. Interestingly, the songs of the Copper family, who over many generations have retained a repertoire of songs comparable with those of the Gypsy families named above, are nearly all in the Ionian mode. Only three out of

2 Cecil J. Sharp, *English Folk-Song: Some Conclusions* (London: Simpkin; Novello, 1907), p. 55.

the forty-seven songs in *A Song for Every Season* show Mixolydian characteristics—namely 'Sweep Chimney Sweep', 'Lemadie', and 'Season Round'. This may be due to the influence of church-type harmonies and the family's familiarity with that type of harmony, as opposed to the harmonization of modal melodies.

Looking in more detail at the Brazil repertoire, there are grey areas that the bare statistics hide. For example, one song, 'The Rambling Irishman', was sung by both Harry and Danny Brazil to a Dorian tune (Figure 1), but their sister, Lementina (known as Lemmie), played it on her one-row melodeon as an Ionian melody (Figure 2). The melodeon itself is probably the 'culprit' here: in common with other traditional English melodeon players, Lemmie played everything in a major key, so perhaps our 'Rambling Irishman' was unintentionally forced into that mode.

Another danger in attaching strict modal labels to tunes is that they can sometimes hover between modes. For example, the Brazil version of 'Thorneymore Woods', which they called 'Limpy Jack', is to all intents and purposes a straight Ionian tune, but Danny sang the first phrase with a telltale flattened seventh, which would indicate the Mixolydian mode (Figure 3)—but this is the only occurrence of that note in the whole song, so are we to classify it as a song in the Ionian mode or the Mixolydian?

There is another point to make here. The modal tunes may be attached to songs that have died out in the current oral tradition. A present-day collector would be highly unlikely to come across songs such as 'The Bold Keeper' or 'Shot like a Bird on a Tree', from the Brazil repertoire, which were sung to striking modal tunes. However, today's collectors might well find songs such as 'The Banks of the Sweet Dundee', 'The Crabfish', or 'An Old Man Came Courting me', and if so they would almost certainly be in the Ionian mode, whereas the Brazil family versions of the same songs were all sung to modal tunes. Figures 4, 5 show further examples of Brazil family songs in the various modes.

Admittedly, this is a small sample, and the subject merits further study, but we can draw out a few generalizations:

- Older collections, such as those of Sharp, Butterworth, and Grainger, all include a proportion of modal tunes—at least one third of the total songs collected.
- Later collections, such as those Kennedy, Yates, and the author, discounting songs from Gypsies and songs collected outside of England, show a vast majority of tunes in the Ionian mode.

- Ergo, the modes apparently once prevalent in English folk song are being used less and less in the oral tradition.
- The exception is found among the songs collected from English Gypsies over the same time frame — second half of the twentieth century — which still show a content of nearly one third modal songs.
- Ergo, the Gypsies retained and were comfortable with modal tunes which gradually dropped out of use among their non-Gypsy counterparts.

Acknowledgements

Thanks to Peter Shepheard and Rod Smith for permission to transcribe their recordings.

Figure 1. *Harry Brazil, Rambling Irishman*

Figure 2. *Lemmie Brazil, Rambling Irishman*

Figure 3. *Danny Brazil, Limpy Jack*

Figure 4. *Harry Brazil, Bold Keeper*

Figure 5. *Harry Brazil, The Gown so Green*

How Good a Music Transcriber was Cecil Sharp?

VIC GAMMON

Cecil Sharp's importance in the history of the collection of traditional song is widely acknowledged and in many ways self-evident, even to those who have disapproved of the man himself or aspects of his work. His collection amounts to about five thousand items from England and the USA. His statements on the nature of English folk song have been common currency for many years. He bequeathed an enduring legacy in terms of ideas, assumptions, and institutions. Notwithstanding the naysayers who declare that Sharp is not worth bothering about any more, interest in his work remains vigorous.[1] Sharp is arguably the most significant individual in the history of the preservation and revival of traditional song in England, and his influence extended, and continues to be felt, much further afield. Yet his substantial collection was made overwhelmingly by a pencil and paper method, in immediate personal interaction with his singer-informants. Tunes were noted directly into field notebooks and then copied into volumes of fair-copy books. Later, they might be arranged and published for popular use, or exhibited, for those particularly interested, in the *Journal of the Folk-Song Society*.

In the light of the importance of Sharp's collection, it is vital to ask how good as an aural transcriber of musical material he actually was. In the course of writing an collaborative article on five-time in English traditional song, we came to the view: 'No work has yet been done (to our knowledge) to assess how good a transcriber Sharp actually was, and until it is done—if the materials exist to enable it to be done—an important question mark has to remain over the quality of this aspect of Sharp's collection. We do not say this to cast doubts on Sharp's

---

1 I am recalling an exchange between myself and Philip Bohlman, an American ethnomusicologist, at a conference and I may be misrepresenting his position. It may also indicate an increasing distance I have felt between myself, a traditional music specialist with a background in history, and much (though not all) ethnomusicology as practised today, which seems to me often shallow and lacking in historical depth.

ability, but merely to record the present state of our knowledge.'[2] This essay is an attempt to provide a response to that observation. Unlike Percy Grainger, Sharp left very few audio recordings of his source singers. Using five recordings that he did make, and one made of one of his key singers after his death, I have tried to assess the quality of Sharp's transcriptions. Throughout the work I have reflected on the issues it raises, the qualities and limitations of Sharp's methods, and the validity of my own investigations.

Transcription and Publication in the Edwardian Revival

It was widely understood that there were inherent difficulties in notating tunes directly by ear. As Frank Kidson, a pioneer of the late Victorian revival attested, 'very great difficulty attends the notation of irregular old melodies from untutored singers'.[3] In the early days of the Folk-Song Society, Kate Lee encourage a wider public to become involved in the activity of song collecting, but was reported to have said, 'Tunes should be noted as well as words; but the tunes, it must be confessed, are sometimes hard to distinguish.'[4] Francis Barrett felt, 'A good ear is necessary to grasp the curious intervals which abound in some of the melodies.'[5]

But transcription, if it could be done well, could also be an act of revelation, as Sharp's collaborator, Charles Marson, attested:

> Would-be collectors however must expect a great many difficulties and discouragements. It is not everyone who can write down a tune correctly, and even of those who possess the power to do so, only a few have the ability to recognize a treasure when it is contained in an earthen vessel. A ballad bawled from a lusty throat which has been already used copiously for other purposes, a ballad heard in a stable or barton, particularly if it is both modal and intricate, does not at first appear to be the jewel that it is. It is often a venture of faith to transcribe it, and it is only when the collector transcribes it into the purer tones of thought, or of the piano, that he realizes how lucky a finder he has been.[6]

2 Vic Gammon and Emily Portman, 'Five-Time in English Traditional Song', *Folk Music Journal*, 10.3 (2013) 319–46 (p. 328).

3 Frank Kidson, ed., *Traditional Tunes: A Collection of Ballad Airs, Chiefly Obtained in Yorkshire and the South of Scotland* (Oxford: Chas. Taphouse, 1891), p. v.

4 Anon, 'Country Notes', *Country Life Illustrated*, 109 (4 February 1899), 131.

5 'Chorister', 'Musical Notes', *Falkirk Herald*, 16 April 1902.

6 Cecil J. Sharp and Charles L. Marson, *Folk Songs from Somerset*, [first series] (London: Simpkin; Schott, 1904), p. xv.

This is quite strange in a way, and rather suspect. The song may not 'at first appear to be the jewel that it is', and the realization of value only comes when the piece is transcribed — that is, removed from context and objectified in what is an alien form of representation. The question of valuation is in the mind of the collector and has nothing to do with the singer's use and experience of the song.

Sharp's method was what we could describe as 'stanza with notable variations'. Sharp made very clear statements as to what he was trying to do with his transcriptions, and he felt that his methods were superior to those of previous collectors, 'because English folk-tunes, owing to their collection in more recent times, have been taken down with great care, and have, consequently, suffered but little from editings and "improvements".[7] Contemporaries supported Sharp's view. Harry Plunket Greene felt that tunes were 'most properly noted down by the present-day collector',[8] by which he meant Sharp. W. M. K. Warren remarked, 'I can vouch for the trouble Sharp took to take down the songs exactly as they were sung.'[9]

Sharp, addressing his students at the Hampstead Conservatoire, commented on the skill needed to undertake aural notation: 'some knowledge of practical music is necessary before you can take down a tune from the lips of a singer — not that I wish to overrate the musical accomplishment required; there are several students in this conservatoire, who, with a little practice, would easily qualify themselves for the work.'[10] We must bear in mind that Sharp is addressing here an audience of music students in a conservatoire, and even so, only 'several' would 'with a little practice' be adequate to the task. We should be clear, whatever Sharp's extravagance of thought, we are dealing here with a significant, high-level skill.

Sharp did not notate tunes from his singers at the pitch at which they actually sang. In her foreword to her edition of Sharp's collection, Maud Karpeles wrote, 'I have not indicated the keys in which they were originally noted as this is of little significance. Cecil Sharp did not necessarily note the tunes at the pitch at which they were sung but wrote them in a key which lay conveniently within the staff.'[11] This is misleading, as Karpeles generally does reproduce the songs in the keys in which they appear in the manuscripts, where there is no indication of the keys in which the singer actually performed.

7 Cecil J. Sharp, *English Folk-Song: Some Conclusions* (London: Simpkin; Novello, 1907), p. 82.

8 Harry Plunket Greene, *Interpretation in Song* (London: Macmillan, 1912), p. 219.

9 London, EFDSS Archives, Cecil Sharp Correspondence, Box 4, Folder A, Item 20, W. M. K. Warren to Maud Karpeles, 15 November 1926.

10 London, EFDSS Archives, Cecil Sharp Manuscript Collection, Miscellaneous, CJS/5/1, p. 11.

11 Maud Karpeles, ed., *Cecil Sharp's Collection of English Folk Songs*, 2 vols. (London: Oxford University Press, 1974).

It is in this context that we can start to understand the promise (or threat) that the Edison phonograph presented to folk song collectors in the early twentieth century. The argument that there was a great falling-out in the Folk-Song Society over the use of the phonograph has been subject to some recent controversy. C. J. Bearman musters some good arguments on the matter, to the effect that the heroism of Grainger and what he terms the denigration of Sharp has given us a false impression of the issue and of the relationships between the individuals concerned.[12] Leading collectors may have simply agreed to disagree and then got on with what they did.

Sharp stated his own position with regard to Percy Grainger's methods and the use of the phonograph in a long letter. Here are some brief extracts to give the flavour and the issues. With regard to the phonograph, Sharp was 'unable to endorse all that you [Grainger] said in its praise'. When confronted with the machine, singers were 'quite unable to sing into it in their usual un-selfconscious manner'. The phonograph was likely to give 'a false impression' of a song and of a singer's qualities, and it should not be used exclusively. Some good songs have been recovered from singers 'far too frail in body and weak in voice to sing into a phonograph'. The machine was 'untrustworthy in the matter of words'. Sharp continues, 'But my chief objection to the phonograph does not lie only here. In transcribing a song, our aim should be to record its artistic effect, not necessarily the exact means by which that effect was produced.' Slowing down the recording to facilitate transcription would bring into prominence sounds 'which in practice were scarcely heard at all or were quite inaudible'. Notating these would, in extreme cases, give an 'utterly erroneous impression of the artistic effect produced', and 'it is not an exact, scientifically accurate memorandum that is wanted, so much as a faithful artistic record of what is actually heard by the ordinary auditor'. The facilitation of hearing detail in the performance that the phonograph provides creates a further problem: 'The difficulty, which is perpetually confronting the collector, is to decide which of these small aberrations he should record and which he should omit.'[13]

There is obviously some, but perhaps variable, substance in the points Sharp makes here. No doubt the production of a phonograph could be intimidating to a singer, and we know

---

12 C. J. Bearman, 'Percy Grainger, the Phonograph, and the Folk Song Society', *Music and Letters*, 84 (2003), 434–55. See also David Josephson, 'The Case for Percy Grainger, Edwardian Musician, on his Centenary', in *Music and Civilization: Essays in Honor of Paul Henry Lang*, ed. Rika Maniates and Edmond Strainchamps (New York: W. W. Norton, 1984), pp. 350–62; Graham Freeman, '"That Chief Undercurrent of my Mind": Percy Grainger and the Aesthetics of English Folk Song', *Folk Music Journal*, 9.4 (2009), 581–613.

13 Letter of Cecil Sharp to Percy Grainger, reproduced in Michael Yates, 'Percy Grainger and the Impact of the Phonograph', *Folk Music Journal*, 4.4 (1982), 265–75 (pp. 268–69).

that Sharp was very skilled and very successful in attaining the confidence of reluctant singers. Yet in a number of ways he protests too much. The decisions about how much or how little of the detail to record in a transcription exist whether one is working from a live singer or from a recording—one is just more pressured in the live situation. The recording gives the transcriber the ability to recall the fleeting moment, to reiterate difficult or questionable passages, but the decisions about what to set into notation, and how to set it, remain.

Perhaps most interestingly, Sharp proposes a distinction between 'the song itself' and its performance. There is an important philosophical issue here, which I do not intend to pursue, other than to say that I find it strange that such a thought should come from a theorist who saw variation as a vital element in the ongoing life and evolution of oral song. Sharp stated explicitly, 'as a general rule, evolution can only take place in a song or tale for any length of time in the absence of an authoritative original'.[14] If the song does not exist in its evolving performances, then where does it exist? In a sense, that is the only time that it is tangible, the only time it can be captured in the process of what Atkinson calls its 'constant and multiple production'—all the rest is potential, be that in words on a page or a melody and text preserved in memory.[15]

Significantly, Sharp tells us, 'I have never tried to collect with the phonograph, but only to secure records of songs which I had previously noted down, and which I wanted to have by me in permanent form for scientific purposes.'[16] This is verified by the dates of notation of individual songs and the subsequent dates of phonograph recordings. It is important to remember that a transcription taken from one of his recordings is not a transcription of the same performance that Sharp took down in his field notebook. Thus in my re-transcriptions of these songs we should not expect identical results but rather should be satisfied with a high degree of similarity, given that Sharp and I are transcribing different performances. Sharp did at least try using the phonograph and we know of five songs that he recorded which are extant and available for listening at the Vaughan Williams Memorial Library:

> William Wooley, 'No John' (also known as 'O No John') (C37/1558).
> Alfred Edgell, 'All Among the New Mown Hay' (C37/1556).[17]

---

14 Sharp, *English Folk-Song: Some Conclusions*, p. 13.

15 For a recent and excellent discussion of this and related important areas, see David Atkinson, *The Anglo-Scottish Ballad and its Imaginary Contexts* (Cambridge: Open Book Publishers, 2014) (quotation from p. 23).

16 Yates, 'Percy Grainger and the Impact of the Phonograph', p. 268.

17 Also available at <http://sounds.bl.uk/World-and-traditional-music/Ethnographic-wax-cylinders/025M-C0037X1556XX-0100V0> [accessed 31 March 2014].

Jack Barnard, 'Lady Maisry' (C37/1637).[18]
Priscilla Cooper, 'The Basket of Eggs'(C37/1581).[19]
Priscilla Cooper, 'The American Stranger' (sometimes incorrectly labelled 'The Indian Lass') (C37/1628).[20]

These five recordings form the centre of this study, with the addition of a recording made by Douglas Clevedon of the BBC in 1942 of one of Sharp's key singers, Louie Hooper, singing 'Hares on the Mountains', which I have also considered for the light it sheds on aspects of the issue.[21]

Method

Music transcription is not an exact science—it is more of an art, more like a sketch than a photograph. Different individuals will produce different transcriptions of the same piece, the output being dependent on the skill of the transcriber and the way he or she perceives the material. Here, predispositions and mental structures can have a determining effect on the outcome. Hearing can be determined by acculturation—just as there are 'ways of seeing', so there are ways of hearing.[22]

A very significant, reflective, and insightful discussion of these issues was written by Ruth Crawford Seeger in the 1940s, and ultimately published as *The Music of American Folk Song* long after her death. It is brutally honest, considering she is dealing with her own work as well as that of other transcribers: 'Each individual will have his or her own preferences in respect to what should be lost, modified or preserved. A transcriber is no exception, and consciously or unconsciously expresses his own preferences.'[23] Crawford Seeger details the inaccuracies and distortions that can creep in during the transcription process, as well as the ways notation simply fails to capture some aspects of musical performance. She makes what could be con-

---

18 Also available at <http://sounds.bl.uk/World-and-traditional-music/Ethnographic-wax-cylinders/025M-C0037X1637XX-0100V0> [accessed 31 March 2014].

19 Also available at <http://sounds.bl.uk/World-and-traditional-music/Ethnographic-wax-cylinders/025M-C0037X1581XX-0100V0> [accessed 31 March 2014].

20 Also available at <http://sounds.bl.uk/World-and-traditional-music/Ethnographic-wax-cylinders/025M-C0037X1588XX-0100V0> [accessed 31 March 2014].

21 My great thanks go to Andrew King and Malcolm Taylor of the Vaughan Williams Memorial Library for helping me locate and giving me access to these invaluable recordings.

22 John Berger, *Ways of Seeing* (Harmondsworth: Penguin, 2008 [1972]).

23 Ruth Crawford Seeger, *The Music of American Folk Song*, ed. Larry Polansky, with Judith Tick (Rochester, NY: University of Rochester Press, 2001), p. 29.

sidered a startling statement: 'it must be apparent what a small part of the original song and its manner of singing is represented to the reader in customary notation.'

Yet transcription into musical notation and subsequent publication was *the* way Edwardian collectors represented and communicated their findings to both the general public and those with a more particular interest in the subject. It therefore behoves us to look critically at their achievement and, in a sense, to meet them on their own ground. I therefore started by attempting rough aural transcriptions of the six recordings noted above. These were pencil and paper transcriptions, which I did without reference to Sharp's notations (although I must state prior familiarity with some of Sharp's published versions of these songs).[24] I then compared my transcriptions with those of Sharp. If my transcriptions were substantially the same as Sharp's, I simply recorded the fact and did nothing else with that particular song. If there were significant differences between my transcriptions and Sharp's, I used two software packages to check and help improve my transcriptions:

1. Sibelius—used to set the music into notation and for checking my own work by the use of MIDI playback.[25]

2. Melodyne (music production software)—used to display a graphic representation of the performance in terms of pitch and duration.[26]

---

24 The initial transcriptions were done purely aurally without the aid of an instrument, sitting in the Vaughan Williams Memorial Library with a computer and headphones. I should say something about my own transcription skills. My school music teacher, Edmond Semmons, valued aural skills very highly. Studying O- and A-level music, each lesson would start with ten to fifteen minutes of aural transcription. This pedagogical emphasis coincided with my own developing interest in traditional music. I knew from an early age that this was the method that the early twentieth-century folk song collectors had used, and I was motivated to try to be good at it. By the age of seventeen (when I left school) I could notate moderately complex melodies with a high degree of accuracy. I think my facility has waned since then, but I still have some ability in the skill.

25 Sibelius is a widely used music notation software package <http://www.sibelius.com/home/index_flash.html>.

26 An introduction to Melodyne can be found at <http://www.celemony.com/en/start>. This software, which is basically a music technology tool for audio manipulation, gives a readout that shows intensity, pitch, and pitch fluctuation on a time/pitch matrix. In this it is similar in a number of ways to the systems of recording graphic representations of song that people such as Metfessel and Charles Seeger tried to develop in the twentieth century. There are difficulties in using the software for this purpose; it runs into the potential difficulty of what Sharp described as giving an 'erroneous impression of the artistic effect produced'. The visual representation it provides depends to some extent on the choice of the user: for example, as to where one note ends and another begins. Nevertheless, I used this software to check my own work and to see if other interpretations of the material were viable. This sometimes involved manipulation of the material: for example, adjustment of the whole segment to a specific pitch base in order to enable comparison. Ultimately, I chose not to present any Melodyne representations in this paper, but I still believe the software has uses in this area, if more as a background

Finally, I undertook a more detailed comparison between my transcriptions and Sharp's in order to address the research question and to reflect on the issues involved.

William Wooley and Arthur Edgell: Uncomplicated Transcriptions

Put to the test, some of my transcriptions turned out almost exactly like Sharp's.[27] The regularity of rhythm and the clear, mainly crotchet, melodies of William Wooley's 'No John' and Alfred Edgell's 'All Among the New Mown Hay' made for an easy transcription process. My transcription of William Wooley's song is almost identical to Sharp's, so there is no need to reproduce either.

There were, however, some differences between the two transcriptions of Alfred Edgell's song (Figure 1). There is a blank page in Sharp's fair-copy manuscript book headed 'New Mown Hay—Alfred Edgell—Dec. 26 1907'; this contrasts with the date of 11 January 1907 given elsewhere in the manuscript book and in the printed collection.[28] It looks very much as if Sharp intended to make a detailed transcription from the phonograph recording but never got beyond writing in the heading. This does suggest that he felt there might be more to be learned from a further transcription of this tune from the recording. Sharp's transcription and my own have many similarities. Yet there are significant differences, too, considering that the two versions of the song were not chronologically far apart. First, Sharp's transcription is very four-square on the page; he gives no indication of the pauses the singer makes (which I have indicated by fermata and irregular bars). Secondly, while the two versions are clearly the 'same tune', there is considerable melodic variance between them—look particularly at bars 3–5. It could be that Edgell moved musical material around in the period between the initial collection and the recording, or it could be that Sharp made some mistakes when he first noted the song.

Sharp notated 'No John' in the key of G, and Wooley sings the song in G on the recording. Sharp notated 'All Among the New Mown Hay' in the key of D, but Edgell sings the song

---

tool than a means of communication. See Milton Metfessel, *Phonophotography in Folk Music: American Negro Songs in New Notation* (Chapel Hill: University of of North Carolina Press, 1928); Charles Seeger, *Studies in Musicology, 1935–1975* (Berkley and Los Angeles: University of California Press, 1977), esp. 'Prescriptive and Descriptive Music Writing' (pp. 168–81).

27 In what follows I refer the reader both to the digitized Sharp manuscripts and to Karpeles, ed., *Cecil Sharp's Collection*.

28 Cambridge, Clare College Archives, CCPP/SHA, Cecil Sharp Collection of Folk Song Manuscripts, Folk Tunes 1527, 1163; Karpeles, *Cecil Sharp's Collection*, I, 145.

The New Mown Hay

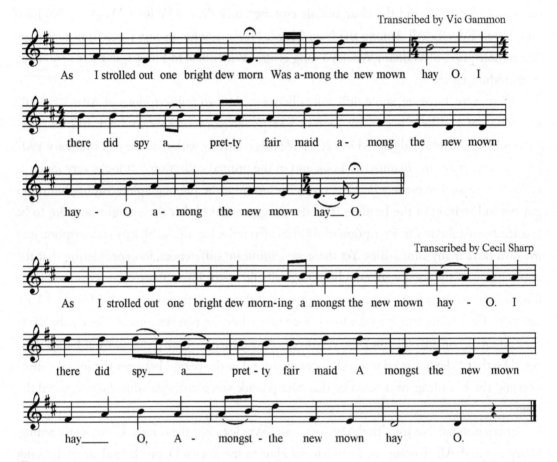

Figure 1.

near to E-flat.[29] In these two instances, Sharp, in his manuscripts and subsequently in his posthumously published collection, gives a good indication of the actual pitch at which the songs were sung.

Jack Barnard: A Case of Misrecognition

Jack Barnard (also known as John Burnett) is most probably the singer that Sharp described in his letter to Grainger:[30]

> In my own somewhat limited experience I have found singers, although not at all unwilling to sing into the phonograph, yet quite incapable of singing into it in their usual un-selfconscious manner. I remember spending an hour or more last Christmas holiday with a singer (from whom I have, in the course of the last few years, taken down a very large number of songs) in the vain attempt to secure an accurate phonographic record of his singing of 'Lady Maisry'. He was a young man, a very first-rate folk-singer, and not by any means a nervous subject. His first attempt failed dismally; he forgot his words, pitched his song too high, sang much faster than usual, and altogether fell far below his usual standard of performance. I then stopped the phonograph and made him sing through the song in the ordinary manner. This he at once did in his accustomed way, without hesitancy, or mistake. Then I put him at the phonograph again, with precisely the same disastrous result as before. I repeated the experiment yet once more, but with no better fortune. Finally I gave up the attempt as hopeless.

This is certainly a reminder of some of the difficulties the collectors faced in using the phonograph, although the recording, poor quality though it is, conveys a confident performance by a singer who knows and is in command of his material. Sharp first notated the song from Mr Barnard in April 1906, so he could well have made the recording in December 1907 (he wrote to Grainger in May 1908).

Sharp published Jack Barnard's version of this song a number of times and I was familiar with it before I undertook this project. In terms of the type of classification Sharp favoured,

29 In citing keys it should be kept in mind that the processes of copying recordings in analogue formats can lead to alterations of pitch and speed. My impression is that the recordings are running at the correct speed, but this cannot be verified as reference tones were not sounded.

30 Yates suggests this identification and I agree with him. The only other possible candidate appears to be William Hitchman, from Farringdon in Berkshire, from whom Sharp obtained the song on 1 August 1907, though only a tune seems to survive in the manuscripts: Cecil Sharp Collection of Folk Song Manuscripts, Folk Tunes 1369.

we would describe the tune as being in the Aeolian mode, or natural minor scale. My previous familiarity with the tune and the secure pitch clarity of the singer did not stop me (internally) quite suddenly hearing the tune as being set in a major scale but ending on the third note of that scale. I resorted to using Melodyne to try to sort out what was happening and the evidence was that the song was indeed in a natural minor scale. Once I realized this, my perception switched back to hearing the song this way and I came up with a transcription very close to Sharp's. The switch was immediate and total—just the sort of thing one experiences in seeing a Rubin's vase picture. I recount this anecdote not to point up my own inadequacies, but to show that our perceptions of auditory phenomena are not necessarily stable. Such difficulties may well have faced the collectors who used the pencil and paper method.

Jack Barnard sings the song at about C-sharp minor. Sharp wrote down the song in E minor in the manuscript, and also printed it in that key in *Folk Songs from Somerset* and in his anthology *One Hundred English Folk Songs*.[31] In Karpeles's published collection it is given in G minor.[32] It is hard to account for this raising of the pitch other than in terms of Karpeles's notion of 'a key which lay conveniently within the staff'. Printed on the page at an augmented fourth higher than he actually sang it, the transcription conveys nothing of Barnard's insistent and guttural, heightened-speech type of ballad singing.

Apart from this important question of pitch and voice placement, Sharp's transcription is substantially correct (in a generalized way), although there are rhythmic subtleties he fails to capture in all their complexity, so I have not reproduced comparative transcriptions.

Priscilla Cooper: Challenging Transcriptions

The two recordings of the Gypsy singer Priscilla Cooper are the most interesting and rewarding performances I consider in this study. They are also the most complex and problematic.

In the case of 'The American Stranger', Sharp makes a musical transcription of only one verse of the song—and to add to our difficulties, it is a verse of the song mostly not on the recording. It is highly likely that he heard a very different performance of the song on 2 September 1907, when he notated it by hand, from that which he later recorded on the cylinder.

---

31 Cecil Sharp Collection of Folk Song Manuscripts, Folk Tunes 912; Cecil J. Sharp and Charles L. Marson, *Folk Songs from Somerset*, third series (London: Simpkin; Schott, 1906), pp. 56–57. Cecil J. Sharp, ed., *One Hundred English Folksongs* (Boston: Oliver Ditson, 1916), pp. 26–28.

32 Karpeles, *Cecil Sharp's Collection*, I, 65.

Sharp notated the September version of the song in an unusual three-line verse form, and this is how it appears in both the manuscript and the Karpeles collection.[33] The state of the recording is too poor for me to be able successfully to transcribe the words, but musically, despite some phrasing variation, it is absolutely clear that Mrs Cooper sings four-line stanzas with an ABBA musical pattern throughout. What can be heard, however, clearly locates the song as a version of 'The American Stranger'. Five verses are recorded, of which three are known from other versions of 'The American Stranger'.[34] Verse four is so indistinct that I cannot decide whether it is commonly part of 'The American Stranger'. Verse five is clearly an interloper, comprising the concluding 'health' verse of 'The Indian Lass' (thus the confusion over the title of the song). The last line Mrs Cooper sings on the recording is clearly 'And we'll drink a good health to a beautiful lass'.

Perhaps Mrs Cooper had only half-remembered the song when Sharp first heard her sing it. Karpeles adds an editorial note: 'This tune appears to be incomplete. Probably the second phrase should be repeated.'[35] She is correct, but she seems not to have been aware of, or had access to, the recording when she compiled her edition.

Sharp's transcription misses the variable upper thirds that are a striking characteristic of the performance, though his notation may have been correct so far as the particular verse he transcribed went. (No third is hit in the lower part of the tune, so in terms of modal classification we would have to describe the tune as Mixolydian/Dorian.[36]) It is impossible to transcribe the same verse because of the incomplete recording, but even a comparison of different verses tells a story. Sharp's transcription looks very four-square on the page; he captures little of the rhythmic flexibility and subtlety that must have been there in the original performance. What he sets down is an inadequate rendition of what on the recording is a lively and well-sung performance, which we can hear in spite of the terrible state of the audio. Perhaps the problem is one of occasion. Maybe the performance for the phonograph was much better, more

---

33 Cecil Sharp Collection of Folk Song Manuscripts, Folk Tunes 1456; Karpeles, *Cecil Sharp's Collection*, II, 577–58.

34 Verse 1 starts 'I'm a stranger in this country / From Americay I came'. Verse two contains the lines 'In the middle of the ocean / There will grow a maple tree'. Verse three starts 'Some say that I'm rakish'. Verse four is indecipherable. Verse five belongs to 'The Indian Lass'.

35 Karpeles, *Cecil Sharp's Collection*, II, 578.

36 Sharp was well aware of the variability of the third interval in some performances. See: Sharp, *English Folk-Song: Some Conclusions*, p. 71: 'It must be understood that the third is not a fixed note in the folk-scale, as it is in both of the modern scales. The English folk-singer varies the intonation of this particular note very considerably.'

rehearsed that the one originally heard and perhaps dredged up from memory. We cannot know for certain.

Given that this is a competent singer and a creative performer, we cannot be too pedantic about the inadequacies of Sharp's transcription. Given the problems of aural transcription in the field, it may be as good a transcription as was possible, and it is clear that the singer performed the song differently on the two occasions. This said, even the sad thing that is the remaining audio recording seems to indicate that there was so much more to this singer's rendition of the song than Sharp began to capture with his pencil and paper. All the musical material in the Sharp transcription is on the recording somewhere, but the transcription seems like a distant recollection of something that is much more coherent and vibrant.[37]

I have chosen to ease comparison by basing my transcription on the key note of D, as Sharp did (Figure 2); the singer actually sang about a perfect fifth lower than that, with an approximate G as key note. A testimony to the misleading nature of Sharp's preservation of this song is a recording made by my friends Shan and Martin Graebe.[38] Their recording is a good realization of Sharp's transcription, but one tries hard to hear it as the same song Priscilla Cooper recorded—it is more like a distant version

This idea of a distant recollection also applies when we consider Sharp's other recording of Priscilla Cooper, 'The Basket of Eggs'. In this case Sharp transcribes what seems to be the last verse of the song (Figure 3),[39] but unfortunately the recording breaks off after the first line of this verse. Rhythmically, Sharp's transcription again looks very pedestrian—it seems more like an outline than a fully worked-through transcription. As set down, it is in the Dorian mode with a variable cadential third (I do not hear these sharpened thirds at all in the recording). Sharp wrote his transcription with the key signature of D major (f-sharp and c-sharp), necessitating the naturalization of every f note except two and every c note in the piece. When Karpeles published the song she uncharacteristically deviated from Sharp's manuscript and chose not to set a key signature, which necessitated much less use of accidentals. She also chose to simplify Sharp's bar structure.[40]

There is a hidden problem with Sharp's rendition of the tune, which the recording reveals. Verses 1 and 2 are sung to a melodic pattern related to, but significantly different from, the

---

37 Sharp transcribes with bars of three and four pulses but does not indicate alterations of time signature. I hear the performance as a coherent seven pulses, though clearly seven is an addition of four and three.

38 <http://www.martinandshan.net/page12.htm> [accessed 29 March 2014].

39 Cecil Sharp Collection of Folk Song Manuscripts, Folk Tunes 1459.

40 Karpeles, *Cecil Sharp's Collection*, II, 112.

American Stranger

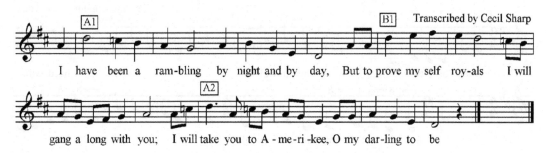

Figure 2.

one that Mrs Cooper settles into from verse 3. Even when she settles into this second phase of the tune, there are unexpected cadences and turns of phrase. Figure 4 shows my transcription of verse 1 and one later verse; sadly, few of the words are distinct enough to transcribe. I have set this at the actual pitch at which Mrs Cooper starts the song, in order to show the different look of the melody on the page when giving the pitch a more accurate representation. I could refine this transcription further (what I did took an entire working day and its accuracy could still be improved), but it reflects some of the rhythmic subtlety of this outstanding performance.

The nuances of the performance are hardly broached by Sharp's single-verse transcription. It is hard to find a metaphor to describe what has happened here. It is not only that in making a museum exhibit of Mrs Cooper's song the life has gone out of it, but it has been pressed into a shape that shows none of the exuberance and irregularity of the original. It brings into

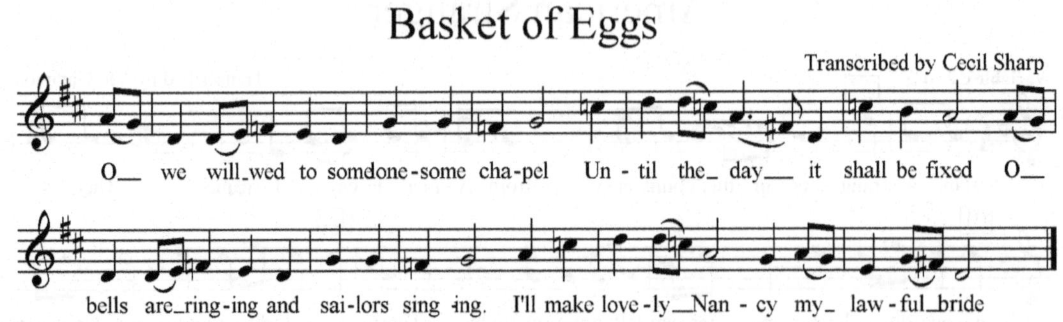

Basket of Eggs

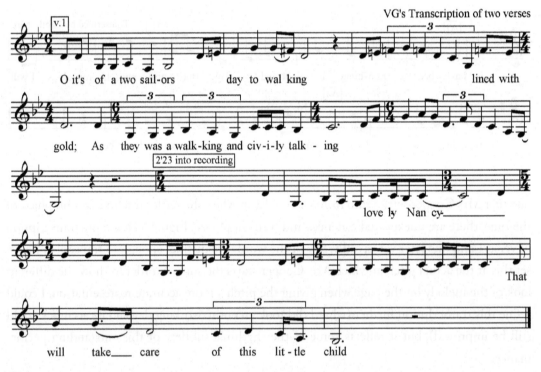

Figure 3.

Figure 4.

question the whole purpose of transcription when so much musical and artistic information is lost in the process. Sharp's difficulty in setting an accurate key signature perhaps points to his more general difficulty in transcribing the piece. He made a space in his fair-copy manuscript book to transcribe the song from the phonograph recording, but the page remained blank.[41] Sharp has the key centre at D; Mrs Cooper sang the song a fifth lower, in the key of G minor, but over the course of the song she crept slightly over a semitone sharper.

The Reassuring Case of Louie Hooper

About forty years after Sharp collected songs from Louie Hooper she was visited by Douglas Clevedon of the BBC.[42] He recorded a number of songs from her. She was in her old age but still singing well. One of the songs Clevedon recorded was 'Hares on the Mountains', which Sharp had collected from her in 1903.[43] There are some differences between what she sang to Clevedon and what Sharp set down in 1903, but they are minimal compared to the equivalences. It is almost as if Sharp were transcribing from the 1942 recording. Mrs Hooper sometimes repeats the second half of the verse on the recording, which is not indicated in the manuscript; there is a slight rhythmic difference in the chorus; and she starts with the anacrusis on the lower dominant note, not the key note—otherwise the tune is the same. Sharp, however, transcribes it in the key of F, whereas Louie Hooper sings in B-flat, gently but mostly in a chest voice low in her vocal range. It is unlikely that her customary pitching of the song went down a perfect fifth over the space of forty years when so much else remained the same.

*

The evidence points to fact Cecil Sharp was a skilful musical transcriber, and he certainly had considerable practice. I write this in spite of all that I have analysed above. Generally, we can place a high degree of confidence in his ability to set down a good notational representation of a song—given the limitations of that form of musical mediation. However, on the limited evidence presented here, we cannot rule out the thought that Sharp's ideas and preconceptions may have shaped some of his interpretations, and that he found some transcriptions technically challenging and only achieved partially successful results.

Sharp's achievement was limited by certain self-imposed factors. Most significantly, his choice of the 'stanza with significant variations' method gives us a limited record of more complex song performances, as the case of Priscilla Cooper shows. It is a somewhat facile

41 Cecil Sharp Collection of Folk Song Manuscripts, Folk Tunes 1549.
42 BBC RPL 4014 [archival copy at London, Vaughan Williams Memorial Library, BBC CDA 44].
43 Cecil Sharp Collection of Folk Song Manuscripts, Folk Tunes 9; Karpeles, *Cecil Sharp's Collection*, I, 430.

conclusion to say that the more complex the musical material, the more difficulty Sharp had in transcribing it, but that is what the evidence suggests and such a conclusion would be both logical and human.

It has been said many times, and in many ways, that the best way to encounter traditional song is aurally—an old idea, but one I would not want to disagree with in any way. It is to be regretted that Sharp did not make more audio recordings of his singers. I think his reluctance to use the phonograph when collecting from an informant for the first time is understandable, but we know he created long-term and mutually respectful relationships with some of his singers, like Louie Hooper, and these relationships could have led to recordings. One thought is that he was perhaps in too much hurry to accumulate the items of his extensive collection. He felt he had an urgent task to rescue the material from oblivion, and clearly recording and through-transcription would have been inconvenient and time-consuming. But equally, we cannot avoid nagging doubts about Sharp's own confidence in his abilities—notwithstanding his public declaration, quoted above, about the superiority of the collectors of 'recent times' who have taken down tunes 'with great care', eliminating the 'improvements' of earlier collectors. Why, when he had made audio recordings, and had even created space in his manuscript books for transcriptions from them,[44] did he not carry through with that intention? Was he simply too busy, or did he not wish to have his work compared with that of Grainger (or, in one notable case, Lucy Broadwood's transcription from a Vaughan Williams recording)?[45] Was Sharp reluctant to have latter-day investigators like me probe his competence? I honestly do not know the answer and, because of that, refrain from judgement.

I have suggested before that Sharp was conflicted because of two rather different roles he saw himself fulfilling, that of scientist and that of popularizer. He uses the word 'scientific' regularly in his writings. Consider this optimistic statement from 1907:

> Subtleties of intonation can best be noted and studied on the phonograph. The attention of the collector is ordinarily occupied with other matters, many of which are at the moment of greater importance, and it is, therefore, very difficult to record with scientific accuracy delicate shades of pitch variation. Now, however, that English col-

---

44 We have evidence of this for three of the five recordings considered here, but, to my knowledge, we have no evidence of Sharp making a full transcription from a recording.

45 Percy Grainger, 'Collecting with the Phonograph', *Journal of the Folk-Song Society*, 3 (1908) pp. 147–242; Lucy Broadwood, *English Traditional Songs and Carols* (London: Boosey, 1908), pp. 113–15.

lectors are using the phonograph, material for the study of this particular branch of the subject is being rapidly accumulated.[46]

In the light of the richness of the Sharp collection as a whole, his contributions to the accumulation of material for such a projected study are meagre. Notwithstanding the ravages of time, five audio recordings from a collection of about five thousand pieces is scarcely even a pin-prick. It compares very unfavourably with what Grainger has left us. It seems that, in practice, the popularizer won out over the scientist, and the 'one verse with variations' method of pencil and paper collection suited the popularizer well. It was relatively quick, easy, author-itative, and largely unquestionable.

This point about the tension between popularizer and scientist is also relevant to the pitches at which Sharp notated tunes. Let us recapitulate: [47]

Song	Singer	Actual pitch on recording	Notated/published pitch	Notated/published version(s) higher/lower
'No John'	William Wooley	G (d to d¹)	G	Same
'All Among the New Mown Hay'	Alfred Edgell	E-flat (e-flat to e-flat¹)	D	Higher (one semitone)
'Lady Maisry'	Jack Barnard	C-sharp minor (g-sharp to a)	E minor; G minor	Higher (three semitones; six semitones)
'The Basket of Eggs'	Priscilla Cooper	G minor (f to a¹)	D minor	Higher (seven semitones)
'The American Stranger'	Priscilla Cooper	G minor (g to b-flat¹)	D minor	Higher (seven semitones)
'Hares on the Mountains'	Louie Hooper	B-flat (f to b-flat¹)	F	Higher (seven semitones)

Based on this limited evidence, a pattern emerges here. When committing tunes to paper, Sharp sometimes reported them at or about the pitch at which the singer sang them, but more usually he wrote them down or published them significantly higher—as Karpeles put it, 'in a key which lay conveniently within the staff'. This would have been quite acceptable if he had indicated the actual pitch at which the song was sung in the manuscript, but he did not.

46 Sharp, *English Folk-Song: Some Conclusions*, p. 72.
47 I am using Helmholtz pitch notation: middle c is notated as c1. 'Minor' here references the third note of the scale, not the actual mode or scale.

In *Some Conclusions*, Sharp makes the surprising generalization: 'Folk-singers like to sing in as high a pitch as possible, and they will often apologise for not being able, on account of age, to sing their songs high enough.'[48] The evidence of these recordings totally refutes this statement. Are the singers on the recordings an unrepresentative sample? I think not, for the sound they make is of a piece with other traditional singers of their day and since, who, though showing considerable individual differences, tend to sing in a chest voice quite close to the natural speaking voice.

Of the women singers, Priscilla Cooper never comes out of her chest voice in 'The Basket of Eggs', basing her songs around a tonic of G. In 'The American Stranger', she sings across her vocal break using her head voice for the upper notes above the top octave. Similarly, Louie Hooper in 'Hares on the Mountains' sings across her vocal break in B-flat, starting and finishing in her chest voice. Of the male singers, Wooley and Edgell are both forthright singers who perform in a full-voiced way within what we could describe as a tenor range, but never going above the notes of d or e-flat. Jack Barnard's performance is altogether more intimate, using the low and middle range of his voice in an urgent but almost conversational tone.

In truth, Sharp shows little demonstrable interest in the pitch at which the singers sang, but instead presented his songs at the sort of pitches that would be acceptable to the conventional notion of voice ranges prevalent in his day. In a cumulative way, he misrepresents how traditional songs were performed, and this can perhaps be seen as the popularizer winning out over the 'scientist'.

There has been some careless talk in recent years about either 'praise' or 'denigration' of Cecil Sharp. I wish to do neither. I wish to understand him and the value and limitations of his work. It might come as a surprise to some readers after the detailed criticisms above that I am an admirer of what Sharp achieved. He was an energetic man who found a purpose in life and pursued it with tremendous vigour. Our knowledge and understanding of traditional music and dance would be greatly impoverished had he not done his work. But whether you dislike the term or not, he was a 'mediator', and in the act of transmitting what he collected, he coloured, emphasized, ignored, and even distorted some aspects of the material. He worked within limitations, historical, technical, methodological, and ideological—we all do. Some of them were self-imposed, some were unconscious. It is in trying to understand those limitations that we gain the fullest appreciation of what he did and achieved.

48 Sharp, *English Folk-Song: Some Conclusions*, p. 108.

Modal Scales in English Folk Song:
An Analysis with Reference to the George Butterworth Collection

LEWIS JONES

This study summarizes the modal theories of Heinrich Glarean. It then takes a random 25 per cent sample of tunes collected by George Butterworth and categorizes them according to the modal scales identified by Glarean and others. Categorization is facilitated by music notation software that transposes the tunes and removes the sharps and flats from their key signatures. The findings show that, of the one hundred or so tunes in the sample, forty-four are Ionian (i.e. in the modern major scale), twenty-six are Dorian, nine are Mixolydian, and seven are Aeolian. The other tunes are hybrids. Two modulate between Aeolian and Dorian; and one, for a single note, between Dorian and Mixolydian. The most common hybrid group, however, consists of thirteen tunes that modulate between Ionian and Mixolydian.

The conclusions would seem to challenge the interpretations of Percy Grainger, since the majority of the tunes can be definitely and unequivocally allocated to a specific modal scale. However, with regard to phonograph transcriptions as opposed to direct notation on to paper, there is evidence to support Grainger's case. The study concludes with a brief consideration of whether modal theory, and analysis of the musical modes, is worthwhile today.

Heinrich Glarean and Modal Scales in Music

Heinrich Glarean (Henricus Glareanus) was born in 1488 and died in 1563. His most famous work, the *Dodecachordon*, was published in Basle, Switzerland, in 1547, and established him as a famous and influential musical theorist.[1] Since Glarean's full analysis of musical the-

---

1 The *Dodecachordon* and other works by Glarean are available from the International Music Score Library Project at <http://imslp.org/wiki/Category:Glareanus,_Henricus>.

ory is too long and complicated for present purposes it has been simplified and adapted here. For example, tunes are not classified as authentic or plagal, and gapped scales are ignored.

In an octave of music there are twelve notes, separated by semitones. These (marked off by commas) are:

> A, A-sharp (or B-flat), B, C, C-sharp (or D-flat), D, D-sharp (or E-flat), E, F, F-sharp (or G-flat), G, G-sharp (or A-flat).

Some avant-garde composers in the twentieth century, notably the Austro-American Arnold Schoenberg (1874–1951), developed a so-called chromatic scale that included all twelve of these notes. Most composers, however, employ scales of eight notes, although they may sometimes modulate to a different key without changing the key signature, or add accidental sharps, flats, and naturals to give a pleasing or interesting sound or dissonance. In classical music there are three main scales: the major, the melodic minor, and the harmonic minor. In English folk song the melodic and harmonic minors are not usually used.

The four musical scales most usually encountered in English folk song are as follows.

1. *Ionian*

This scale, which is identical to the major scale, was, according to Glarean, the one most frequently used by composers in his day. It is the scale most commonly used by classical composers and most often found in English folk song.

The notes of the Ionian scale are C, D, E, F, G, A, B, C'—and you can get it if you play upwards from C to C' on the white notes of a keyboard or, in tonic sol-fa, if you sing the familiar scale of 'do, ray me, fa, sol, la, ti, do'. Note the distribution of tones and semitones in this scale:

> C–(tone)–D–(tone)–E–(semitone)–F–(tone)–G–(tone)–A–(tone)–B–(semitone)–C'

2. *Dorian*

The notes of the Dorian scale are D, E, F, G, A, B, C, D'—and you can get it if you play upwards from D to D' on the white notes of a keyboard or, in tonic sol-fa, if you sing a scale of 'ray, me, fa, sol, la, ti, do, ray'. Note the distribution of tones and semitones in this scale:

> D–(tone)–E–(semitone)–F–(tone)–G–(tone)–A–(tone)–B–(semitone)–C–(tone)–D'

3. *Aeolian*

The Aeolian scale is similar to the modern minor scales in their melodic and harmonic forms, but without the accidentals that sharpen or flatten some of the notes of those scales. The notes of the Aeolian scale are A, B, C, D, E, F, G, A'—and you can get it if you play upwards from A to A' on the white notes of a keyboard, or, in tonic sol-fa, if you sing a scale of 'la, ti, do, ray, me, fa, sol, la'. Note the distribution of tones and semitones in this scale:

A–(tone)–B–(semitone)–C–(tone)–D–(tone)–E–(semitone)–F–(tone)–G–(tone)–A'

4. *Mixolydian*

The notes of the Mixolydian scale are G, A, B, C, D, E, F, G'—and you can get it if you play upwards from G to G' on the white notes of a keyboard or, in tonic sol-fa, if you sing a scale of 'sol, la, ti, do, ray, me, fa, sol'. Note the distribution of tones and semitones in this scale:

G–(tone)–A–(tone)–B–(semitone)–C–(tone)–D–(tone)–E–(semitone)–F–(tone)–G'

The Mixolydian modal scale differs in but one note from the Ionian: the seventh note of the scale is flattened to make the final interval of the scale a tone instead of a semitone, and the penultimate interval a semitone instead of a tone.

There are two other modal scales: *Phrygian*—if you play upwards from E to E' on the white notes of a keyboard or, in tonic sol-fa, if you sing a scale of 'me, fa, sol, la, ti, do, ray, me'; and *Lydian*—if you play upwards from F to F' on the white notes of a keyboard or, in tonic sol-fa, if you sing a scale of 'fa, sol, la, ti, do, ray, me, fa'. The Phrygian and the Lydian modal scales, however, are rarely encountered in English folk song.

It was Heinrich Glarean who gave to the six modal scales the names of Ionian, Dorian, Aeolian, Mixolydian, Phrygian, and Lydian. He believed that this was what they were called in the ancient world. He was quite wrong in this belief, but the nomenclature has been retained nonetheless.

Note that the modes are all about the distribution of the intervals between the notes of a scale, and whether these intervals are tones or semitones. The modes are not about pitch—that is determined by the key. For example, a tune in the key of F major has the same Ionian mode or scale as a tune in the key of C major, but the pitch of the notes is two and a half tones higher.

Modal Scales of Folk Song Melodies Collected by George Butterworth

My colleague Simon Furey and I have transcribed all of the tunes from the Butterworth collection and posted audio, PDF, MusicXML, and abc files of them on to Folkopedia.[2] Our main aim was to open up the collection to people with limited musical skills and/or who are uneasy about deciphering a raw notation. However, it was also possible to use the transcriptions as the basis for this short study.

Butterworth noted over four hundred tunes, mainly of songs but also of folk dances, many from the county of Sussex. The present research selected a random 25 per cent sample, a total of 103, of the transcriptions of these tunes. These are the archival reference numbers:

> GB/6a/6, GB/6a/13, GB/6a/18, GB/6a/28, GB/6a/32, GB/6a/36, GB/6a/42,
> GB/6a/51, GB/6a/56, GB/6a/60, GB/6a/64, GB/6a/74, GB/6a/79, GB/6a/86,
> GB/6a/90, GB/6a/95, GB/6a/99, GB/6a/104, GB/6a/108, GB/6a/112, GB/6a/116,
> GB/6a/120, GB/6a/130, GB/6a/134, GB/6a/138, GB/6a/145, GB/6a/149,
> GB/6a/156a, GB/6a/160, GB/6a/164, GB/6a/175, GB/6a/179, GB/6a/184,
> GB/6b/1, GB/6b/5, GB/6b/9, GB/6b/12, GB/6b/16, GB/6b/20, GB/6b/25,
> GB/6b/29, GB/7a/2, GB/7a/4A, GB/7a/6, GB/7a/10, GB/7a/14, GB/7a/18,
> GB/7a/22, GB/7a/26, GB/7a/30, GB/7a/33B, GB/7a/37, GB/7a/41, GB/7a/45,
> GB/7a/49, GB/7a/53, GB/7a/57, GB/7a/61, GB/7a/65, GB/7a/69, GB/7a/73,
> GB/7a/76A, GB/7b/2A, GB/7b/4, GB/7b/4D, GB/7b/5C, GB/7b/7, GB/7b/9A,
> GB/7b/11, GB/7b/13, GB/7b/16, GB/7b/19, GB/7b/21, GB/7b/23, GB/7b/26,
> GB/7b/30, GB/7c/2, GB/7c/5, GB/7c/7, GB/7c/9, GB/7c/10, GB/7c/11, GB/7c/14,
> GB/7c/17, GB/7c/20, GB/7c/23, GB/7c/27, GB/7c/31, GB/7c/35, GB/7d/4,
> GB/7d/8, GB/7d/12, GB/7d/16, GB/7d/20, GB/7d/24, GB/7d/31b, GB/7d/37,
> GB/7d/41, GB/7e/4, GB/7e/8, GB/7e/12, GB/7e/16, GB/7e/21.

Music notation software was used to transpose these tunes and remove the sharps and flats from the key signatures. Pure modal melodies were thus rendered into the keys of C Ionian (C major), D Dorian, A Aeolian, and G Mixolydian. (There were no Phrygian melodies and GB/7b/3A, the single Lydian melody, was not included in the random sample.) If, after the transpositions, there were tunes with notes the pitch of which had been altered by accidental sharps or flats, this would indicate that the tune was not a pure modal melody but, in most cases, a hybrid form. The melodies were then categorized as follows.

---

2   To access the transcriptions go to <http://folkopedia.efdss.org/Take_6_Transcription_Programme> and follow the links.

Pure modal

Ionian (44 tunes)

GB/6a/13, GB/6a/32, GB/6a/51, GB/6a/56, GB/6a/60, GB/6a/99, GB/6a/108, GB/6a/116, GB/6a/120, GB/6a/130, GB/6a/134, GB/6a/138, GB/6a/149, GB/6a/160, GB/6a/164, GB/6a/175, GB/6b/12, GB/6b/20, GB/6b/25, GB/6b/29, GB/7a/2, GB/7a/6, GB/7a/10, GB/7a/37, GB/7a/41, GB/7a/65, GB/7a/69, GB/7a/76A, GB/7b/2A, GB/7b/11, GB/7b/21, GB/7c/5, GB/7c/7, GB/7c/9, GB/7c/14, GB/7c/17, GB/7c/20, GB/7c/23, GB/7c/35, GB/7d/12, GB/7d/16, GB/7d/20, GB/7e/4, GB/7e/21.

Dorian (26 tunes)

GB/6a/28, GB/6a/74, GB/6a/79, GB/6a/90, GB/6a/104, GB/6a/145, GB/6b/5, GB/6b/9, GB/7a/45, GB/7a/49, GB/7a/61, GB/7a/73, GB/7b/4D, GB/7b/5C, GB/7b/7, GB/7b/13, GB/7b/16, GB/7b/19, GB/7b/23, GB/7c/2, GB/7c/10, GB/7c/27, GB/7d/31b, GB/7d/37, GB/7e/8, GB/7e/16.

Mixolydian (9 tunes)

GB/6a/179, GB/6b/1, GB/7a/14, GB/7a/22, GB/7a/30, GB/7a/57, GB/7b/9A, GB/7d/41, GB/7e/12.

Aeolian (7 tunes)

GB/6a/6, GB/6a/42, GB/6b/16, GB/7a/18, GB/7a/33B, GB/7a/53, GB/7b/26.

Hybrids

Ionian with Mixolydian influence (10 tunes)

GB/6a/86, GB/6a/95, GB/6a/112, GB/6a/156a, GB/6a/184, GB/7b/4, GB/7c/11, GB/7d/4, GB/7d/8, GB/7d/24.

Mixolydian with Ionian influence (3 tunes)

GB/6a/64, GB/7b/30, GB/7c/31.

Aeolian with Dorian influence (2 tunes)

GB/6a/18, GB/7a/26.

Dorian with Mixolydian influence (for a single note) (1 tune)

GB/7a/4A.

Total: 102 tunes (one melody, a pure Dorian mode replicate that is identical in GB/6a/36 and GB/6b/5, was only counted once.)

The large number of hybrids (thirteen out of the sixteen) that modulate between Ionian and Mixolydian is explicable by the similarity of those two scales—they are identical except for one note (the seventh) of each scale.

Percy Grainger and the Modes

In 1908 Percy Grainger wrote in the *Journal of the Folk-Song Society*:

> My conception of folk-scales, after a study of them in the phonograph, may be summed up as follows: that the singers from whom I recorded do not seem to me to have sung in three different and distinct modes (Mixolydian, Dorian, Aeolean), but to have rendered their modal songs in *one single loosely-knit modal folk-song scale*, embracing within itself the combined Mixolydian, Dorian and Aeolean characteristics.[3]

Following this there came a reply: 'The Editing Committee [...] wish to point out that the general experience of collectors goes to show that English singers most rarely alter their mode in singing the same song.'[4] On both sides the debate was courteous and respectful, with Grainger adding that his suggestion was 'put forward in all tentativeness' and the *JFSS* editors praising his 'most careful observations'. But the question is: who was correct?

A possible answer to that question lies within the Butterworth collection. A clear majority of the tunes, as the preceding analysis indicates, can be unequivocally allocated to a specific mode. It would seem, therefore, that on that basis Grainger's editors were right and he was wrong. But before hasty conclusions are drawn, the case of 'The New Garden Fields' (GB/7b/13) should be considered. Figure 1 shows the first verse of the melody, fitted to the appropriate words, as transcribed by Simon Furey and myself. This was the tune as it was taken down by Butterworth, on the spur of the moment, directly on to paper, as it was sung to him in April 1910 in Norfolk by Mr Locke. Clearly Butterworth did not have much time to cogitate on the exact interval between every note. He reached approximate conclusions, but he did the best he could in the circumstances, and the tune, as noted in this initial take, is pure Dorian.

However, Butterworth later had Mr Locke sing the song again, and he made a phonograph recording of it. Then, in October 1910, he enlisted the help of Ralph Vaughan Williams to transcribe this phonograph recording into musical notation. Figure 2 shows the result as transcribed by Simon Furey and myself. In this second notation, the clear, simple Dorian melody of the first version is lost. Two of the most eminent musicians and composers of their

---

3   Percy Grainger, 'Collecting with the Phonograph', *Journal of the Folk Song Society*, 3 (1908), 147–242 (p. 158).
4   Grainger, 'Collecting with the Phonograph', p. 159.

day collaborated to produce an accurate version and they tried to catch every nuance and variation in rhythm and the exact interval between each note. The result is that the purity of the Dorian mode has been sullied by the presence of accidental sharps, there are a number of melodic variations, and the transcribers could not reach any definite conclusion as to the exact intervals between some of the notes. Indeed, what they transcribed from the phonograph recording could arguably be described as a melody in the '*one single loosely-knit modal folk-song scale*' described by Grainger.[5] It is also possible that the uncertainties and ambiguities that Butterworth and Vaughan Williams attempted to reconcile and unravel were exacerbated by the quality available from the phonograph. In the opinion of the *JFSS* editors, 'whether it [the phonograph] is sufficiently perfect as yet to be preferred as a substitute for the human ear is still a disputable point'.[6]

The conclusion, therefore, is that Grainger was correct with regard to transcriptions from phonograph recordings, but his editors were correct with regard to songs transcribed directly into musical notation. The vast bulk of what has come down to us from the early collectors was noted directly on to paper from the source singer. Grainger's analyses are largely inapplicable to these notations, but may well have a value in the analysis of sound recordings, many of which were made after the First World War. A more detailed musical analysis may be possible when the Carpenter collection is at last made readily available to the world.

*

Modal theory, as it has come down to us from Glaraen, is sound and still valid — but does it matter? In some cases, perhaps it does not. Those who listen to folk songs may consider Dorian, Mixolydian, and Aeolian melodies old-fashioned, unfamiliar, and unappetizing, and modal theory uninteresting and baffling. But for singers and performers the case is arguably different. Broadwood, Sharp, and other great collectors made frequent references to the modes, and they were extensively identified and flagged up in the early volumes of the *Journal of the Folk-Song Society*. Today, in contrast, they generate little serious or extended attention, and when they are mentioned at all they are often dismissed — sometimes by leading practitioners — as tiresome, irrelevant, and unimportant. Perhaps a greater awareness of the modes would open the way to a better understanding of the nature of English folk melody.

For those who transcribe archival folk song manuscripts the modes cannot be ignored. With abc notation there is a key field (K:) that must be filled in, and if conversion software is

---

5   Grainger, 'Collecting with the Phonograph', p. 158.
6   Grainger, 'Collecting with the Phonograph', p. 159.

used to create abc code from MusicXML files, the conversion emerges in the Ionian or major key for the respective number of sharps or flats in the key signature. Thus a tune that is clearly D Dorian, with no sharps or flats in the key signature and no accidentals, and that ends unequivocally on D as the key note, would be converted into C major or Ionian. This makes no difference to the melody, but it is theoretically wrong it is thus necessary to edit and correct the key field as appropriate.

The modes are distinctive and they set English traditional music apart from popular song and from the compositions of singer-songwriters as well as so-called folk hymns and mass settings. They modes have a role to play in helping to explain and illustrate what folk song is and what it is not.

GB/7b/13 New Garden Fields Version 1 of 2

Text: Bodleian Broadside Collection (online)   Singer: Mr. Locke (c. 70), Rollesby, Norfolk, IV. 10.
04600 Harding B 11(3678)

GB/7b/13 New Garden Fields Version 2 of 2

The same (i.e. New Garden Fields Version 1 of 2), from phonograph record (x. 10)

R. V(aughan) W(illiams) & G.S.K.B(utterworth)

Sabine's Tunes — *summary*

PAUL WILSON

We looked briefly at the context and background of Sabine Baring-Gould's collecting and reminded ourselves that—unlike some significant contemporaries such as Cecil Sharp, Lucy Broadwood, *et al.*—he was largely self-taught as a musician, We noted how he involved others in attempting to achieve really accurate transcriptions of the tunes, notably H. Fleetwood Sheppard and Frederick W. Bussell. We were looking at tunes specifically and not texts—there has been much more written about Baring-Gould's editing of texts than of tunes and this talk aimed to redress the balance a little. We re-stated that Baring-Gould wanted to collect the songs of the peasantry and to bring the old English modes back into popularity and we know he was highly selective as to which tunes he collected.

Summary and Method

To decide how reliable a record the notations of the tunes provide, we borrowed a method used by other commentators on textual matters and compared the notation given for a dozen variants he collected for one song—'The Trees They Do Grow High'. We chose this song because it exists in all levels of transcription

- Rough Copy notebooks
- Personal Copy notebooks
- Working notebooks—different versions
- Fair Copy notebooks—different versions
- *Songs of the West*—first and subsequent editions, including the 1905 edition under Cecil Sharp's musical editorship.

Although the smudges on the Rough Copy notebook, and the absence of any bar lines and the accompaniments provided in the published versions, gave cause for discussion in their respective ways, we found that the tune shape remained very consistent throughout all these levels. We displayed on screen examples of the original manuscripts for delegates to view and also played these examples 'live' to indicate how the tunes would strike the ear, and to include fully in the discussion delegates who did not read music.

We briefly focused on the mode Baring-Gould assigned to one of the variants and showed how the same set of notes could equally legitimately be given two modal names, depending on which method was used to establish the mode—either that used by Western classical musicians of taking the final note as the 'key' note or tonal centre, or a method similar to Alan Lomax's 'weighting' of the tones in the melody to find the tonal centre. We illustrated this by playing the same tune against two different notes representing the different tonal centres.

We found that Baring-Gould had revisited, or arranged for his collaborators to revisit, singers and noted the same tune on different occasions, in order to collect any variations in the shape of the melody or ornaments. In contrast to some other collectors' methodology of 'bare boning' a melody and omitting the ornamentation, this was to be welcomed.

We briefly looked at variants from around the country and found that the tune for this song appears in a striking number of modal colours—Ionian, Hypodorian, Mixolydian, Dorian, Aeolian, and, if you accept Baring-Gould's own theorizing, Phrygian. In addition to James Parsons, whose versions provided the backbone for the talk, we looked at transcriptions collected from

> Mary Langworthy—collected by Bertha Bidder
> Roger Hannaford—collected by H. Fleetwood Sheppard
> Matthew Baker—collected by F. W. Bussell
> Henry Stansbridge, Lyndhurst, Hampshire—collected by George Gardner
> Mr Whitehead—collected by Anne Gilchrist
> Mrs Russell, Upwey, Dorset—collected by H. E. D. Hammond.

Conclusion

While we openly question some of the more fanciful commentary Baring-Gould indulged in around the origins of melodies and his assigning of modal names to tunes, we must thank him for

- his collaboration—involving others where he felt his own musical skills were lacking
- his transparency—leaving us a record of what tunes he was going out to collect
- his honesty—in trying to notate the tunes as accurately as possible
- his breadth and flexibility—showing a capacity for learning and for revising his opinions
- his persistence—in collecting the same tune several times from the same singer and noting more than one stanza from several singers.

We conclude that, compared to his altering of texts (often for good and openly stated reasons of popularizing the songs), his editing of tunes was more transparent and less pronounced. This, coupled with the fact that he was specifically on the lookout for old and modal melodies, gives this beautiful collection of tunes an unrivalled place in the canon of English folk song.

Sources and References

S. Baring Gould and H. Fleetwood Sheppard, *A Garland Of Country Song: English Folk Songs with their Traditional Melodies* (London: Methuen, 1895).

S. Baring Gould and H. Fleetwood Sheppard, *Songs & Ballads of the West* (London: Methuen, [1889–91]).

S. Baring Gould and H. Fleetwood Sheppard, *Songs & Ballads of the West* (London: Methuen, [1891–95]).

S. Baring-Gould, H. Fleetwood Sheppard, and F. W. Bussell, *Songs of the West*, music ed. Cecil J. Sharp (London: Methuen, 1905).

Devon Tradition, online resource created by Wren Music, 2010

Malcolm Douglas, introductory to Classic English Folk Songs, ed. R. Vaughan Williams and A. L. Lloyd (London: EFDSS, in association with South Riding Folk Network, 2003).

E. David Gregory, *The Late Victorian Folk Song Revival: The Persistence of English Melody, 1878–1903* (Lanham, MD: Scarecrow Press, 2010).

IV. Revivals

IV. Revivals

In Defence of Revivals:
Tradition and Community in a Contemporary English Folk Club

FAY HIELD

Contemporary English folk clubs are broadly viewed as part of a revival movement—a revival movement in decline. Built on socialist ideologies that rejected mainstream music industries in favour of grass-roots music making, and fuelled by the collections of rural song made around the beginning of the twentieth century, this particular performance environment spread widely during the 1960s. The folk club model is found in all corners of England, and surrounding countries, with events sharing similar organizational structures, performance ideals, and social mores. Activity peaked in the 1970s and 1980s, and has since been steadily reducing in scale and impact. In order for this tradition of folk singing to regain some of its past exuberance, as is widely called for by those still practising it, new audiences must be sought. This is problematic, as newcomers cannot simply be plunged into existing practices, and more gradual means of integration into established mores must be developed.

As a performer and club organizer I am often called a revivalist. Perhaps I am a product of the revival movement, but the 1980s folk club scene is my tradition. The revival movement has developed its own identity through shared behaviours and ideological connections, and a tradition has emerged. The matter has come full circle, however, and, somewhat ironically, there is a need for a revival—a restoration to use—of the revival tradition itself. Royal Traditions was developed as a conscious act to address the problems highlighted in previous studies and in my own research into the English folk singing scene, an experiment to develop new ways of working with the aim of helping people make new connections in order to strengthen the community at the heart of the study. In the process, it has shed new light on the role of revival within tradition. This paper explores the tensions of the terminology and its empirical application. I begin by describing the methods adopted for the study, followed by an examination of the wider literature on traditions and revivals. I then present a more detailed explanation of the English folk scene at large, before focusing on the Royal Traditions club in particular and outlining the conscious changes we have made in order to revive behaviours, and their impacts. I conclude with a view of tradition and revival as interrelated and dynamic, as a necessary intervention for the continuation and development of musical community over time.

I have drawn on the results of three periods of data collection utilizing diverse methods. Firstly, my doctoral ethnographic fieldwork (2005–10) encompassed participant observation at ten events in Sheffield; the maintenance of participant diaries by twenty-seven singers throughout October and November 2006, inclusive; a focus group with sixteen participants; and interviews with seven professional folk singers. This generated data concerning behavioural patterns and personal identification with folk repertoires and a local folk singing scene.[1] The second period involved a survey generating network data on the activities of participants in the Sheffield folk scene. Alongside basic demographic information, participants were asked about their attendance at seventy-seven folk-related events in the Sheffield area between April and June 2012, inclusive, and they were invited to add further local events attended during the specified period. From this, 188 usable responses were generated, and 101 events with at least one attendee each were identified. These events were categorized by type and compared with the demographic data, illuminating differences in participation patterns.[2]

Building on the findings of the two earlier projects, the third element employs action research methods. This involves a cycle of activity commencing with the development of new models of practice, implementation, and reflection. These findings in turn contribute to the development of new models and the process begins again. Widely utilized in the fields of education and business studies, the method has been little explored in the arts. To model my enquiry, I lean heavily on David Coghlan and Teresa Brannick's guide to action research.[3] They propose two distinct outcomes as desirable: a change in practice within the field; and the advancement of knowledge about the process.

1 Fay Hield, 'English Folk Singing and the Construction of Community' (unpublished PhD thesis, University of Sheffield, 2010).
2 Fay Hield and Nick Crossley, 'Tastes, Ties and Social Space: Exploring Sheffield's Folk Singing World', in *Social Networks and Music Worlds*, ed. Nick Crossley, Siobhan McAndrew, and Paul Widdop (London: Routledge, 2014).
3 David Coghlan and Teresa Brannick, *Doing Action Research in Your Own Organisation*, 3rd edn (London: SAGE Publications, 2010).

Thus Royal Traditions, an environment designed to explore new ways to facilitate folk singing, was established and observed. This research has no clear start date, as the interventions were developed through the earlier periods and advanced over the five years since 2009 when the organization was established. Throughout this period I have maintained a journal reflecting on the process and documenting adaptations within the endeavour. The data collection and analysis methods are roughly integrated, and include personal reflection on my activities, evaluative discussions with key members of the organization, and reflective discussions with artists and other participants, alongside analysis of materials generated through the practice, including social media sites and email correspondence. These various data sets are drawn together here to illuminate current activity occurring within the contemporary folk club scene.

Developing the Discourse on Tradition and Revival

There is a small but useful literature on the English folk revival. Most significantly, Niall MacKinnon quantifies the scene of the 1990s and provides ethnographic observation on the unspoken governance guiding performance rituals, clarifying some of the economic, social, and musical structures supporting this musical scene.[4] Though researched in the 1990s, his findings remain surprisingly current. The participant demographic has shifted in line with the attending population. Constancy in personnel has maintained relatively stable structures for many folk clubs, though some areas have altered due to the twenty-somethings of the 1970s now being sixty to seventy years old. A second study, by John Smith, describes a live music club in the North East of England through an ethogenic analysis.[5] This work maps the proceedings as a script, providing a helpfully transparent transcription of an event's structures and practices. Though a development from the traditional folk clubs described by MacKinnon, Smith finds similar issues facing his organizers. These include the problems of cliques and social exclusion, and concern over the ageing demographic and lack of new recruitment.

The latter has led to mixed predictions for the future of folk clubs. Some academics portray the folk club scene as defunct, giving way to new environments (festivals or gigs).[6] How-

---

4   Niall MacKinnon, *The British Folk Scene: Musical Performance and Social Identity* (Buckingham: Open University Press, 1993).

5   John Smith, 'The Ethogenics of Music Performance: A Case Study of the Glebe Live Music Club', in *Everyday Culture: Popular Song and the Vernacular Milleu*, ed. Michael Pickering and Tony Green (Milton Keynes: Open University Press, 1987) pp. 150–72.

6   Simon Keegan Phipps and Trish Winter, 'Contemporary English Folk Music and "the Folk Industry', in *The Oxford Handbook of Music Revival*, ed. Caroline Bithell and Juniper Hill (Oxford: Oxford University Press, 2014); Michael Brocken, *The British Folk Revival 1944–2002* (Aldershot: Ashgate, 2003), pp125.

ever, there remains an impressive quantity of activity in this area, with many major towns and cities maintaining at least one folk club. *English Dance & Song* magazine has devoted a series of articles to examining folk clubs, especially the newly founded events springing up around England over the past few years.[7] It transpires that many existing and new organizers feel these revival events are worthy of reviving.

This leads us on to the debate concerning revivals and the maintenance of tradition. A body of literature developed in the 1980s presenting constructionist notions of revived traditions. Eric Hobsbawm and Terence Ranger's seminal *Invented Traditions*, Benedict Anderson's *Imagined Communities*, Richard Dorson's *Fake Lore* and Dave Harker's *Fakesong*, and Carole Pegg's notion of 'neotraditionalists' influenced three decades of research into traditions in contemporary society.[8] Through these frames, revived practices were put under the microscope and found somehow wanting.

The notion of distinct 'natural' and 'unnatural' traditions needs to be questioned, however. The main basis for differentiating between 'authentic' and 'non-authentic' traditions seems to be situated in the participants' level of consciousness about the aspects of tradition with which they are involved. Burt Feintuch, in a study of a Northumbrian piping tradition in the late 1990s, challenges this approach, stating that to label the field 'an invented tradition [. . .] always left me uneasy. It seemed arrogant. It felt as if a body of theory trivialized its subject.'[9] His unease is shared by Henry Glassie, who challenges even more strongly the notion of difference between natural and invented traditions: 'The fact that cultures and traditions are created, invented—wilfully compiled by knowledgeable individuals—seems a surprise to scholars who cling to superorganic concepts and who invent, in order to sharpen spurious contrasts, uninvented, natural traditions.'[10]

Alternative understandings of tradition can now be considered. Tradition has been widely associated with stability, a process of preserving historical practices. This association with the past has been challenged with Richard Handler and Jocelyn Linnekin, who assert that

7   'Derek Schofield, 'Folk Clubs in the 21st Century', *English Dance & Song*, 76.1 (2014), 13–15.

8   Eric Hobsbawm and Terrance Ranger, eds, *The Invention of Tradition* (Cambridge: Cambridge University Press, 1983); Benedict Anderson, *Imagined Communities: Reflections on the Origins and Spread of Nationalism* (London, Verso, 1983); Richard M. Dorson, *Folklore and Fakelore: Essays towards a Discipline of Folklore Studies* (Cambridge, MA: Harvard University Press, 1976); Dave Harker *Fakesong: The Manufacture of British 'Folksong', 1700 to the Present Day* (Milton Keynes: Open University Press, 1985); Carole Pegg, 'Factors Affecting Music Choices of Audiences in East Suffolk, England', *Popular Music*, 4 (1984), 346–50.

9   Burt Feintuch, 'Longing For Community', *Western Folklore*, 60 (2001), 149–61 (p. 152).

10 Henry Glassie, 'Tradition', *Journal of American Folklore*, 108 (1995), 395–412 (p. 398).

tradition is more concerned with activities in the present.[11] This is taken one step further by Barry McDonald's assertion that, rather than being of the past, or even the present, tradition is directed towards the future.[12] Activities of the past are performed in the present, with the goal of preserving both performance context and material for future generations.

Breaking down the boundaries of what constitutes a tradition, however, leaves the term at risk of redundancy. Simon Bronner poses the question: 'If tradition [. . .] is indeed both invented and inherited, individual and social, stable and changing, oral and written, of past and present, of time and space, about authority and freedom, then what does it exclude?'[13] He continues with a proposal that considerably shifts the perspective on tradition: 'Is it shorthand for a feeling of connection rather than a process of transmission?' My research suggests that it is, and that, viewed in this light, tradition sheds light on the links between community and practice. All human activity could be viewed as traditional, but it is the viewing lens that is of central importance. Activity must be perceived to belong to a practice or to a group of people for it to qualify as traditional. Where a group of people, a body of material, or a mode of behaving, or an ideological link between these things, becomes weakened, a tradition comes under threat. In such cases, new connections need to be developed in order to restore the health of the ideological community and to ensure the survival of its practices. We have come full circle to revival again, but are now viewing revival as a part of a community's tradition.

There have been calls to abandon the term 'revival' on account of its historical associations, but I am reluctant to abandon the idea it suggests. Perhaps our saviour will come in the form of the *Oxford Handbook of Music Revival*.[14] Caroline Bithell's approach chimes with those presented here, and she claims that the book 'presents new theoretical perspectives on processes of revival' and that the chapters 'reveal the potency of acts of revival, resurgence, restoration and renewal in shaping musical landscapes and transforming social experience'.[15]

Here, I favour 'revival', because 'resurgence', favoured by some, suggests a re-emergence in the same form after a period of absence. I find, conversely, that significant interventions are called for in order to increase the amount of activity on the part of those unaccustomed to the

---

11 Richard Handler and Jocelyn Linnekin, 'Tradition: Genuine or Spurious?', *Journal of American Folklore*, 97 (1984), 273–90.

12 Barry McDonald, 'The Idea of Tradition Examined in Light of Two Australian Music Studies', *Yearbook for Traditional Music*, 28 (1996), 106–30.

13 Simon Bronner, 'The Meanings of Tradition: An Introduction', *Western Folklore*, 59 (2000), 87–104 (p. 96).

14 Caroline Bithell and Juniper Hill, eds, *The Oxford Handbook of Music Revival* (Oxford: Oxford University Press, 2014), forthcoming.

15 Caroline Bithell <http://www.manchester.ac.uk/research/caroline.bithell/research> [accessed 26 May 2014].

practice. There is a need for a renaissance of accessible modes of interaction, rather than of musical repertoires themselves — though often tacitly segregated from wider popular culture, the practice of folk singing continues to flourish in many environments.

The English Folk Scene

While 'traditional' or 'folk' repertoires may be performed in many contexts, including classical recitations, community choirs, and rugby matches, a discreet set of participants identify with what they commonly call the 'folk scene'. These people form a network, both directly through mutual acquaintance, and indirectly through mutual participation in various events that are themselves important elements of this musical world.[16] Defined thus, the folk scene can be identified and analysed at local, national, and international levels. Furthermore, it can be differentiated according to styles and according to the emphasis placed upon, for example, singing, dancing, and instrumentation. My focus here is upon folk singing in Sheffield. This regional scene is in rude health, with high levels of participation, attracting claims in the national specialist press that 'Sheffield has become the new centre of English folk music.'[17]

The events that contribute to this network are disparate. Predominantly voluntarily run, there is no overarching organizational structure, and individual event organizers operate independently in their preferred areas. A wide variety of tastes is catered for, ranging from participatory to performance activities and displaying a range of musical repertoires.

At the grass-roots level are singing sessions. The Sheffield Ballads Club meets monthly in a private room of a public house and members take it in turns to sing around the room. The artistic motivation for this group is to promote the art of storytelling through song. There is no expense incurred in its organization, and consequently no entry charge is made. Raise the Roof similarly meets monthly in an ancillary room of a pub, though a low fee is charged to cover room hire and to contribute towards biannual guest bookings. The focus here is on group singing and choruses are strongly encouraged. At Rivelin Folk Club the material leans towards singer-songwriter, and features both original compositions and 1960–70s American pop covers. The club also meets in a public bar and there is no entry charge. While these events present different repertoires and musical styles, they all provide amateur performance opportunities and promote participation over consumption.

16 For more on 'art worlds', see Howard Becker, *Art Worlds* (Berkley: University of California, 1984). For the remainder of this chapter I substitute the term 'scene' for 'world', as that is how many of the participants themselves refer to it.

17 Chris Nickson, 'Folk Industry', *fRoots*, 276 (2006), 39–41.

Complementing these participatory events are concerts. These typically operate in 100-plus capacity venues and tickets are sold in advance to cover the costs of performers, PA equipment and engineers, and marketing. At Bright Phoebus, for example, audiences contribute to choruses and can be made to feel involved through attempts at de-staging on the part of performers.[18] However, the main musical activity is provided by professional musicians and the social mores of folk concert audiences are similar to those of attendees at concerts in a wide variety of musical genres.

Occupying a halfway house between these structures is the folk club. A professional, semi-professional, or amateur guest performer, performs as the main act in two performance blocks, or 'sets', during the evening. These sets are preceded by 'floor singers', members of the club who provide one or two songs each in two or three slots before the main act. Folk clubs meet regularly, typically weekly or monthly, and have, in some cases, been running for over thirty years. Their longevity, regularity of attendance, and interactive engagement in musical practice facilitate the development of strong social bonds and feelings of community.

The folk scene consists of a variety of events following versions of the formats described above, as well as others, such as festivals, a burgeoning recording industry, and media channels including TV, radio, and a variety of specialist paper and web-based publications. Within this mass of opportunity, people choose a pathway and those of similar tastes attend similar events. Over a period of time, taste cultures, or social cliques, can develop. This is explored in more detail elsewhere.[19] Suffice it to say here that, while the folk scene contains a great deal of variety, and sub-groups can be readily identified by those who participate in it, in terms of social network analysis the relationships between events and participants in this socio-musical context are exceptionally dense.

That density promotes a strong sense of community for those within the environment, but it also generates barriers to participation for those outside. Despite its portrayal as an 'anything goes' environment, over time performance expertise (both musical and social) has developed and behavioural traits have become unspoken rules of governance. Identified as 'structured informality' by MacKinnon,[20] and branded as a more sinister 'hidden authority' by Brocken,[21] it is hard to ignore the paradox that environments designed to be accessible in actuality cause alienation and exclusion. Newcomers can feel out of place, not possessing the skills to partic-

18 MacKinnon, *British Folk Scene*, p. 93-4.
19 Hield and Nick Crossley, 'Tastes, Ties and Social Space'.
20 MacKinnon, *British Folk Scene*, p.79.
21 Brocken, *British Folk Revival*, p 118.

ipate, or even necessarily to understand what is happening around them.[22] In order to break the downward spiral of decreasing participant numbers, new people need to be educated in the mores of performance, a process that needs active intervention if it is to occur before they are discouraged from continuing attendance — a challenge that has been accepted in our case study, Royal Traditions.

Revitalizing the Folk Club Format

After settling in Sheffield in 2009, my partner, Jon Boden, and I established a new event at the Royal Hotel, Dungworth, on the outskirts of the city. Our motivations were various. Supporting the local rural public house was high on the agenda, and keeping an element of the established group singing that takes place in this pub around Christmas going throughout the year was a further consideration.[23] We also wanted to bring 'revival' folk singers to the area, as folk clubs and concerts were a format less widely adopted in Sheffield than the predominantly locals-led singing sessions.

We were, however, loath to adopt the established folk club format. Having both toured on the national folk club circuit as performers over the previous five years, we were well acquainted with the prevalent organizational systems, audience demographics, and social behaviours associated with established folk clubs. While we celebrate and hold many of the attributes of folk clubs in high regard, there were elements that we felt acted as barriers to success on various levels. We were keen to experiment with new ways to maximize the positive aspects of folk clubs and to reduce the elements that might exclude younger singers or newcomers to the scene. Royal Traditions was established in order to address some of the barriers to participation identified through my research, and to provide a way for newcomers to access the benefits of participation in folk singing.[24]

Meeting on occasional Saturday nights, roughly monthly, with breaks over the summer, we typically hold between eight and ten events per year. Guests are advertised in advance and tickets sold through a web ticketing agency <www.wegottickets.com>. Guests are paid a low guarantee against the door and 'hat' takings, and a raffle is held the proceeds of which cover

22 Fay Hield, 'Negotiating Participation at an English Folk Singing Session', in *Taking Part in Music: Case Studies in Ethnomusicology*, ed. Ian Russell and Catherine Ingram (Aberdeen: Elphinstone Institute, University of Aberdeen, 2013) pp 99-120.

23 For more on the Sheffield carols, see Ian Russell, 'Sacred and Secular: Identity, Style and Performance in Two Singing Traditions from the Pennines', *The World of Music*, 46.1 (2004) 11–40.

24 For more, see Stephanie Pitts, *Valuing Musical Participation* (Aldershot: Ashgate, 2005).

the minimal overheads of advertising in the local press and maintaining a website <www.soundpost.org.uk/royal-traditions> (Figure 1).

Ticket holders are entitled to sit directly in front of the performance area, where we can comfortably accommodate between thirty-five and forty people, depending on the space requirements of the guest, and tickets usually sell out in advance. The performance occurs in the main bar of the pub, which remains open to public entry. Therefore, while the privileged seats are sold for a fixed price, other supporters are welcome to attend and stand in two areas with good sight and sound lines to the performance. For this audience we pass the 'hat' around. Others also attend the pub, paying little or no attention to the music, and usually sit or stand around the back corner of the bar or in the side room.

Figure 1. *Advertisement for Royal Traditions in* Stirrings *magazine (2014)*

The evening begins around 7.30 p.m. with tunes played by Jon and anyone else who has brought an instrument and is inclined to play. Those who have reserved seats settle into place and others gather round the bar. At 8.00 p.m., the first 'house song' is sung. The 'house songs' are preselected and provided on printed sheets distributed around the room. They are begun by whoever is taking charge of the evening (usually Jon or myself, occasionally others in our absence), but the whole song is sung as a group by the majority of those present. The guest(s) are then welcomed and they perform their first set, lasting between thirty-five and forty-five minutes. The set is closed with another 'house song' and there follows an interval for conversation, buying drinks, and selling CDs and raffle tickets. Around 20 minutes later, another 'house song' signals the start of the second half, and the raffle is drawn. A fourth 'house song' heralds the guests' second set, which again lasts between thirty-five and forty-five minutes. The final 'house song' is sung to close the guest performance, and there follows a brief break during which the pub provides free sandwiches. The time is now around 10.00 p.m., and the singing session commences. Three or four songs are led by regular singers at the club, and the guest(s) are invited back to deliver their 'encore' of two more songs. This is usually less formal than their set, and often performed from another space other than the designated 'stage' area in front of the fire. After this, anyone may contribute a song and the singing session lasts as long as there is still enthusiasm for it. The club often runs until past midnight, though on quiet nights singing can cease around 11.30 p.m.

While there are elements in common with the established folk club model, there are also intentional differences. Similarities include an appreciation for traditional unaccompanied chorus singing, the presence of guests to perform two sets, a mixture of performance by guests and regular singers, advertising in the specialist folk press or privately held mailing lists, and the ever-lovable raffle. Table 1 provides a comparison of the prevailing folk club model and Royal Traditions.

Established folk club model	Royal Traditions
Floor singers perform before the guests	Floor singers perform after the guests
Little whole group singing beyond choruses	'House songs' frequently performed
Held in private rooms within public houses	Held in the main room of the bar
Fixed price entry	Graduated ticketing

Table 1. *Salient differences between the established folk club model and Royal Traditions*

The impacts of these changes have been monitored over the five years the club has been in existence, with some of our initial aims being met and others proving elusive. Several positive effects can be noted. Reversing the floor singer and guests' time slots reverses their roles. In our case, the professional guests warm up the audience, who are notably eager to contribute to the singing session by 10.00 p.m. Potential insecurities are loosened later in the evening by the effects of alcohol. This exuberance is not reserved for the closing section of the evening, however, and throughout the night energetic singing occurs at numerous points, as Arthur Knevett, a guest performer, notes: 'I particularly like the novel way you get everyone involved with the "house songs".'[25] By providing the words the expectation is created that everyone will

25 Email communication, October 2013.

join in, and many people who do not normally lead songs, or readily sing choruses, feel able to contribute. This is especially notable among groups of younger people, who are enthusiastic to participate but do not necessarily possess the skills to assimilate quickly into choruses.[26] Along with other enthusiastic newcomers to communal singing, they appreciate the support and explicit invitation to join in.

The atmosphere is affected by the general noise levels of the pub. Background noise is created by audience members and other pub users going to the bar, by the organizers', landlord's, or audience members' children playing in the back room, and by conversation among those in the standing areas of the pub, who dip in and out of listening to the music, and more constant conversations among other pub users paying no attention to the music. Occasionally a TV in the back room can be heard drifting through. By situating the singing within a mixed culture, some of the ideals associated with folk singing are rehabilitated. Mixing audience types has the effect of blending music with the everyday sounds of speech, laughter, and a generally sociable soundscape. This is in direct contrast to the quiet environment promoted in many folk clubs in order to prioritize the music. While we greatly respect the music and the art of singing, at Royal Traditions we also regard the social environment as central to our enjoyment of the music. It has been remarked by older guests that this atmosphere is reminiscent of the folk clubs of the 1960s, when audiences were younger and more jovial.

The wide entry policy affects the atmosphere, but it is also pertinent to address the ways it affects the people involved. Committed, experienced folk enthusiasts from around the city of Sheffield and beyond are able to buy tickets and to behave in relatively conventional folk club ways. Dungworth locals who know it as 'folk night' at the pub, and groups of young people from the city who have been encouraged to come along, also attend. These people stand on the fringes of involvement, with less financial and participatory commitment. Others who are not aware there is a planned event at the pub participate to a greater or lesser degree. Regulars at the pub continue their usual habits of drinking in the back bar regardless of our presence.

While this structure permits a wider range of roles than the standard folk club model, it is also evident that these roles are not static. For example, John, a local teacher, happened across the club one evening when he popped in for a pint. He is now on the mailing list to receive advance notice of events and makes a point of attending when he knows Royal Traditions is on. Claire, Stella, Rich, Julian, Sarah, Mark, and Frazer are locals, whose children attend the same school as ours. While all have an interest in and aptitude for folk music, to varying degrees,

26 Hield, 'Negotiating Participation', pp.112-3.

none regularly attends folk clubs or sessions in the wider Sheffield folk scene. As their interest develops, people move physically closer to the performances, and in three cases, after three or four years of gradual acclimatization, locals have learned songs and contributed to the singing session. While they are yet to make the jump to visiting another folk club, it is no longer beyond the realms of possibility, as they have acquired the key skills to facilitate integration.

People gradually build from behaviours they are familiar with (standing chatting at the bar) to new behaviours (joining in choruses, leading a song). Providing different layers of physical and participatory positioning means that outsiders have the opportunity to observe from a liminal space how more experienced members of the group behave. This creates a safe environment for the necessary knowledge to be developed to enable more involved participation—an incremental movement inwards through increasing levels of involvement, which Liz Garnett describes, among barbershop singers, as a 'centripetal compulsion towards greater engagement'.[27] Individuals do not move from one circle to another, however, but rather increase their participatory options, which map approximately on to their physical positions within the pub (Figure 2). A guest performer for example, can participate as a back-room drinker at other points in the evening—but that shift in positioning is not reciprocal. As people acclimatize to the mores of the environment, they feel a deeper connection and adopt the prevalent behaviours. A strengthening, or at least a broadening, of the tradition is taking place.

27 Liz Garnett, *The British Barbershopper* (Aldershot: Ashgate, 2005), p. 163.

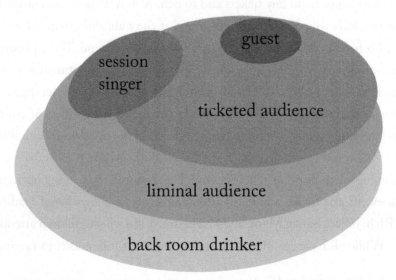

Figure 2. *Roles available to clientele at the Royal Hotel on club nights.*

These are important and valuable achievements for our event and we are pleased with the results. There are, however, elements that have not been as successful as we had hoped, aims that were not fulfilled by the interventions and new issues that have arisen as a result of the changes. Depending on the ratio of focused audience members to non-interacting pub clientele, the background noise levels can vary from friendly and informal to rowdy and intrusive. This can prove challenging for guest artists who, though warned of the potential for noise beforehand, are not generally used to performing in this kind of environment. This can cause embarrassment for me as an organizer. However, following an apology, artists have invariably said it was not a problem and that they actually enjoyed the difference in atmosphere from their usual gigs, emphasizing how special they find the environment. However, this is not always shared by audience members, some of whom may shuffle in their seats or turn around to give disapproving looks at the noise-makers or the organizers. To my knowledge, no one has left mid-performance, or requested their money back, though I am sure some have been discouraged from returning. Similarly, there are active singers on the Sheffield folk scene who do not attend because they prefer singing in a quiet environment and do not wish to 'shout' above the background noise. These are perfectly acceptable preferences, though they cannot be addressed without affecting other, positive, changes. This serves to illustrate the importance of having a variety of environments available to satisfy different tastes.

Particular social groups are absent from the club. There are other Sheffield-based singers who share similar aesthetic and ideological ideals to ours who we had hoped would attend our event regularly. Various factors have precluded this, including commitment to their own events and established social lives. The Royal Hotel is located out of the city centre and is difficult to access without driving; several singers have had young families since the club began, and, of course, there may be other factors unknown to me. The vision that our club would centre around a social group, reminiscent of our previous experiences in Keighley, Oxford, and Newcastle, has not yet been realized. Though there are regular attendees, and a generally friendly environment, a core group has not developed. This leads to the hypothesis that, in order to achieve a genuinely open environment, some of the closeness associated with shared knowledge has been diminished. Royal Traditions may be less cliquey, but it is also less familiar.

Lastly, we made efforts to connect with the local carol traditions, but this has not transpired as we had hoped. While some locals attend regularly and have been brought into the singing, other respected singers from established local traditions attend sporadically but have not become central components of the club. We had hoped the 'house songs' would function as a bridging device since the local traditions are based more on group singing than on individually led songs, but while they have had proven benefits, as outlined above, they have not facilitated the transition to regular singing for those who come out at Christmas. While efforts have been made to move away from some folk club models, that tradition has remained strong for a large proportion of our core audience. Perhaps because the seats tend to be secured by those familiar with folk club mores, those behaviours have prevailed; while locals have integrated, this has been on the established terms of folk scene participation.

Overall, Royal Traditions has successfully addressed core issues preventing participation, and provides a model that could be replicated elsewhere. This raises a contentious question. What is the difference between galvanizing a tradition through the widespread execution of stable structures, as the folk club tradition has developed to date, and what we are encouraging through sharing our model, and institutionalization? Simon Keegan Phipps's analysis of contemporary folk education addresses this point when he writes, 'an institution is such if it is recognized as an "organized element" by the members of its own culture [...] "institutionalization" not only illustrates the process of creating an institution [...] but also implies the intention or desire held by those involved that the result of that process should be an institution'.[28] This returns us once again to the distinction between natural and conscious activities, a distinction that continues to be blurred here.

The folk scene is fluid and open to multiple approaches — there are as many ways to structure events as there are events themselves. I am not attempting here to present a fixed model to be rolled out and applied wholesale; rather, this chapter seeks to encourage those involved with active traditions to analyse their environment and consider changes in order to maintain a connection with the wider pool of potential audiences. If similar changes are deemed necessary, or popular, a shift in the tradition may occur, a new institution may arise. Rather than observing whether actions are conscious or not, the pertinent difference is that the change is instituted by the collective actions of a mass of individuals, rather than enforced through a hierarchical structure. Shared behavioural rules develop through practice, rather than being imposed on a practice. In healthy traditions these changes occur incrementally, perhaps imperceptibly, but not unconsciously. Where traditions are in decline, more dramatic changes are

28 Simon Keegan Phipps, 'Déjà vu? Folk Music, Education, and Institutionalization in Contemporary England', *Yearbook for Traditional Music*, 39 (2007), 84–107 (p. 85).

made, with the resulting jolt in behavioural practice more easily observed as a conscious act of revival.

'Revival' suggests there has been a break, a discontinuation of something that needs to be reinstated. The folk club movement has not died out. Nevertheless, while the folk club continues to function well for those who participate in it, there is a discontinuity between folk club behaviours and the ability of potential participants to adopt those behaviours. Where there is a discernible rift of this kind, two options are available: (i) to develop new environments for participation; or, (ii) to create stepping stones into the established tradition. These options are not mutually exclusive. The relatively new festival and concert circuits are flourishing; however, attention needs be paid to folk club movement if it is to be sustained. The model presented here, whereby audiences move through the available roles at Royal Traditions, could be extended. Royal Traditions itself could be seen as a liminal space between wider participation through new environments (festivals, consumption of recorded music) and the traditional folk clubs. Rather than suggesting a change to the folk club formula in its entirety, complementary events can act as stepping stones to deeper involvement with existing practices.

Traditions are not inanimate objects. The folk scene is commonly viewed as a collection of events tied to a musical repertoire. The shift of perspective generated here, however, suggests that it is rather constructed of people, their behaviours, and their ideas. It is the process of accessing those ideas and behaviours that needs consideration. Where behaviours and ideologies are shared, people perceive themselves to be connected. That connection, the sense of community and its resultant behaviours, in this case the singing, is the nucleus of a prospering tradition.

Lightning Source UK Ltd.
Milton Keynes UK
UKOW05f1959031117
312116UK00005B/545/P